DATE			

D1418167

© THE BAKER & TAYLOR CO.

What You Aren't Supposed To Know About Writing And Publishing:

**An Exposé of Editors, Agents, Publishing Houses and More ...
An Insider's Report**

by Laurens R. Schwartz

SHAPOLSKY PUBLISHERS, INC. *** NEW YORK

What You Aren't Supposed To Know About Writing And Publishing: An Exposé of Editors, Agents, Publishing Houses and More ... An Insider's Report.
Copyright © 1988 by Laurens R. Schwartz. All rights reserved. Printed and bound in the United States of America. No part of this book may be reproduced in any form or by any electronic or mechanical means, including information storage and retrieval systems, without permission in writing from the publisher, except by a reviewer, who may quote exceptional passages in a favorable review. Published by Shapolsky Publishers, Inc.
For information, write: Shapolsky Publishers, Inc., 136 West 22nd Street, New York, New York 10011.

Library of Congress Cataloging-in-Publication Data
Schwartz, Laurens R.
What you aren't supposed to know about writing and publishing: an exposé of editors, agents, publishing houses and more -- an insider's report
/by Laurens R. Schwartz -- 1st ed.
       p.   cm.
Includes index.
ISBN 0-944007-03-1
1. Authorship -- Humor.   2. Publishers and publishing -- Humor.
I. Title.
PN6231.A77S38   1988
808' .02'0207--dc19   88-16909
                                               CIP

Manufactured in the United States of America

691 70969

Dedicated to my editor, without whom ....

No, no, no, I never met an editor for this book.

Dedicated to my father, who supported me through ...

I always say that.

To my mother, who ...

But she didn't dedicate her last book to me!

For my beloved wife ...

It's ex-wife now ...

My dog, who has never ...

Oh yes she has.

To the Nobel Prize committee, composed of the most brilliant, objective people I have ever ...

They'll never fall for that.

Dedicated to myself, without whom I wouldn't exist.

Too philosophical.

Als Gregor Samsa eines Morgens aus unruhigen Traumen erwachte, fand er sich in seinem Bett zu einem ungeheueren Ungeziefer verwandelt.

Was hab' ich gesagt?

To everyone who paid suggested retail for this book.

Publisher's Central Bureau, eat your heart out!

Dedicated to those wishing to exploit the ancillary rights, which are still available.

Contact me whenever convenient.

To R.G., A.B., C.F., T.S.E., J.W. and the rest of the gang.

But particularly former girlfriends.

Other books by the author:

TABLE OF CONTENTS

What You Aren't Supposed To Know ...

APPENDIX

DEDICATION

Dedications serve a number of useful purposes. Of course, there are those who take the easy way out and just dedicate everything to relatives and even spouses. As in: *To my father*. What is often left out of those dedications is the following:

"To my father, who supported me during the past twenty years while I tried to get this book published."

Or, "To my wife, who put up with me sitting around the house picking my cuticles for fifteen years while she worked as a waitress to support us while I tried to get this book published."

The more sophisticated dedication is to the letters of the alphabet. "To K.R." No other hint. This device is typically used by two kinds of writers. First, the well-published author who knows that academia is waiting for him or her to pass away so that all those treatises and biographies can be written. The letters often stand for nothing, but are tossed in to lead scholars astray and give them something to quarrel over for decades to come.

Second, the notorious author who wishes to make it seem that he or she has been or is leading a wild life. This is a good way to get onto *Entertainment Tonight*, *Lifestyles of the Rich and Famous*, or *Merv Griffin*, as in "To K.R., B.G., L.Z. and T.S.W." This tactic is even better where the author is married and the spouse is known to be writing his or her own book, which of course will be an exposé. Dedicated to "A.M., R.K. and all the guys at the gas station." Then their children will begin drafting their books, preselling ancillary rights to a music video company.

But authors sometimes use dedications to pay back people. As where an author dedicates the book to the editor who effectively destroyed its word flow. Or to the multinational corporation which has signed the author to a contract guaranteeing more income than any book ever generated. "To American Express, I wouldn't have a home without you." A dedication with this purpose becomes a preface or introduction where there are hundreds of people to thank, regardless of their association with the book itself. The editor, the spouse, the secretary, the children, the dog, the swimming pool, the view from the hotel, the second spouse, the agencies providing grants, the neighborhood bar, the second set of children, the typewriter, the psychiatrist. These dedications are often as long as the text of the book.

The final classification for dedications is where the author mentions the name of someone the author wants to meet, hoping the book will do well enough to attract attention. As in, "To Jacqueline Bisset, the most beautiful woman in the world." My address, by the way, is ....

DEDICATION REDUX

This book is dedicated to the great author and Pulitzer Prize winner, Irving Smith, whom I met on the Bowery and spent the next three years trying to get rid of. He taught me everything I know about writing while drunk. To the grammarian, Harvey Fuxner, who discussed the use of prepositions with me over many meals that he fed to pigeons and not to me. To Mary Oungfest, my writing instructor in school, who told us to keep writer's diaries containing our deepest thoughts and who, upon reading mine, expelled me from her class. To Joe Harrington, whose real name is Moishe Shummel, who showed me why pseudonyms have more to do with success than artistic ability. To the editors at the *Foreign Nite Press*, who illustrated for me the best manner in which to destroy a copy of a manuscript before rejecting it, as by leaving coffee cups and burning cigarettes on it.

This book is also dedicated to Mary Fawn, my first wife, who left after a year. And to my second wife, Melissa Hall, who left me after six months. And to my third wife, Alberta Mulzac, who unfortunately stayed with me for four years. To John, a child by one of my wives or maybe someone else, who tells everyone I'm a waiter instead of a writer. To Katherine, his speech therapist, with whom I've had an on again, off again affair while she pursues her real career of being a television announcer.

And to Barbara Suthington, the seventy year old widow who lives down the block and who recently had her first, only and last book published by a major house, picked up by a major book club, and nominated for numerous prestigious awards, and who donated her royalties to the Animal League. To my parents, who keep telling me that it's still not too late to go to medical school. To the various manufacturers of typewriters and microcomputers, who know that I'm a sucker for anything they put out that promises to help one's writing. Not to mention the many small copying stores that I have supported through the years, and the United States Post Office, which has transported one hundred thousand manuscripts back and forth around the world for me without a single complaint. And to Arlene Shostak, who types my manuscripts when I can afford her, and who does not say outright that my stuff is trash, although she changes commas on me.

But certainly no dedication would be complete without expressing the extreme gratitude and heart-felt thanks every unsuccessful writer must feel at being unsuccessful, for otherwise one might hit it big enough to have writer's block.

CHAPTER ONE

OVERVIEW

This book is intended for the five published and twenty million unpublished writers in this country who wonder why they have or have not succeeded. Unlike those countless magazines, manuals, books, videocassettes (*The James Joyce Workout*), and directories that purport to tell you how to write, how to get published, and how to invest your royalties, this book is going to explain why you have not succeeded and how you still may.

Before delving further into this book, it is suggested that you pull out that green trunk you keep in your closet or basement, unlock it, and reread those form rejection letters you have received over the years from The Editors. Then glance at the fifty thousand dollars' worth of xeroxes of your creations and see how many of those pages are now yellow. With that as a back-drop, you will be able to continue reading this book in the proper mood.

If you truly are an unsuccessful writer, your first question is: How did this guy get this book published? And your second question is: Why didn't I think of this? The answer is this: It doesn't really matter to me, since you bought the book and I'm getting some royalties, and you aren't.

But don't think it was an easy route from concept to publication. This book was written fifty years ago and was rejected by every publishing house in the known world at least four times each before some editor broke down and accepted it just to get rid of me. Actually, I also had to enter into a contract where I get royalties only if this book sells one million copies of the English edition in hardcover in Nairobi. My real money is coming from the film rights, which were just sold to Golden Legs Cinema on the assumption that the book is an X-rated musical.

This book contains useful insights into the world of writing and screenwriting, and the underworld of publishing, agenting and motion picture production. They are all based on experience. The first thing you have to get out of your mind is the thought that publishing is not business, but a glamour industry. If you have ever attended a party at which the guests were writers and editors, you will know that playing bridge by yourself is often more entertaining and that talking to your dog or goldfish can lead to a more erudite discussion on turns of phrase and quality of paper and binding.

The second thing you have to get out of your mind is that publishing a book leads to wonderful rewards, such as large royalty payments, television appearances, and

1

the opportunity to have affairs with renowned and beautiful people.

The third thing you have to get out of your mind is that reading the *Oxford English Dictionary* will do you any good. I used to do that and got nowhere; now that I dwell on words like "thing," I find that I am in a publishable mainstream. If you think that James Joyce (anagrams), William Faulkner ("scoriated"), or Virgil (writing in Latin) would be published authors today, you are definitely in trouble.

The fourth matter you have to divest yourself of is that you can devote yourself primarily to writing, as opposed to devoting yourself primarily to trying to sell what you have written. You cannot get an agent unless you have published, but you cannot get a publisher to read your material unless you have an agent, and you cannot .... There are ways of getting editors to read your material without having an agent, but you have to work at it. You have to devote your creative talents to innovatively getting your foot in the door.

The fifth thing you have to forget is that writing is fun or can be fun. It never is. If it were, more than twenty million people would call themselves writers.

Now for the things to learn. The first thing to learn is that having a sense of humor is extremely important, not for success, but for the sake of not destroying your marriage, your typewriter, or your income-producing career as a waiter or secretary.

The second thing you have to learn is that a change of name and a nose job can often be as important as having a masters' degree in creative writing.

The third thing you should learn is that ideas are frivolous.

The fourth thing you have to understand is that your time may never come and if it does you won't know what to do with it.

The fifth thing you have to know is that committing suicide only works once every thirty years, if you are contemplating a posthumous publication.

All the other things, big and small, will be detailed later on. At this conclusive point, however, let's pause for a moment and acknowledge the essence of writing as a career: postage.

CHAPTER TWO

BIRTH

By Any Other Name

Writers are always born with catchy names. Many times, their first and last names will rhyme; sometimes, their last names will sound literary; the rest of the time, their names will just be plain imposing. Since a name is a writer's most important asset, you can tell right off the bat whether or not you are a born writer. If your name is Joe Smith, or Irving Cohen, or Mary Klunk, you are not a writer. But if you were born John R. Oxford, George DeBeer, or Maria Quanto Valdez-Garcia, you have a fighting chance.

A bad family name is not the kiss of death, however, since you can later change your name. Struggling writers like to accumulate pseudonyms or, as they are known in the trade, a/k/a's. To give you an idea of pseudonyms which have worked over the years, consider these: Mark Twain; Moliere; Saki; Lewis Carroll; Stendhal; Joseph Conrad; E.V. Cunningham; Ed McBane; Brooks Stanwood; Isak Dinesen; George Sand; George Eliot; O. Henry (who eventually gave up writing to become a candy bar); Ellery Queen; John le Carre; and Woody Allen (who ended up in analysis for most of his life due to the guilt engendered by changing his name).

In some situations, you may be born into a name that has already been used. As in acting, you will then have to change your name. This is not because the original author can sue you on the ground that he arrived on this world first, but because if you don't change your name, all your relatives in the Midwest will celebrate every publication of your senior twin and tell everyone they know that they are related to a famous writer. They will expect you to appear at their door dressed in a white suit and wearing a wide-brimmed straw hat with either a slinky blond on your arm or a young man dressed in black leather. You can fake that, but the kicker is that they will also expect you to hand out dozens of copies of "your" book for free, and that can financially wreck you.

The popularity and necessity of name changes have led to a number of computer programs which permit you to randomly generate possible nom de plumes. In my case, my surname was given my predecessors by an Irish officer at Ellis Island (it was shortened from the Austrio-Hungarian *Woods*). I selected my first name from a Latin dictionary because my birth-name was Stephen. When Stephen Schwartz became famous for the play *Godspell*, I still felt secure because my relatives lived too far away to ask for theater tickets. But then I wrote a screenplay for a documentary and Eli Wallach was selected as the narrator. After going over the script with the producer, he announced that he was having lunch with Stephen Schwartz the next day and would continue the discussion with him. So now I have a name which no one can spell and which results in people addressing letters to "Ms. ..."

Except that a few months ago, a French woman asked if I was the famous (published) French mathematician, Laurens Schwartz. I add about as well as I speak French.

To legally change your name, if you feel you need some stolidity to it, you petition a local court and then appear for a hearing. A name change is looked upon as a possible means for evading creditors, so the judge will call you up to the bench and say, "Why do you want to change your name?" Your answer is, "To win the Pulitzer Prize." That response will usually put the judge into enough hysterics that he will stamp the petition and dismiss you. Of course, your real reason is to evade your creditors, such as the copying store, the typewriter store, and the Post Office.

Developing Childhood Enigmas

After you have your name straight, you must establish yourself as being strange. Later on in life, in the event you do get published, you will maintain your fame only if you are and were strange. As a baby, you should be shipwrecked and spend your first ten years living on a desert island. If you cannot achieve that, then you should be known for reading Freud at age two, Joyce at age three, and for writing your first book at age four. Attempting suicide by age seven is usually good for a later pictorial (always have someone taking photographs of everything you do). Meeting a famous writer by age eight and entering into a lengthy correspondence that can be published as "The Letters of ..." is also commendable.

In the event you neglect all of the above, at least pretend you are left-handed and a Virgo.

At elementary school, you should act withdrawn yet sophisticated; unathletic yet forceful; sensual but not overly sexual; and you should be impeccably dressed yet willing to dirty yourself at the drop of a hat. By the age of ten, you should be having a notorious affair with the wife of the principal. She will later become a symbol in many of your books, denoted by the sound of surf breaking through the morning dawn and landing on the smooth sand of the silent, silky beach. This will be so even if you are a nonfiction writer.

To set the stage for your autobiography, you will flunk every English course you take. This will permit comparisons to other geniuses who supposedly flunked their areas of later specialization.

Your creativity will be such that as you are introduced to each new writer, you will

CHOOSING A NAME

You may select any combination of names from the list given below, in any order, and with any addition of hyphens, apostrophes and accent marks you find appropriate.

Chertok	Weinbach	Amidon	Lapper	Pridgent
Elia	Resident	Sack	Dunn	Crutcher
Kidd	Kill	Bakker	Swaggert	Lecker
Licker	Bellow	Yell	Whoop(s)	Smith
Angle	Angle	Silvershlotz	Warshauer	Yavitz
Yeoh	Flesher	Brozman	Bro'	Mouth
Vermont	Sleeper	Seller	Zoogman	Paar
Nicklaus	Saint	Sain	Kooper	Pet
Spritzer	Wine	Vine	General	Sarge
Babitt	Hepner	Yristanslaus	Minkin	M.
W.	R.	Dante	Danto	Ralli
Jr.	Sr.	Tops	McN.	Gates
Tufo	Tugg	Cotti	Petty	Marks
Alva	Gulino	Goetz	Spanbock	Zief
Zweibel	Lapatine	Ken	Kenny	Len
Lenny	Ard	Ark	Arc	Spock
Aard	Aaard	Derek	Zuk	Charen
Petschek	Itallie	Sviss	Simone	Shea
Goodson	Gooddad	Doodad	Dike	Thumb
Downdike	Yorker	Marcus	Josh	Phlegm
Rahm	Blechman	Bicker	Finewrite	Strum
Wasser	Davey	Strawberry	Zonana	Weil
Zifchak	Ched	Waks	Kezsbom	Dunne
Fox	Foxy	Bigman	Ship	Stern
Mother	Mothra	Thorner	Corner	Hall
Rover	Pepper	Aluminum	Mailman	Gore
Ottensoser	Pine	Wilsker	Monty	Moses
Slim	Doctor	Zed	Volet	Viol
Violate	In	Producer	Award	Sase
Jan	Bordeaux	Francois	Jonemann	Sue
Sal	Groult	Grout	Blondeel	Kong
Katrasz	Lunding	Ripp	Lewkow	Chung
McGurn	III	IV	Turnage	Flog

take on the persona of that writer. When you read Camus, you will sit beneath trees and stare unblinking at the space before you. When you read Kafka, you will wake up one morning as a television antenna. When you read Mann, you will hack and cough terribly. When you read Tolstoi, you will find yourself tilling the soil in your backyard and growing wheat. When you read Joyce, you will hide behind fences and shout out anagrams in seventeen languages. When you read Hemingway, you will grow hair on your chest, walk around in winter with your shirt unbuttoned, and shoot anything that crosses your path, including yourself.

What is most important for your later public relations' releases is that people remember you as being an enigma.

By the time you are twelve, you will be such an enigma that you will have absolutely no friends in the world. You must convince yourself that being alone is the best thing for you because now you can spend all of your time dwelling in your imagination. Enigmatic people always dwell in their imaginations. If you have never dwelled in your imagination, you are not a writer and you should change your name back to whatever it originally was.

For the young writer, dwelling in your imagination means manipulating all the people who hate you so that they end up being killed while you have affairs with their girlfriends or boyfriends. Thus, the seeds for your first twenty novels or first six thousand poems.

Writers-to-be are also hypersensitive. That means bursting into tears at the slightest suggestion of emotions, bringing home bees to train because otherwise they would starve in the wilderness, and spending all of your money to give other people pleasure.

That also means that when you enter puberty, you will not fall in love, you will discover Love. The object of your first true love will be some ugly, disgusting, filthy, idiotic person everyone else hates, but your hypersensitivity and dwelled-in imagination will elevate that person to the height of beauty, truth, serenity, philosophical insight and religious fervor. Your initial impulse to write something lasting will burst forth in the fevered love you bear for this person.

If you write something five hundred pages long, you will be a novelist. If you write something exactly seven hundred and fifty words in length, you will be a journalist. If it is twenty lines long, you will be a poet.

You are not going to succeed as a writer if you strive to receive A's in English classes or care much for grammar, plot or style. A true modern writer knows innately that following the same form is the means to later achievement. If any experimentation takes place, it is in filling a blank page with as few meaningful words or just as few words as possible. For example, the first pubescent poem will read as follows:

ALGAE

Algae

oh algae
Floating across your white body
Beautiful

in its green

its green
ness

Oh algae, algae, *algae*
As it floats
across the body

of my
love.

The first short story will read as follows:

DEATH

George Trumbull, successful, handsome, a man for all women, slowly pushed open the door to his bedroom. Inside, sitting on the velvet sheets, was Brigitte. She was beautiful. She was naked. George had met her only briefly at the cocktail party. He approached her, untying his tie as he always did.

"How are you?" she asked. She gently stroked her breasts, breathing heavily. [Which part of her anatomy is breathing heavily is left to the reader to guess, thus introducing concepts of allegory and symbolism.]

"I am fine," he said.

"I have been waiting for you," she said. "Ever since that night."

"I know," he said. He tossed his silk tie onto the bed, next to her. Then he slowly unbuttoned his silk shirt. His blue monogram caught the light from the overhead chandelier.

"I have been waiting for you," she repeated in English.

7

"I know," he said. He heard her panting. Slowly, he flexed his shoulders and slid his smooth, expensive shirt from his body. She sighed unable to contain herself. [What "containing" oneself really means is left to the imagination.]

"I want you," she said.

"I know," he said, approaching her. He kissed her passionately on the lips. His tongue flirted with hers. She could stand it no longer.

"I want you now," she said, pulling him toward her.

"Yes," he said, giving in slightly.

"And then I want you to kill me and hide the body," she said, pulling his hands to her vibrant, hot and full chest.

"I know," he said, kissing her, then slowly raising his hands to her neck and squeezing.

So it goes. Perhaps you are a budding nonfiction writer. In that case, you will have a formula for your history essays, such as:

The Trials and Tribulations
of King Arthur During
The
Occupation

Few people have considered the implications inherent in the revolution that expanded across the expanse of Europe during the Twelfth Century A.D. This is a shame, for that period, of all periods, is the essence of what later became modern civilization. As the great historian and philosopher, George Schlep, wrote at the time (translating from his original Latin): "These were times of merriment but, certainly, also of insights. Scientific advances were unparalleled. Political upheavals were constant. Life was a mixture of love, lust and plague. Starvation was rampant. The stars were salvation."

Perhaps being a copywriter is the bent of the adolescent writer. In that case:

8

My Summer Vacation

If *anyone* at **any** time were ever going to spend *their* summer at a camp, the camp to be at is **Camp Wanna Go Home**. This camp not only costs less, it offers more! **Much more!** So much more, you won't *believe* it! But if you want to become a Camper Wanna, you have to act now, yes, **now**, for enrollment is limited, so limited that if you don't call now, you will lose out forever and for ever. Major credit cards accepted!

DO IT! AND DO IT NOW!

For the television and movie addict, screenplays and teleplays will be attractive.

DOVE

EXT., MARIE'S HOUSE -- DAY

It is a small house in a suburban setting. The front door opens and . . .

EXT., SAME -- DAY

Marie appears. She is twenty and gorgeous.

EXT., SUBURBAN WOODS -- DAY

POV Marie: she watches Peter approaching. Peter is seventeen and into music. He is snapping his fingers and bouncing to a tune. Music up: a hard rock song.

EXT., MARIE'S HOUSE -- DAY

Marie is smiling and waving. Peter jumps up the steps to the porch and kisses Marie on the cheek.

MARIE [*breathlessly*]

I have been waiting.

PETER [*nonchalantly*]

I know you have.

INT., MARIE'S KITCHEN -- DAY

Peter and Marie, arm in arm, walk toward the counter. Peter lifts Marie onto the counter. He kisses her.

PETER

Good girl.

MARIE [*breathlessly*]

That feels so good.

PETER [*manfully*]

Have some more.

Peter kisses Marie for a long time. Marie sighs and breathes heavily. They kiss madly.

MONTAGE OF:

Peter and Marie making love on the counter; dancing to hard rock music; making love on the table; dancing; Peter chasing Marie; Marie giggling. [In the forties and fifties, this scene would have been described as a "lap dissolve to an ocean wave."]

MARIE [*caressing Peter's face*]

That was so good.

PETER [*idly*]

I know. The best.

MARIE [*purposefully*]

I want you to kill me now.

PETER [*thoughtfully*]

I know.

The budding journalist will have none of that. All of the above themes will be abbreviated into a column reading:

Our Founding Father:
Julius Aldus Guttenburgus.

THE DAILY KLONDIX $1.13

DEATH STRIKES SUBURBS
DA THREATENS SUITS

Mid Town -- Marie Blatowsky was an unpretentious woman in her thirties who lived in a neatly kept two-story white house nestled on a tree-lined street. All neighbors who were interviewed described her as being lovely, quiet, someone who was not seen much but who also contributed a great deal to the community and her Church.

Then one day Marie Blatowsky's life was taken by a stranger and this small, quiet community will never be the same.

Continued on B-14

11

In reality, today's incipient author will probably be unable to link more than one or two words together in any form. The attention span of the contemporary adolescent seems to be limited to a fifteen second commercial. And everything else is now geared to that time period. A two minute music video is actually composed of eight scenes. A one hour and fifty minute long motion picture contains four hundred and forty scenes (no more the uninterrupted six minute dance scene between a Fred Astaire and a Ginger Rogers, or the close-up ten minute monologue of a Humphrey Bogart). More likely than not, today's adolescent writer will first attempt the craft by drafting a music video which reads: Lots of different shots of lots of men and women in leotards jumping around like maybe they were dancing to the music.

The budding writer will be somewhat averse to showing or reading his material to others. He may purchase a rubber printing press and spend hours slipping in words backwards and upside down, but when his first limited edition does not bring in the thirty dollars a book he charges, he will toss the machine away and revert to using his oddity as a form of charisma. He or she will soon learn that saying you are a writer may have certain sexual benefits.

Sexual Underpinnings And Dirty Wash

If there is one genetic element in being a writer, it is the need for sex. One writer once told me it was actually a need for procreation, but with all the birth control devices around today and during his day, I tend to doubt that. Besides, neither he nor the prospective mother would particularly want to be burdened with a baby on a writer's often non-existent income.

It is not that sexual experience will come early to a writer. A writer would rather dwell for years in his imaginary sexual habitat. His or her first sexual experience will be a complete disaster because of that. If that disaster is repeated, the writer will then go on to produce numerous rape scenes, S&M scenes, and walk in on your lover in bed with best friend scenes for R-Rated films.

In most instances, however, the writer will mold the first experience over a period of months into one of the most astonishing events ever to be recorded, over and over again, in the history of sex. He, a child of fifteen, walked slowly into the room and there she was, a virgin of seventeen, her hair long, straight and ebon, the sunlight flashing against her pale face and brilliant eyes. Her lips quivered. He gently touched her shoulder. His heart pounding, he took her into his arms and slid her backward so that they reclined on the mellow bed.

And on and on for another twenty pages, when finally: He held her face between his hands and gazed into her deep eyes. She smiled and sighed and he could feel her stretching beneath him. It had been an experience neither of them would ever forget, although neither of them would ever meet again.

For her, of course, she is on the top or on the side, both teaching him and learning from him, and the initial sensations radiating through her uterus quickly vibrate into guiltless, multiple orgasms.

If the above do not occur at an early age, the repression will eventually burst out as a middle-aged author's quest for sexual bliss. Such as the zipless you-know-what, or those interminable highlights of men walking into lakes bearing women.

Ultimately, the need for sexual expression will become merged with the need for literary expression. One reason is that much of writing involves sex, sexual tension, or just plain people who are capable of having sex with each other. Note that books, stories and poems never begin with any character being sexually incapacitated, although they might end up with someone being sexually incapacitated, who will then go on to murder everyone in the summer camp.

Sexual organs will also be anthropomorphized when one runs out of a plot line or has forgotten about plot lines altogether. A number of years ago, a somewhat famous Italian author wrote a rather long book which detailed a lengthy argument between a man and his penis. It often seemed that the penis was more well-educated than its owner. (The desperation of the motion picture industry was fully realized when this book was actually made into a film. I don't recall who played the penis.)

Similarly, the concept of a "zipless" fling is nothing more than an argument between a woman and her vagina. But at least this form of "art" is somewhat more interesting than the repetitive quality of potboilers, romances and gothics. There (as in pornographic novels), the author is required to follow an explicit form, detailing words (lust, passion, white, limbs, thighs, negligee, sweat, tongues, teeth, toes) to be used in the ten pages per each twenty page chapter which contain the obligatory sex scene. In that context, it would make sense to have the sexual organ interrupting and lodging a complaint or two.

The problem with writers is that the sexual pursuit can never be simple. The older married writer will inevitably leave his wife to live with the teenaged nymphet next door. The young unmarried author will live with the old actress who has seen better times. The unpublished writer will seek out the published writer. But no writer in his or her right mind will go to bed with an agent.

Overdoing It

Another aspect of developing into a writer is that everything must be experienced while one is extremely young. This is the writer's syndrome known as "fear of burning out" before one has developed a pit of memories.

A budding writer, therefore, will travel to Europe while young; hitchhike through the United States; drink; discover drugs; walk through neighborhoods late at night where he is the minority member; read every book he can; see every movie he can; fall in love with every person he can; flunk or fight his way through every school he is shipped off to; and then worry intensely that he has lost his touch. After worrying awhile about that, he will latch onto some poor soul who is impressed with his being a writer, and he will then proceed to rant and rave about how he has lost it. The young writer will contemplate suicide but, since he is not yet at the stage where a real suicide would yield him anything, he will use his imaginary suicides in later works about paraplegics and the misunderstood.

The Possibilities And Impossibilities Of Childhood Publication

The born writer will have his first short story published when he is seventeen. Back in the old days, this was because it was relatively easy to get published if you knew someone or were somebody. I am discussing the twenties and thirties in this context. This was a time of few literary agents, many literary magazines (that paid writers), and few writers. This was also a time when there really was not that much around to read and, of course, television sets had not invaded every known brain.

Writers of that generation all knew each other, drank together, smoked together, and rambled through Europe together. They had all been expelled from their private schools, or had dropped out, and knew they were going to write and get published. These writers will say to the struggling unpublished writer: "My first story was published when I was seventeen. If you write well, you will get published."

As will be seen in later chapters, nothing could be further from the truth nowadays but, when you think about it, those halcyon days of easy publication produced some of the best writers this country has ever had.

In contemporary times, that first adolescent publication will arrive because: 1) one's parent or close relation is a famous writer; 2) one's parent or close relation is an editor-in-chief; or 3) one's parent or close relation, as a birthday present, buys a magazine or publishing house as an outlet for the budding writer.

Sometimes, it is hard for the novice to track down these relationships, although gossip mags will attempt to do the job for you. That nice large glossy photograph of son and daughter and father and mother all tapping away at their word processors in the family den while their agent works at the ledger book on the wet bar. This arrangement is no different than that found in acting, where child follows in parents' footsteps. The best quote from these siblings is: "I changed my name so I would know I made it on my own." The public name may be different -- i.e., you and I might not immediately know why such and so is getting so much publicity while shooting to the top -- but the private name is known to everyone: the agent who is godfather, the publisher who is the next door neighbor, the critic who plays canasta at the family pool.

Power and money are another depressing reality. For example, the child of a publishing empire who decides, after nineteen years of not writing, that he wants to be (or is) a writer. He applies for one of those "fellowships" certain houses give out annually. These are supposed to be awards for the best writing talent, permitting that talent some freedom for a year, at the end of which a manuscript is supposed to be produced amenable to publication. A thousand struggling writers apply along with our newcomer. The newcomer "wins." The losers receive form letters stating that because of the number of submissions received, no personal comments are possible, but you should rest assured that the board of editors put a great deal of effort into selecting the best talent.

This budding writer will then take the money, buy a car, and bum around. He realized the day the check from the house cleared that he wanted nothing to do with sitting in front of a typewriter attempting to compose anything. The money remains his in any event.

Thereafter, he tires of driving the car and decides it is time to marry. He marries the daughter of another publishing empire and, as their wedding present, the newlyweds receive their own national publication to run. After a year or two of running the publication into the ground, they divorce. He finally writes that book, all about what an idiot she was. The book is, of course, promptly published to both critical acclaim and a lawsuit that yields a tremendous amount of publicity. He is photographed at a new discotheque on the arm of another famous person. She flies to an island off Spain and is photographed naked on a deserted beach. She eventually sells the film rights to her life story while he announces that he has begun work on another book.

A major tip that someone has connections in the business is when that person goes from childhood directly into publishing and lives solely on the income from advances. As is common knowledge, advances are not that large anymore for first publications since most house money is tied up with "name" writers. If a first writer is able to live on an advance without also working as a waiter or insurance salesman, and he is not otherwise independently wealthy, then he is connected.

Since you are not connected, after changing your name you should seriously consider a nose job. Wrong names and wrong noses seem to go together. You must also dress the role of the writer, which means wearing clothes that are casual, yet expensive. As you cannot afford the latter, you can pick up imitation clothing on most street corners of big cities. You should also streak one braid of hair purple or pink and hang outside the offices of PR people on your local Madison Avenue. Even though that will probably lead to nothing, you will at least keep out of trouble while getting a chance to watch all the beautiful people hurrying to limousines.

If you believe that names, plastic surgery and clothing are not essential aspects of making it as a writer, then I suppose you won't believe me when I add that acting and voice classes have become just as necessary. Writers nowadays are actually

15

submitting videotapes of themselves along with book proposals. Both books and their authors have to have commercial appeal. The purpose of the videotapes is to prove to publishers that the author can handle himself in an interview situation. Some of these tapes are of television interviews held to promote a previous book by the author, while the rest are staged in a studio rented by the author.

Another form of authorial promotion occurred a year or two ago, when the female screenwriter of a motion picture posed nude for some film promos. She later did an entire spread for *Playboy*. As I understand it, her videotape is used as the standard against which all others are measured.

CHAPTER THREE

EDUCATION

The Invaluable Writing Degree

Back in the old days, writers didn't have degrees. Times have changed in that one often comes across writers who have accumulated at a minimum one masters' degree in writing, and perhaps a Ph.D. One plausible purpose for obtaining a degree in writing is so that one can teach writing while trying to get one's own work published. Another reason is that, particularly in areas such as nonfiction treatises and poetry, being affiliated with a university in one capacity or another helps to get one's work published by a university press.

The primary purpose, however, is to escape reality for a few more years. Parents are more likely to provide financial support when one is still in school, as opposed to starving to death in a garret.

Otherwise, the value of a higher degree in "writing" is essentially nil. One obvious reason is that most of the required courses are usually taught by writers who either have one minor work published or no works published. Even worse is the course taught by a critic for, although writer-professors will often attempt to understand and promote styles different from their own, a critic has an established system of rights and wrongs that he will never vary from.

The Famous Writer As Professor

Sometimes, a famous writer will come to a writing program for a one year period. This creates a number of problems within a school. First, the regulars will be upset, especially when all the students try to get into the famous writer's classes and ignore theirs.

Second, the famous writer more likely than not decided to teach to get away from something, such as a bad marriage. This can lead to scenes in the classroom, as where the abandoned wife suddenly appears wielding a meat cleaver.

Third, the famous writer, having left his wife, will be on the lookout for sex. For example, writing "conferences" will be held in the privacy of the writer's apartment and, if he is expecting a beautiful young student, it is likely that he will open his door and be stark naked. Or buck naked, depending on the writer.

Fourth, the writer, having left his wife, not having found a nymphet, and being broke, will eventually end up drinking large quantities of alcohol. This will begin to lead to black-outs that will occur more and more frequently in the classroom. The writer will be discussing a class project and suddenly launch into a glassy-eyed attack on Ralph, his cousin who had died ten years previously.

Fifth, the writer will sometimes draft a quick story or poem as an illustration of what he wants the students to do as an assignment. The writer's piece, however, will also appear in a major publication during the semester, thereby leading to mass depression in the classroom.

Sixth, the writer, being alone and drunk and feeling quite sorry for himself, will then commit suicide in the middle of a semester. The students will be forced into finishing the semester under the tutelage of the jealous, irate professors whose classes they had originally ignored in favor of the famous writer's. The irate professors will proceed to rip apart everything the students bring to class, while praising

---

PHRASES FOR USE IN WRITING CLASSES

Your word flow is not only unremarkable, but egregious.

I wish you would bathe more often.

You certainly write the sort of [trash] things most people want to read.

I think your spacing is off.

Everyone is invited to the party except for ...

People do not fall *into* a chair, they fall *onto* a chair.

Just because you have a computer and laser printer does not mean ...

Your pagination is off but it doesn't really matter.

Using aliens from outerspace having only three fingers on each hand as an allegory for Mickey Mouse-ism was a stroke of genius.

If you were as a brilliant as you think, you would have committed suicide by now!

The meaning of life has nothing to do with writing.

I couldn't get *into* the story, I couldn't *identify* with the characters, I didn't *laugh* or *cry*, I was left *drained*.

That's been done before.

You misplaced every single comma and period in the entire manuscript.

Writing is a craft, like a skateboard or helicopter.

I never did like your personality and this story shows why!

No one in their right mind has written like this for fifty years.

Just because you're going for your fifth M.F.A. doesn't mean ...

You've missed the point completely.

You can take your dangling modifiers and _____.

---

everything the loyal students read aloud.

Writing classes themselves are an experience that has nothing to do with writing, but with one upsmanship. As stated in the previous chapter, budding writers tend to over-identify with known writers. Entering a writing workshop for the first time will shock the uninitiated with a row of doubles. The hulking man in the rear with his shirt unbuttoned, probably with a rifle at his side. The thin man wearing spectacles. The chunky woman wearing tons of hippy beads. The depressed dark woman with a tote bag full of liquor bottles collected on airplanes. The short solicitous man drinking vodka. Of course, if you happen to be in a costume too, none of that will bother you.

Likes and dislikes will become apparent as soon as the professor shows whom he prefers. Then camps will sprout up. Regardless of what is read and by whom, those in the opposing camp will roar into action. If the reader is preferred by the professor and the professor steps in at each objection by the opposing camp to support his protege, the opposing camp will hit at grammar. "Well, then, I don't like your commas, your semicolons, or even your periods!" Grammar is used as the objective weapon.

Many times, however, the professor can turn aside grammatical attacks on the ground of poetic license. In those instances, the opposing camp may resort to an even more objective frontal attack, as by beating up the protege.

If You Haven't Done It

Writers in writing courses, besides being hypersensitive, always on the verge of outrage, and strange, are "intense." The intensity is an outgrowth of the enigmatic childhood, and its purpose is to prove to other members of the class that one can stare without blinking. But behind that icy glare is the ultimate weapon of those who have not yet matured into the craft of writing: "If you haven't done it, you can't write about it!"

One cannot read about it, research it, ask others about their experiences, or rely on imagination. If you want to write about drugs, you have to experiment with drugs. If you want to write about orgies or homosexuality, you have to visit Plato's Retreat or a turkish bath. This kind of idiocy has also become prevalent among "intense" actors, whose PR agents will announce upon the release of a motion picture that so-and-so, to develop her role as a prostitute, lived in a whorehouse for six months; or that the famous actor studied Bowery bums for a year by drinking Muscatel.

The concept that one has to have *done* it prior to writing about it, in summarily tossing out the possibility of using one's imagination, is one reason why so many novels, poems and short stories are autobiographical. (The other reason, as will be discussed later, is to get back at people.) But it is also a great lead-in for retorts when it arises during a seminar. The opponent hisses out, "It's obvious you don't know what you're writing about because it's just as obvious you never experienced it." The response can be, "I guess you'll never write about love, then." Even better: "Why don't you write about a person who pours gas over himself and then lights a match?"

My Protégé

Having summarized writing classes, it is only just that I toss some embellishments at you. Famous writers, for example, tend to latch onto one student in particular. This is the protégé syndrome which is related to the procreation urge. It does have its ups and downs.

One writer I know became the protégé of an extremely well known author. Let's call them Nouveau and Setinway. Setinway, being of the old school, was a wonderful alcoholic. Nouveau used to go to his apartment every morning at nine sharp to get Setinway dressed and lead him to a nearby bar for breakfast. Setinway would sit on a barstool trying to drink a double vodka. Nouveau's job, as protégé, was to make sure the drink did not fall on Setinway's pants, that Setinway did not fall from the stool, and that Setinway made it to the class he was supposed to be teaching. The former two acts were generally satisfied by Nouveau gently lowering Setinway's head toward the bar until lips touched glass, and then Setinway would sip until he decided to rear his head back. The scene was like those wooden birds which, set near a glass of water, begin an eternal round of bend, sip, up, bend, sip, up.

The last act was harder, for Setinway, no longer eating solid food and depending solely upon vodka for his sustenance, had a very small grasp of reality that was not helped much by downing five doubles before a ten o'clock class. Nouveau would gently prod Setinway, sometimes paying the bar bill himself since Setinway was accustomed, in his own bar far away at his home (he was a visiting professor), to end a session with a strong, "Put it on the tab!"

During class, Setinway would praise Nouveau, defend him from attack, and then shoo away everyone except Nouveau, who would lift Setinway from his chair and guide him back to the bar for lunch.

The actual learning process is this. Setinway, once settled in his university apartment, a lit cigarette burning a hole through the crotch of his pants, would reminisce. "Upstart," he said, referring to another famous writer, "was my first protégé. I worked with him on his first stories. I got him published in X. Upstart is a wonderfully creative person. He only fucks seventeen year old girls."

Setinway had had a second protégé. "Bubblehead," he said, "published the first long story on homosexuality ever taken on by a major magazine. I wrote that story with him." Then Setinway stumbled up from the couch and wandered to his typewriter stand while Nouveau frantically stamped out the cigarette embers that sizzled on the couch and the rug. "Come here," Setinway said.

When Nouveau reached the desk, he was confronted with Setinway blinking his bloodshot eyes over one of Nouveau's manuscripts next to the portable typewriter. Setinway put a piece of yellow paper into the roller and brought it up crooked. He sat down on the chair. "Watch," Setinway said as he typed away. After a few minutes, he pushed the chair back and tugged Nouveau forward. "Read," he said. What Nouveau read was the beginning of his story written in Setinway's exact style.

The point is not that a famous author can maintain his own writing style while obliviously drunk. It is the realization that being a protégé means either letting the master rewrite your material or rewriting it yourself, and is a crucial moment in the educational process of a writer. In this instance, Nouveau knew that if he objected, Setinway would probably not get him published, but that if he did not object, Setinway would merely be publishing himself. Established writers seem to dwell on the idea of molding others into their imagery and style, even to the point of retrieving dead souls from prisons, "editing" their poorly written manuscripts, getting them published, and then testifying at the inevitable trial concerning the writer's most recent murder or rape. Established writers also like to claim that other established writers always send them their manuscripts for rewrites.

Setinways do have other techniques they use when they adopt a student as a protégé. Take another Nouveau and place him in a professorial room bedecked with books, leather and polished wood. Nouveau, week after week, is seated on a high backed red leather chair facing an open window. Setinway paces back and forth behind the chair, occasionally circling it, but all the time speaking in rapid, high pitched tones. "You are not to write fantasy. You are not to write science fiction. You use too much explicit sex in your work. You are the born writer, the person who pops out of the womb capable of achieving more with words than most people will even contemplate. But you need to rein in your skills. Some writers are taught, some writers are born, but even the born ones, like you, have to learn." The question, of course, is learn what, for it is quite possible that Setinway's type of writing and style would never be published today but for the fact that Setinway has a reputation from years before. To learn is to read, and to read is to know that editors want you to write their way. Or to become involved in a different form of sexuality.

While being a protégé can be a stunning and sometimes psychotic process, not being a protégé seems to have an even more astonishing effect on a person wanting to be a writer. As a literary representative, I have discovered that fifty percent of the people who submit manuscripts to me claim to have been someone's protégé. Since ninety-nine percent of those can't write beans (spelling it instead "beens" or "biens"), I suppose they mean they were protégés outside of the context of writing.

Post-Enigma Sexuality

When one conceives of a "glamour" industry, the general impression, which is certainly promoted, is that those at the top date whomever they wish. Morality never becomes an issue unless one then decides to run for political office. The implication is that those who have made it to the top did so in some manner involving a "prostitution."

Sexual favors are not as prevalent in the publishing world as in, say, movies (for one thing, it makes sense to readers of the *National Enquirer* that an actress practice a nude scene nude with a director, whereas it is not quite as impressive to contemplate an author illustrating a zipless fuck to an editor or agent). The sexual kinks of the publishing world have always been more literary than in the rest of the entertainment industry. If, for example, certain actors are known for molesting girls, the prize-winning author will be known for wooing girls who are one day past the age for statutory rape. If, in the music world, there is a woman who goes around taking plaster casts of famous musicians' penises, in the writing world that becomes the wife of a magazine editor who has made a career out of postcoital photographs (probably shot with a disk camera or Polaroid; nothing fancy).

The almost laid-back nature of sexuality in the publishing world has a great deal to do with the "enigmatic" nature of writers. A Madonna-Sean Penn relationship is always newsworthy because either is capable of answering a question with a four-letter word or a physical attack. An author, on the other hand, will always try to respond with something literate, which makes it less printable than the curse.

The student-mistress, on the other hand, will never denigrate the experience of having been a betrayed, sexual protege with a writing professor by blubbering out the story or filing a lawsuit. Being the betrayed, sexual protege adds to the patina of the enigmatic and is a decent source of plot lines and character descriptions; more, if the writing professor sent love letters (which writers are prone to do), the protege will either publish those letters (apparently, now against the law should the writer himself sue), or hold onto them until the writer passes away, at which time she will auction them off.

And there are those who build entire careers based upon a one night stand with someone famous. A number of professors of English literature boast about their trysts with authors and use that hour of nudity to cut off any analyses of an author's body of work which departs from their position.

English?

Curiously, writing programs do not teach English as a language. Whereas in law school, the professors will drill the students until they are brainwashed into thinking "like a lawyer should," writing schools follow the dictates of "poetic license." No one wants to be responsible for giving someone else writer's block, even if that psychological development might be of benefit to humankind.

Still, languages, including English, seem to have been constructed by our ancestors to have a certain structure permitting communication among people who are supposed to be versed in the same language. Pushing a language to its understandable limits, as Joyce did in *Finnegan's Wake*, is different from modern day authors who garble language for the sake of claiming a linguistic philosophy. These are the people who lack any writing ability whatsoever, but put the fear of God into editors and critics who do not want to make the mistake of shrugging off the writers in the event that it should turn out the rubbish did, after all, have some meaning. (The same absurdity can be seen in the art world, where the acceptance of an artist who merely cuts out photographs of famous artworks from magazines, signs and frames them, represents one of the cultural lows of the universe.)

It is not only the arcane author who distorts language, but also some extremely popular writers. As will be seen in Chapter Five, a technique used in many best sellers is to eliminate as many words as possible on the assumption that the English language is redundant (which it is), and that most people skip over every other word. The arcane writer slows down the communication, while the best selling author speeds up the process.

Since a writing degree often means nothing more than finding a professor who likes you, and handing in a manuscript typed with the appropriate margins, those who want to know something about language should take courses in Teaching English as a Second Language.

Retreats

The remaining aspect of writing programs is the retreat. These are camp-like summer programs in camp-like areas of the country where one usually gets a room or a bungalow, privacy, extended periods in which to write, and extended invitations for acting enigmatically.

Being accepted to a retreat is a completely political process. If you are not a protege -- the Setinways of the world are inevitably on the boards of directors -- you have to find someone who knows someone who can successfully sponsor you. Once in, you should not waste your time at the retreat by writing. The primary reason for going is to make more political contacts. That you might be escaping a bad marriage for the summer is of secondary importance, beneath which you might list finding a new lover, or learning the best way to pose beneath an oak for jacket covers.

CHAPTER FOUR

FREELANCE WRITING AND EDITING

The Sucker Syndrome

Freelance writers are those writers who have either never sold the big one, or sold a big one and spent all the money presuming another big one was around the corner.

Freelance writing does teach some good lessons. To succeed, you have to forget about writing and think about getting business. That means answering advertisements for Writers, even though each letter entails a great deal of work since it is the letter that will sell you. It means trying to generate your own business, as by pounding the pavements to drum up an industrial film, or an audio/visual project, or an educational guide of some sort. Frequently, it also means working as a temporary secretary.

The first lesson is learning how to read between the lines of any advertisement. If the ad calls for a freelance writer or editor who is attractive and can type 60 wpm, or for a freelancer willing to take on a "glamorous entry level" job, be prepared to take home someone else's manuscript to retype.

In other cases, the advertisement will read something like this: "Writer wntd to work with famous author. Call ..." "Author" can also be doctor, historian, scientist, or professor. They are always famous. They will never give you their name over the telephone, nor will they explain what you are to do except in a mysterious fashion that causes them to breathe heavily. If you are a woman, be extremely careful about these ads, for they are related to ads that read: "Models wntd, female, fashion modeling, movies. Call ..."

Sometimes, those ads do end up having a vague ring of truth about them. A friend of mine once answered one and suddenly had a short, black haired, nervous man at his door, carrying a load of elementary school level history books. He wanted my friend to ghost write a book on a certain historical figure. He even mentioned that he had a contract with a major publishing house and, as a sign of good faith, he gave my friend some cash.

Freelancers are always suckers for cash because it helps them to eat and meet alimony payments. It turned out that this fellow was a vaudevillian who had suddenly awakened to the fact that vaudeville was dead (or, in his words, "no longer on the circuit"). So he had turned to persona from history. My friend worked on the book for a year, spending a great deal of his own money on the research, and then was told

25

where to go to drop off the manuscript. The "major" publishing house was actually a place that put out pornography. What they had contracted for was a manuscript detailing the sexual habits of that certain person, even if it meant making up those habits.

The book, of course, was rejected and the vaudevillian tap danced out of my friend's life, leaving him with the manuscript and a huge debt. On top of that, the publishing house began sending him threatening letters, demanding the return of the cash advance.

You see, freelancers are also suckers for the possibility of publication, so they will never ask questions and will neglect to ask for a written contract. They will then spend anywhere from one to twelve months devoting themselves to a task, only to find out that they were being led on, or that the publishing house didn't want the project anymore, or that the co-authorship that had been promised was a lie.

A better understanding of statutory rights will help some. As a writer, you should realize that most of your legal rights rest in the Copyright Act, which is Title 17 of the United States Code. Subsection (b) of section 201 states:

> In the case of a work made for hire, the employer or other person for whom the work was prepared is considered ... the author for purposes of this title, and, unless the ... parties have expressly agreed otherwise in a written instrument signed by them, owns all of the rights comprised in the ... copyright.

What this has meant so far is that an employee and most independent contractors will discover that whatever they write becomes the property of the person who pays the bills and, perhaps vaguely, supervises the work. To some writers, the feeling is that fair is fair, and if someone is willing to give some money, let them have the product. But what has to be remembered is that "title" to a written product represents a number of rights. That the person using the writing may only want to use it once. That your payment scale may well be based on "use" as opposed to what you might believe to be literary merit or marketplace realities. And, most importantly, that most people don't consider the options involved in rights because most magazines and houses -- and this means primarily small and independent presses -- work on an oral basis. But even saying, "You do this and the rights revert to you after publication," has no real legal validity.

Gimmick One -- The Blond

But then again, in the beginning, freelancers tend not to care about ownership or rights. It is the foot in the door which counts. The most successful foot usually belongs to the lithe leg of an imposing blond. There is no one better where the door which has to be opened has a heterosexual male behind it. Sometimes, the woman herself is the freelancer; many times, the woman is living with or married to the freelancer, who makes his entrance meekly, the idea being to let the editor's fantasies take wing in an non-threatening atmosphere.

A problem with this fantasy approach is that if the woman (or team) fails to produce the appropriate article, the editor may nix both the fee and reimbursements for costs. The article itself becomes the symbolic tryst, and if it is not "satisfactory," the editor will not "pay" for it. Instead, he feels betrayed, let down and embarrassed. He is left with the photograph of his family on his desk and an empty space to fill in the next issue.

A variation on this approach entails submitting an article or book proposal which includes 8 by 10's of a nude woman. Photographers have a monopoly on this aspect of the freelance market. Photographers often "help" out ear wet actresses and models by providing headshots for free; in exchange, the women pose nude after signing releases. If a woman becomes famous, the photographer is in the money. Not only do they sell the photographs, they also insist on writing an accompanying article or book on the woman's personality, life and dreams, all based on a three hour session during which the only words spoken were, "Now lift your right arm," and "Now stand on your toes."

Gimmick Two -- The White Lie

Another gimmick is the white lie, known in the trade as the exaggeration. If you are not beautiful and sensual, you have to get in the door in another manner. That means doing things that will make you stand out from the twenty million letters or live bodies already jamming the doorframe.

Name dropping is generally acceptable. In fact, most people in the entertainment industry take courses at the New School in learning the who's, how's and when's. Name dropping always starts out casually and builds up weight and speed as the other person tries to top you.

In answering an advertisement, as another example, you cannot just state: "I am a freelance writer." You have to embellish. "I am a freelance writer with over two hundred publications to my credit." Or, if you have not published but have written two hundred pieces, you would say: "I am a freelance writer with over two hundred articles to my credit."

The next step is to hone in on the needs of the employer. "Most of those articles happen to involve the evolution of dental floss in the Nairobi wastelands." Or, "I am an expert in the infrastructure of the armament industry as it relates to socio-economic shifts during the past four decades." You need not be an expert. The knack of being a freelance writer means developing the ability to become an overnight expert in any area. Is a lack of prior knowledge unethical? Probably not, because it has been an ethical guideline for lawyers for a century. Lawyers, pursuant to their code of ethics, are not supposed to handle a case in which they have no expertise unless they feel sure they can adequately learn the area without detriment to the client. Do you know a lawyer who has ever turned down a case? Why should you, living in Cincinnati with an elementary school degree, be incapable of writing about symbolism in Anglo-Saxon poetry?

Speculation

If the employer is accepting material on spec, the odds are that you will merely receive a package in the mail detailing your project. Writing on spec means spending too much time on something that pays too little and having it rejected anyway. But if the project involves a slight advance or other expenditures that have to be reimbursed, such as travel, you will be called in for a personal interview.

Personal Interviews

Women have it easier here, for they need only look seductive (if the editor is a woman, though, they're sunk unless she's a lesbian). Men, on the other hand, should try and research the company as thoroughly as possible. Not fitting in physically can mean an immediate wave to the door. One time, I answered an ad and dressed in my only suit because the address of the company was a prestigious one. It turned out that the company was new wave and everyone working there was either partially disrobed or wearing things I wouldn't give my dog to chew on. In another instance, the exact opposite occurred. The address was not very prestigious and the company name implied drugs and sex. I wore blue jeans and socks my dog had chewed on. The drugs and sex part was there, all right, but that publication was in another wing. The interview was for the sophisticated financial magazine.

One technique is to call ahead and tug what information you can from the receptionist. You can say things like: "I am taking a survey and hoped that you could tell me whether the editors wear three-piece suits." "I believe I left my Burberry there the other day. Are there many in the closet?" Just having an open telephone connection can often tell you a lot. What sort of music is playing in the background? Is the receptionist sassy, upper class, sexy? Is the receptionist a male who asks you what type of flowers you like?

At the interview, you have to sell yourself and not your writing. If you are a beginner, you have to inflate what you have done and keep the interviewer off the topic of seeing writing samples. There are two reasons for that. First, every writing sample you give means yet another set of samples you have to xerox, i.e., more expense. Second, the odds are that you do not have impressive writing samples. If you are a good talker, the interviewer will give you the assignment, period. If not, and he asks for samples, tell him you left them at home, or that you no longer have any since no one returns them. By the way, the latter is a true point: interviewers never do return writing samples. Samples are either tossed, or they go into the file cabinet for possible rewrites and inclusion in the interviewer's publication at a later date. Those are the "fill" files: samples, cuts from other magazines or newspapers, and odds and ends collected over the years that serve to fill empty spaces.

But interviews and samples do raise another legal issue as to rights. For example, what happens if you attend an interview where the employer doesn't seem exactly sure as to what he or she wants in the form of an article, and after two hours of picking your brain you are sent home? A month later, your ideas appear in print, written by someone else.

Giving Too Much

Ideas are not "protectible" under the Copyright Act. But some ideas are protectible under state law. How concrete the situation has to be for you to win depends upon that state law. If you spend a lot of time with the prospective employer outlining the article, giving sources, defining illustrations, and the like, you may have a possible claim. The problem, of course, is that your claim for damages will in most cases amount to little more than actual damages, which may end up being what the publication paid the other author for the article. And that might be in the range of a few hundred dollars. Your lawyer, in the meantime, will be charging you that by the hour.

As to ideas you have put on paper, and as to those writing samples, you should seek copyright protection. Section 102 of the Copyright Act reads in part:

> Copyright protection subsists ... in original works of ... authorship
> fixed in any tangible medium of expression, now ... known or later
> developed ....

If you call the Copyright Office in Washington, D.C., you can put in your order for tons of information, pamphlets, brochures, lists, declarations, forms -- all for free. Select the appropriate form, fill it in, write out a check in the appropriate amount, and append one copy for an unpublished work and two copies for a published work. This does not, however, work if you are copyrighting a sample of something you wrote for someone else who holds the valid copyright (although you will probably receive back a certified copyright registration, it will be invalid).

In the meantime, just make sure that you write "Copyright ©19__ by X, all rights reserved" on the cover page of your samples. The "C" in a circle is used because it is one of those internationally recognized symbols such as an arrow pointing left or a crossed-out cigarette. As with everything else in life, a C in a circle was selected because almost no one can reproduce it. I suppose you could type a C and an O and draw an arrow pointing from one to the other.

Approaching The Assignment

If you are given an assignment and the interviewer neglects to give you a copy of his publication, ask for one. You have to follow the style and format that he likes. Freelancers, like prostitutes, have to do what the buyer wants. Even if you can write anagrams in seventeen languages, draft free-flow poetry, or bring a reader to tears, none of those skills is going to do you a bit of good when the buyer wants X and not Y.

You also have to keep your wits about you. A common occurrence, for example, is that your assignment might involve interviewing people who would not ordinarily see someone like you. A Jew might be commissioned to research and write an audio/ visual script involving the United Nations. One aspect of the project will be to interview various ambassadors and emissaries, such as from Arab countries. This

---

SOME FREELANCE WRITING POINTERS

1. Clarify the issue of work-made-for-hire -- in writing.
2. Have the employer write down exactly what expenses will be reimbursed. Do not expect to have that list include dog kennels, dry cleaning or the delivery of Chinese food.
3. Many magazines accepting freelance material plan issues by theme. Make sure you obtain a list of themes. There is nothing more embarrassing than sending in a carefully crafted piece on raccoons when the up-coming theme is cows.
4. If you are computerized, think for a moment before including an SASE. What is the cost of return postage, the mailer, and the postage added to the primary mailer because of the inclusion of the return mailer; what is the cost of printing out a copy of the article? If the former is more than the latter, put the money saved into a glass jar and hide that under your bed.

situation once arose during the Thirtieth General Assembly, which spent its time condemning Israel and Zionists approximately fourteen times a day. Arabs were instructed to never speak to a Jew. In that instance, the writer turned interviewer introduced himself as Joe Smith. Not too witty, you might think, but the interviews were held because Joe Smith was the right approach: it was humorous. After all, at that time, half the Arab emissaries were either Christians or were married to Christian and even Jewish wives.

Writing Is Too Cheap

A freelancer, to make a relatively decent living (and most only gross about six thousand dollars a year), must also write rapidly. After awhile, one draft should be enough. Two drafts is the maximum. The goal is to meet the employer's desired style and format by filling in spaces with light, airy words that say nothing while leading the reader to believe that something is being said. The best example is in journalism. If you pick up a newspaper, you will note that the first line gives a suggestion as to what the story is about and the next thirty paragraphs really say nothing. What is most important to a publisher of papers, newsletters, journals and magazines is the "impact" of something, and they don't mean content by that. They mean heads, type size, lay-out, neighboring advertisements, and so on. The person who does the heads for mass publication newspapers typically makes much more than in-house staff editors and writers, because doing a head on the spot supposedly takes a great deal more print and write knowledge than fleshing out the rest of the page. Lay-out artists come next, but their lower income is due in great part to the fact that once an initial pattern (the "dummy") is set for a magazine or paper, it is not varied from that much. There are only so many ways in which columns of type bordered by ads can be laid out: Writers exist at the bottom of the heap, in the dime a dozen crowd.

This calls for some sort of explanation. It is not just that writers are cheap, but that writing is cheap. There's tons of it to select from. If you are doing a mass-circulation newspaper, journal or magazine, you can, for example, subscribe to a variety of AP, UPI and foreign wire services. Every night, these services transmit thousands of articles, all of a certain length. You need an article on cow manure as fuel that runs exactly four and a half inches? Scan through to the article on just that and begin cutting out from the middle, working your way up and down the prepared article. AP and UPI don't have such an article? Go through the fill files and the clipping services until you find the appropriate article, edit it down, and vaguely rewrite parts of it. Then publish it as your own, regardless of copyright issues.

With all of this easily accessible and inexpensive writing floating around, there is little need for in-house writers or freelancers.

31

Writing Isn't The Point Anyway

In many cases, it is not the writing that is important or even the publication itself but the list it generates of subscribers. This is often the most lucrative aspect of a trashy publication. It works this way. Direct mail is a major marketing device for selling products and services. A list is a list of people who fit a certain defined market segment, such as college educated with a high income, or lawyers, or priests. When I was in the business, lists sold for anywhere from fifty to two hundred dollars per thousand names, but I'm sure the price is much higher nowadays.

Developing your own list for resale can take different routes, but two common ones are as follow. In the first, you purchase lists yourself and sell your new product by direct mail. As you gain subscribers and renewals, you end up with what you can now call your list, that you can market.

Another way is to place space ads in publications where you know their readership breakdown. In that way, you gain a list that is already defined for you.

One publisher in New York was renowned for his ability to make millions by generating lists from worthless pulps. The magazines or newspapers contained articles culled from the wire services. To add credibility, space ads were sprinkled throughout -- but they were reproduced from reputable publications without the permission of the advertisers.

Subscriptions were then sold for a dollar.

As an example of how this enterprise could turn a substantial profit, a premier list at the time was subscribers to the *New York Times*. The *Times* was extremely circumspect about who could rent its list, and turned down the publisher. So the publisher placed full-page come-on ads in the newspaper. Since the subscriptions were a dollar, and often included freebies, the response was astronomical. Soon enough, the publisher has his own pseudo-*Times* list which he could rent out.

Pornography And The Freelancer

Returning to prostitution and making that dime, half the ads a freelancer answers will involve pornography. In fact, a freelancer can sometimes come up with a relatively steady income by answering the following ad: "Writer, wrt twenty pg day min, good pay." This is the porno fluff market. You get paid a couple of hundred dollars a week to sit in a cubicle and churn out twenty pages of porno daily while following a defined style and format. In many instances, all you really have to do is change the names of the characters from book to book. It is a steady mindless income. If you are worried about the impact of that background on your later career as a Nobel prize winning poet, the books are not published under your name -- that is one industry which typically provides its own a/k/a's through which numerous writers pass. Besides, look at all the famous actors and actresses who started out as bit players in X-rated films. At least you don't have to sit at the typewriter nude.

Although sometimes that happens and shouldn't. I recall one rather infamous publisher who used to walk around the office wearing a t-shirt and boxer shorts. He never bathed with any frequency and it was always an unwelcome shock to report for work and find the top man winding down a hallway, somewhat odiferous, somewhat nude, waving his arms and shouting that his staff was undercutting him.

One other quirk about this gentleman was that he adored fleshy, school-marmish women. So when he decided that his house would produce a line of erotica, he personally drafted the story line for the premier book. Needless to say, it involved the fantasies of a dashing young man who meets an overweight librarian in a field of wheat. The book required twenty rolls of film just to get through the removal of hair pins, eyeglasses and pencil holders.

But ... the book is still on the market, undiscounted.

Even the government printing office realizes the value of sex. Every so often, our tax dollars are earmarked for the production of utterly ridiculous federal studies on pornography which immediately hit the best seller list.

If you have moral qualms about writing which involves overt sex, oddly enough there are more female editors in this area than others. Of course, strict constructionist feminists would say that female editors who permit this kind of sexual exploitation are themselves exploited, but then again some people who have BA's in English and no other prospects in life frequently find editorialships more pleasing than poverty or serving at a major house as an editorial assistant by title and secretary by trade. Besides, those who work for the truly raunchy magazines have a built-in source for humor, because both writer and editor can visualize the reader and what he is doing with old issues.

Other than becoming an editor for a skin magazine, the female freelancer always has a good shot at writing those gothics, romances and potboilers sold next to white tuna fish and Vanish in the neighborhood grocery store. These are the soaps of the freelance trade, with "lines" written by an "author" who is actually a series of freelancers following printed forms. Female freelancers are invariably selected because, as one editor told me, "Women have a better understanding of what a woman will actually feel in these situations." The situations involve rape, violent rape, romantic rape, general promiscuity, and the ability to thrust hot tongues like sharp swords.

What a writer should remember, though, is that overt sex has been in use ever since man started drawing obscenities on cave walls. (Most primitive art involves outright erotica; editorial censorship protects us from that, giving us humdrum animals with spears being thrown at them.) Sex has always been the historically stable market among both men and women. More, only those who speak directly to an otherwise silent God have been able to define "obscenity" and "pornography." Their definitions typically include everything from D.H. Lawrence's novels to Michelangelo's *David*. What makes one wonder is that these Bible Belt occupants are demolished every so often by tornadoes and hurricanes.

Humor

The only freelancer who is truly in demand is the writer of humor. It is very difficult to sustain humor in the written word. Perhaps because of that, those magazines which do commit themselves entirely to humor (and there is only one decent publication that comes to mind, *MAD Magazine*) tend to emphasize satire, which is easier to create than outright humor because the funniness of it is based upon exaggerating something already known or done, such as a film.

Most of the humor market is relegated to drafting one liners for comedians. Jokes sell for fifty to two hundred dollars each. To break in, a writer has to study a comedian for content, accents and delivery. Jokes should be typed on separate cards and presented directly to the comedian while he is sober.

Final Points

Two final points on freelancing. The first is that whatever you do may be a potential article. For example, the family vacation can become a journal on restaurants in a particular region, an essay on airplanes, or an article on sights to see. If published, you will be able to deduct some of your expenses. Moreover, in some markets, such as the travel market, the magazines don't seem to mind reprints, which means you can have the same article published in a couple of places.

Second, a freelancer can cover all the needs of a magazine by taking photographs. Photography is perhaps the easiest trade to learn. Basically, it means purchasing sophisticated equipment, some of which will talk to you, and then shooting four or five rolls of film for the one or two photographs which, by chance, will turn out to be relatively acceptable. Learning about film speed, filters, lighting, and the rest is not that hard; you can use a how-to book (the ones filled with naked women, as most are, can be both entertaining and informative), or you can keep a notebook detailing the machinations behind each shot. The only real secret is that you have to have the film, generally slides, developed at a professional lab, and not through a mail order house.

Freelance Editing and Editors

Freelance editing is a service industry that was created by necessity when the island off Cuba where former editors used to be sent became filled up. The overflow, having to remain in New York, Chicago and Los Angeles, needed something to do or the rest of us would never be able to get a seat at a local bar.

Freelance editing is an extremely lucrative field. Depending upon the names of editors still employed at houses that the freelancer can drop -- suggesting that he has strong contacts for eventual publication of the work -- these people charge from $500 to $15,000 per manuscript. What they do is read it, synopsize it (just in case you forgot what you had written about), and add up to a ten page critique of your literary failings. They do not rewrite. Often, they will hold onto a timely book long enough for it to be outdated, something they will affirmatively note in the critique.

It is up to the writer to follow the critique. Having done so, the writer often ends up with a costly, critiqued work. End of story.

The exception is where a manuscript has been sent to a publishing house and an editor says, "We would be extremely interested in your resubmitting the manuscript after it has been edited by Flugelhaimisch, who used to be one of our editors." I know of many cases where this kind of buddy-system "advice" has resulted in contracts. If one were of a suspicious nature, one might even think that a kickback might be involved.

But since no one involved in the entertainment field could ever comprehend anything as disdainful as kickbacks, buddy systems or even sexual favors in an area renowned for its morality -- or, at least, being somewhat more moralistic than the practice of law, politics, or the breeding of pit bulls -- one can only think that the entire process is refulgent with coincidences, fate and Zodiacal signs.

In any event, the field of freelance editing, bursting into the forefront of high profit, little work, has become integrated with many literary agencies which, instead of trying to place books, now charge for reading them.

CHAPTER FIVE

BREAKING THE MOLD

The step above the freelance writer is the "author." An author is someone who has published something "big." "Bigness" is correlated with the size of the hardcover advance, the extent of the first printing, the success of the paperback and book club auction, and the size of the second printing. Even though craft has nothing to do with "bigness," we might as well discuss it. If you like, you can subtitle this chapter: "An Afterthought on Publishing."

Tricks Of The Trade

Writing, as with any profession, is mainly a question of learning the craft. Prostitutes learn how to wear miniskirts and permanent make-up; academics learn how to work until they get tenure; politicians learn how to speak forcefully and with conviction without having any idea as to what they are saying; union chiefs learn how to manipulate pension funds from the car phones in their limousines; in-laws learn how to destroy their daughters' marriages; and weathermen learn how to give inaccurate forecasts. There are tricks of the trade for each of those endeavors. To learn how to write, you have to learn how to read. Reading means looking at the work of successful writers and seeing what they are actually doing.

A writer's tricks are applicable to both best sellers and literary works. The difference in how the tricks are used has to do with the fact that best sellers are devolutionary in nature, whereas literary works should be evolutionary. The former seeks out the lowest common denominator with something the majority can feel safe with (having read it before), while the latter seeks out the Pulitzer and Nobel prizes with something the awards' committees can feel politically safe with.

Two basic tricks involve adjectives and death. Adjectives in triplicate, once the domain of authors such as Anatole France and John Cheever, have seeped into best sellers on the assumption that three descriptors is probably better than one prior to the character dying. Thus, "Amy sat at the piano. It was a dark, moldy, untuned piano."

Amy can then die in peace and her mother or lover can imagine her favorite sonata being played on the dark, moldy, untuned piano. "She died" is the extent of effort found in a best seller; a more literary work will often be satisfied with the symbolic death of the protagonist, which means that there must be a scene involving water.

Purification by water was so popular in certain quarters that people often read books by D.H. Lawrence or Cheever while grasping umbrellas. Here, "He died" is replaced with "He walked into the rain and suddenly felt invigorated, as if life had always been simple." Or, "He walked into the pond and suddenly felt invigorated, as if life had always been simple."

Sometimes, death is neither quick nor easy. Someone dying of cancer or AIDs for three hundred pages is one neat way of selling a book for twenty dollars. Even better, as applied in one best seller, is to suggest on page ten that someone innocent (a child, dog or parakeet) must have died, but to focus on the ramifications of the hypothetical death for three or four hundred pages before finally admitting it in the flesh. "The car crashed into Joyce's car, and little Tommy was tossed from the back seat forward with a force that should have been terminal."

Once the plot (rape and revenge; romantic rape and marriage; murder and mayhem; bleeding mirrors in the new house; death) and descriptors have been selected, the next step is dialogue (sometimes spelled dialog, which is also the name of a computer program, so take your pick). Dialogue can fill reams of paper. In literary works from the turn of the century on, dialogue used to be equated with dialect and/or developing a character's personality. In contemporary best sellers, dialogue means putting the narrative between quotation marks.

"What do you want to do today?" he asked.
"I don't know," she said.
"I thought perhaps we would go for a stroll," he said.
"That might be nice," she said, picking at her fingernails.
"Yes. It would be nice," he said, looking at her picking at her fingernails.

Another trick is to repeat what has just been written, as was done above with the fingernails. A subset of that trick is to begin a new sentence with the last word of the prior sentence. This trick is usually accomplished without quotation marks, meaning it is dialogue returned to narrative.

He went to the door. The door was large.

Where a character is actually going to be distinguishable from other characters other than by sexual descriptors (female; male; promiscuous; virginal; hot tongued; close-mouthed), a writer will typically assign a trait to the individual.

Mary blew her nose and crumpled the kleenex before replacing it neatly in her purse.

Every so many pages, Mary will be crumpling kleenex and placing it neatly in her purse. Thus, people are always tapping a cigarette on a table, rubbing their left knee, or stuttering.

Formulas

The introduction to tricks given above lends itself to a deeper analysis primarily because my editor insists that the chapters of this book contain exactly the same number of letters and spaces. Since I have failed miserably so far, I am constrained to embellish much as one would for any publication required to be a preordained length.

When an author, teleplaywriter or screenwriter has sold three hundred works over a fifteen year span, or twenty works over a ten year span, it is because he has a formula. Everything they have written can be synopsized for a fortune cookie. If X murders Y and Z pursues X until X confesses sells a hundred thousand copies, achieves "legs" upon theatrical and video release, or results in an on-going series primed for syndication, keep using it.

I wonder whether you have experienced what I have with increasing frequency. I go to the movie theater (or I used to until the price of admission went to seven dollars, and a kernel of popcorn increased to three dollars), the credits roll, and then I am overwhelmed by the sensation that I have seen this before. Most of the time nowadays, that sensation will have obvious underpinnings, for I will be seeing a sequel to a sequel, or a remake of a remake; but even before then, I had the complete belief that I was watching something stolen from other graveyards. Same thing with sitcoms. After a while, you can even announce what each character will say and what will happen before the first four minutes have run.

Best sellers can present an even more impressive distortion of *deja vu*. I obtain best sellers by rummaging through garbage. Once, a neighbor tossed the entire series by one author, and each book jacket declared "Over twenty million copies in print." I read one book and put it aside, selecting another. I read the first fifty pages and then left the books on my night table. The next day, I picked up the book and read another fifty pages -- before I realized that I had been re-reading the first book. I picked up the second book and read fifty pages. By that point I was utterly confused; had it been that book I had finished, or the other one? Which book was which? *Why is it I didn't know anymore?*

These formulas are often drawn from the Bible. God was foolish not to copyright the book, especially since He would have made a killing on reprints, revisions and motion picture ancillaries. A number of biblical figures would also have claims for invasion of privacy and publicity. Job is a wonderful model for desultory writing, while Christ has been appropriated for almost everything else.

The Job formula entertains us with the person who matures because of inexplicable adversity. After awhile, you don't even have to turn the page to know that something terrible is going to happen. The overall sensation generated by this type of book is the intense desire to scream. The attraction, however, is that the schlep is going to suffer more than we have. In a way, we don't want the character to have anything right occur, we don't want the book to end in triumph. The book is a kind of talisman; if you hold it up at night, God will strike the character instead of you.

The Christ theme, on the other hand, has us yearning for the protagonist's death because we know he is going to come back in triumph. In science fiction, for example, X goes to a planet where he is burned to a cinder but out of the cinder comes X prime who goes on to save the planet. X has a strange disease that debilitates him but because of the disease he has certain powers that permit him to save the planet. X develops an omniscience that permits X to save the universe.

In straight literature, Christ may lose some of His sanctity because of the requisite love affair. X is the misunderstood professor at the university who saves numerous students anyway while having an affair with Y, the wife of the provost. X is the misunderstood architect who builds a masterpiece that saves the world while having an affair with the mistress of Y, the powerful and corrupt politician. X rises up through a multitude of setbacks to become a powerful politician who does good for mankind against the mainstream thought of other politicians, while having an affair with his daughter who turns out not to be his daughter, so they get married.

In murder mysteries, X is killed and Y discovers the killer. Y often has qualities of a godhead -- both prescience and an alcoholic's form of omniscience -- and his triumph, as in science fiction, is of good over evil.

Tricked Again

The difference between a novel and a short story using tricks is about two hundred pages of dialogue and three thousand dollars (unless you have a best seller). A similarity is drafting a piece so that it seems amenable to transformation into a teleplay or screenplay. Short stories tend to read like half-hour long television shows, whereas novels read like one hour fifty minute long screenplays (which is about the length of time it takes to read a novel; the fact that a short story may take less than thirty minutes to read is because the author has left out the commercial breaks). Poems, on the other hand, sometimes read like copy for a thirty second advertisement.

Let's go through the tricks of the trade a third time:

1) The Christ theme. Most obvious in science fiction, it is also prevalent in other forms of literature and entertainment. Although the exploitation of Christ has offended some evangelists, particularly when He is represented as a cuddly alien available on t-shirts and in toy stores, it should be remembered that these same evangelists accept credit cards for the purchase of their ancillary exploitation of Christ.

2) Dialogue. Dialogue is easier to read than "text," and is therefore used to "move along" a plot although no characters would reveal that much information even during a silver wedding anniversary. Dialogue has become so important to the detriment of character development that many modern novels and short stories neglect the characters completely. For example, a quote will end with "he said" or "she said," and then the retort will take up the next line. This is actually a trend back toward oral histories, without the lute or the song. One may recall that oral histories were the way stories were related during those medieval times when everyone was illiterate.

Another aspect of dialogue beloved of the publishing world is that conversations mean short paragraphs. I have always believed that the furor over *Ulysses* was not really about its possible obscenity, but because Joyce dwelled on long paragraphs of internal monologue. The thought is that modern day readers will get eye strain if forced to read more than one or two lines at a time without a definite pause thereafter for refreshments.

Dialogue is, of course, the required form for a teleplay or screenplay, although quotation marks are deleted in favor of the indent. Character development is left to the director and sometimes the actor, using camera angles, lighting, scenery, make-up and, for actresses, the removal of a blouse every fifteen minutes.

3) Length. Short stories are generally limited to ten manuscript pages, whereas novels are limited to two hundred and fifty manuscript pages (which used to be considered a novella). Even Stephen King, before he gained the clout to shove two-thousand page manuscripts down the throats of editors, was forced to cut hundreds of pages from *The Stand* before Doubleday would publish it in 1978. (Needless to say, after King's success with thick books at other publishing houses, Doubleday reissued the uncut version of the novel.)

For magazines, brevity is required in part because of page layouts, as in advertising space. One can always read about a magazine expanding its "pages" for a particular issue, although never for the sake of a long short story; it is always because the ad space sold out and the publisher has to fit in the additional advertisers.

For books, the length of the manuscript is sometimes ascribed to the cost of manufacturing, which establishes the retail price, and partly to the durability of the reader. The latter is also true of the magazine reader. Books and stories aim for those people who want something to read because they are not near a television, that is: commuters; people going to the bathroom; people eating lunch alone; and women getting a dye and a perm. A chapter of a book or a section of a short story should take exactly ten minutes to read. An entire book should consume one visit to the bathroom on a Sunday morning. An entire magazine should make one look busy and content while sweating through a lonely meal.

There are exceptions in the book market. If, for example, a short novel does very well in the market, one will usually come out with volume two. Volume two can be substantially longer because of the marketing concept that a hooked reader will pay

COMPARISON OF HORROR AND MYSTERY TRICKS

HORROR	MYSTERY
Hair stands on end.	Hair itches.
Floor creaks.	Floor creaks.
Blood-stains.	Blood-stains.
Why did the victim leave the door unlocked?	Why did the victim leave the door unlocked?
Victim comes back to life.	Since it was the wrong victim, the intended victim is still alive.
Prolonged discussion of sexual activities.	Prolonged discussion of sexual activities.
Supernatural powers that permit the manipulation of reality.	Use of computerized detecting techniques permitting the manipulation of reality.
Stormy, windy, muddy, dusty, lightning-filled, out-of-gas, godforsaken nights.	Stormy, windy, muddy, dusty, lightning-filled, out-of-gas, godforsaken nights.
It is discovered that the occult is involved.	It is discovered that the occult is involved.
Why did the next victim walk down the deserted forest path?	Why did the next victim walk down the deserted forest path?
A stormy, windy, muddy denouement involving screaming banshees.	A stormy, windy, muddy denouement involving screaming lawyers in the courtroom scene.

more for the follow-up to find out how something ends -- before volume three comes out. Exactly like today's television and motion picture business.

Another exception is where the book is the life's work of someone who is on the verge of death. This makes for good publicity and, besides, everyone knows that the author will not be writing anything else. So in a way the lengthiness of the work is accommodated because one could imagine it as representing the ten books which might have been written during that lifetime.

Otherwise, the length requirements established by magazines and houses have to be met. As an agent, I have had returned to me dozens of stories which were loved by the editors, but the stories were from one to ten pages over the guidelines. Editors at houses will bluntly say that they will not even consider a first novel of more than a few hundred pages in length.

Length requirements are also strictly followed in the entertainment industry.

COMPARISON OF POTBOILERS AND ROMANCES

POTBOILERS	ROMANCES
Establish a setting, such as Hollywood or the suburbs.	Establish a historical setting, such as 18th Century France.
Heroine has a setback in her love for a man because she is raped.	Heroine has a setback in her love for a man, as through economic difficulties.
Heroine learns to cope with the rape while plotting her revenge.	Heroine learns to cope with poverty while plotting her triumph.
Another woman appears who advises the heroine on techniques for revenge.	Another man appears who advises the heroine on techniques of love.
Prolonged discussions of sex in vengeful terms.	Prolonged discussions of love in sexual terms.
Heroine has a series of love affairs, trying to forget the rape.	Heroine has one love affair trying to forget the loss of her true love.
Heroine spots the rapist unexpectedly.	Heroine spots her true love unexpectedly.
Heroine decides only way she can save herself is to fulfill her need for revenge.	Heroine decides only way she can save herself is by getting her man back.
Heroine successfully achieves revenge.	Heroine successfully gets her true love back.
Heroine charges a mink coat.	Heroine gets a diamond ring.

Script treatments should be exactly twenty pages long, while screenplays should be exactly one hundred twenty pages. One-line jokes must be exactly one line, and heavy metal song lyrics must contain exactly three words repeated fifty times each.

4) Death. Someone usually dies or appears to be dying in just about every piece. The goal seems to be to present something crucial and irrevocable -- and death fits the bill -- to draw in the reader. Editors and writers like using the phrase "draw in." I suppose they envision a reader crouched over a book with the face getting closer and closer to the pages until the reader topples into the binding.

One genre of the death theme is the dying protagonist, often the tender hearted, well-beloved woman. But this means spending a hundred pages of dialogue on the wittiness of the woman before she contracts something like cancer.

The quickest "drawing in" route is the death of a child. One need not dwell too much on the character development of a child because, unlike an adult, it is assumed that a reader will readily accept any child as being wonderful and innocent. The context of the death is what is important. An extremely popular book a few years ago involved a child caught in a bad family situation because his parents were fooling around. The child is killed in a car accident. This denouement is particularly helpful in establishing the stage for what is often the ending of a book after a death: guilt.

But for those readers too callous to be drawn in with the death of a child, there is the genre which picks on animals, mainly dogs. The dog rationale is because readers are not expected to be drawn in by the death of a cat -- cats have nine lives anyway -- or a cow -- since the reader may be eating a steak while reading the story -- although for awhile horses were valuable victims. But dogs are the supreme subjects for an animal demise because they are the most anthropomorphized of the other kingdom. Dogs are always wagging their tails, lapping faces, and saving children and freight trains from destruction.

5) Horror. Horror is a technique which can be anything from the reaction of the reader to the price of the novel to whether the reader will be able to sleep at night if a closet door keeps drifting open.

The trick here is in the repetition of certain words. "His hair rose on end at the back of his neck." "He woke up in the morning and there was blood on his pajamas." "There was a noise." Today's authors tend to do no more than what is done in television or films: look to the special effects of the turn of phrase.

What one gets -- and these books sell very well -- is a story about a typical family driving into a typical town which suddenly doesn't seem all that typical because of one or two quirks. Such as the busy highway which everyone lives next to, where trucks run over people and animals. As in television or the movies, the novel will never explain why these idiots don't erect fences.

Or, moving into the wonderful old creaking house but something is wrong with the mirrors. Look in one and you see a ghost! A progressively more vicious ghost on top of that.

But even with those twists of supernatural fate, the novel itself will primarily involve things like bad marriages, the death of children or dogs, and tons of dialogue among the scared victims-to-be and the ghosts.

One trick which is permitted horror books moreso than other genres (discussed below) is the use of italics. An example is, He walked casually down the deserted alleyway. *Don't look back! You know it's behind you. If you look back, it will get you, it will have an edge, you can't show it that you're scared. It feeds on fear.* His footsteps echoed with an eerie quality, something he had never before been aware of. *Because the echo was not from his footsteps!*

The real difference between a Poe and a modern day horror writer is the addition of sex. Sex is sometimes used to represent evil or a method for destroying evil, but in most cases, eight hundred of the thousand pages will be devoted to the humdrum sexual activities of characters who are about to be scared to death or drenched in a bucket of blood.

If you look closely, you will note that this form of writing is almost exactly like that used in mystery novels. Instead of a ghost, though, there is a progressively more vicious next door neighbor, friend, acquaintance, dog or car. But hair still stands at attention, and there is still a collection of "clues." The difference between the horror novel and the mystery is that in the former, it is acceptable if all the people die, whereas in the latter the detective must succeed and live on. This technique is necessary in the event the first book sells well and one wishes to do a follow-up. In the horror book, the dead souls can always come back as ghosts.

6) Simple sentences, repetition. Simple sentences are related to dialogue, since dialogue is generally in such a simple form it can often entail no more than a grunt. "Ugh," he said. Repetition has been mentioned in the context of character development, as in "she crumpled her kleenex." These two techniques are again signs of the times we live in. Faulkner and Joyce, for example, often used sentences which could consume a page or more before ending. The modern reader, being in a rush and existing in defined time segments, needs a quick period for inserting the bookmark. But "simple" here also means using simple words in simple sentences. Returning to Faulkner, he used to toss in somewhat arcane words now and then, and the effect is to make the reader pause and cogitate. Joyce was even worse, tossing in anagrams. Word choice like that is considered absurd in today's culture because it holds up the reader and prevents his being "drawn in."

For the same reason, repetition has become a trick because it is easier to read something the second or third time. This helps memory, builds character, and gives the reader a sense of deja vu. One understands what is going on in the book because one is being hit over the head with it again and again. And that is why repetition has become a trick -- because it is easier to read something the second or third time.

The ultimate simple sentence is the staccato shortening of a thought to its barest essentials. This technique is being used more and more in best sellers as another method of speeding up the time it takes to read something. Since English is a highly redundant language, the first words to go are connectors; the next are pronouns; and then every so many words on a random basis. "It was ten-fifteen. The clock chimed from its shadowy corner. He knew it was time to go," becomes, "Ten-fifteen. He left." "I could have done that," is shortened to, "Could have." The response to learning the most startling revelation in the entire book is, "Really? Thought so."

7) Scenery changes. Scenery changes involve continuing exactly the same story with the same characters in different parts of the world. By shifting the bad marriage, or the prolonged death, or the horror from city to city and country to country, one can quadruple the length of a manuscript through the device of describing the new culture, including its foods, religion, and architectural failings. One can also introduce a character, such as the tawny guide, who will be left behind as the major characters hop a flight to yet another place.

8) The historical novel or story. This trick means establishing generations of families, from start to finish, from the great grandparents fleeing oppression, to the grandparents building towns and cities, the parents erecting airports and oil tankers, and the children having that bad marriage during which one of their children dies.

A recent twist to the historical novel is where some of the characters, or the major character, is a known person. Just as Walt Disney brought Abraham Lincoln back to life, the fiction writer is now permitted to do the same. Giving him, of course, extensive dialogue in simple sentences. This technique is merely a clarification of what has been done in the past, that is, taking the life of a well-known person, fictionalizing it, and giving that person a new name although everyone who reads the disclaimer at the front of the book will know who is really being written about.

Oddly enough, some recent court decisions have upheld the right of a fiction writer to use the names of living public figures, including the right to have them speak words composed entirely by the author. The rationale seems to be that living figures have an extremely limited right to sue over libel, and rather than extend even that right to novels, one can gut it entirely because a reasonable reader will assume that although the character is real, the fictional setting safely declares that whatever the character says or does is also fictional.

Which is similar to saying that the reader of a gossip magazine can't possibly believe the gossip.

9) Autobiography in the guise of fiction. This trick is an expression of the reality that people, including editors, tend to be most interested in gossip. What better source of gossip than a writer's own life, which is why one should never befriend a writer. The more famous the writer, or the more famous the people the writer knew, the greater the chance that the book will be published and will sell well.

But autobiography is also the simplest form of writing because it entails absolutely no use of imagination. Most first novels, short stories, and books of poems are in this class, and tend to use a first person narrative. "While trying to finish my first novel, who should drop by but [name resembling that of one's former lover]. She was wearing [description of that former lover's usual garb]." That sort of thing. This "trick" of writing, however, is detrimental to those creative writers who are always confronted by those relatives or spouses exclaiming, "How could you have written about me!," since it is no longer possible to respond, "But this is all from pure imagination! All writing is!"

By the way, there is a legal problem associated with autobiographical writing, and that involves issues of right to privacy and freedom from libel. In other words, your ex-mistress, former psychiatrist, cult leader or Latin teacher can sue you if you reveal them to the world in the derogatory manner in which you currently perceive them. Unlike the use of public figures in historical novels, the autobiographical novels attack the private lives of private people, who have strong legal rights. As will be discussed in Chapter Seven, the fear of litigation has created a new form of censorship: "review" editing by insurance companies and libel lawyers.

10) Biography in the guise of fiction. Related to the historical and autobiographical, biography in the guise of fiction consists of an author acting as a journalist. The author lives with murderers on death row, attends court in the Bronx with lawyers, or moves to an exotic locale and follows the daily activities of the maid. These books are hyped as being better than fiction because they teach us something about real people living in a real world (much like the historical novel which is supposed to teach the reader about history in a painless way by forcing characters to say things like, "It was 1776, and for those of us living in New York City, it was a restless time. Revolution was in the air."). In real life, murderers can win numerous PEN awards, but the profits from their books would under many state laws go to a fund for vicitims. Having a writer in attendance is a nice way to pass the time. Lawyers who practice in the Bronx love to have writers troop along with them for protection. Maids in exotic places don't speak English, but are usually not pleased when the writer pops up during a quickie with the gardener.

Why would an author turn journalist for the sake of fiction? Because the closer fiction is to nonfiction, the happier the editors. They avoid arguments with authors which normally go like this: "A murderer [lawyer, maid] would never act that way in real life!"

11) Plagiarism. You may have noticed that during the past ten years, television and movies appear to have reached a creative standstill. Not in terms of technological advances, such as wonderful special effects, but in terms of stories. Looking deeper into this, one finds that not only are most shows and movies remakes of the same themes and plots, but the rest are actually remakes of remakes of remakes. In some instances, these are "legitimate" remakes in the sense that the copyright has expired, or the studio has been assigned the appropriate picture or television right; in other instances, the remakes are plagiarized, in the sense that the names have been changed but everything else remains relatively the same. Both the legitimate and the perhaps unlawful remakes try to "update" this material, by injecting it with those wonderful special effects, name stars and hot sex scenes that make the remake into a modern day film indistinguishable from any other modern day film.

This pattern also exists in publishing. We are not involved here in "revisions," as in, "lost sentence of Faulkner discovered, entire work to be re-edited," or, "the third definitive final edition of *Ulysses* to be released, seven commas changing import of work discovered beneath sofa." We are discussing, for example, the use of an Ambrose Bierce horror story in a prestige magazine a few years back under the name of a known author who had merely changed the names and placed the occurrence

---

ELEMENTS FOR A BEST SELLER
Select and Mix and Match:

Who dies: baby; toddler; devoted wife; dog; devoted husband.

Manner of death: run over by car; torture; drowning; own child transformed into a horrible entity; prolonged disease; loss of blood.

Sex: rape; loss of virginity to true love; easy conquest; affair.

Descriptive words: tall, dark, handsome; voluptuous; sprang to life (nipples); hot (tongue, thighs); blond; muscular; rustling (clothes, sheets, bed, murderer approaching, monster behind bushes); sudden; suddenly; unexpected; unexpectedly; fated; fateful; fearfully; anticipated; renewed; glaring; distant; hypnotized; mesmerized; paralyzed; spacious; cramped; restrained; unrestrained; loosely; tightly; damp; moist; wet; sweaty; remembered; recalled; ingested; regurgitated; secretly.

Plot settings: something lost; something (to be) gained; something threatened.

Alternating scenes: sex; death; marriage; divorce; clue; sex; violence; luxury; sex; death; affair; confession; marriage; death; sex.

---

in a New York apartment. There is no copyright protection for Bierce's work (there is, however, copyright protection for edited versions of older works, so don't confuse the two), but that was plagiarism nonetheless. There are also instances of known authors redrafting and updating otherwise arcane works which are validly copyrighted.

But we are entering a new world of absurdity when publishers, following in the footsteps of motion picture studios, decide to provide sequels to books solely for the sake of trying to make a buck on what is perceived to be an ardent audience. *Gone with the Wind* is one example. One wonders what might be next. In-house sequels to successful books written by still-living authors who refuse to write their own sequels? The colorization of books because some editors decide the original edition is too depressing?

Overall, it is apparent that in many corners of culture, we have reached dead-ends. There is the urgency for output, the urgency for survival, and the belief that people are satisfied with reading or seeing the same thing over and over. In this light, the plagiarized work is not much different from the formula book or the remake or update. And the issue is not so much homogenization of culture (which is used as both an excuse and a sneer), as a fear of art. Because art sometimes is not understandable. So we can take a poorly written novel and claim it is art because it was written by someone whose PR agent has suggested to us is an artist. Or we can permit a museum to exhibit telephones, screwdrivers and a splotch of yellow paint on a canvas as "art."

Beyond Writing

Before moving on to nonfiction writing and poetry, about which there is not much to say, take a glance at some areas of the craft of writing which are currently in the cultural doghouse.

The first is internal rhyming or rhythm in prose. This is where the writer carries a beat within each sentence and may include actual rhymes. Related to that is the word play, such as using anagrams. So that you do not get confused, these have nothing to do with giving characters names that "symbolize" what they are, such as Joe Wisdom, Arthur Kill, or Doctor Disc. Those choices have as much inner meaning as the brief chuckles one gets noting, in real life, that Coffin runs a funeral home, Foot is a podiatrist, or Kidney is a nephrologist.

The third technique is to use the symbols to denote movements of the symbols that are even more powerful than the symbols themselves. This is the allegory. A straight allegory has two levels: the literal one (Joe and Mary marry and die), and the symbolic one (Joe is Adam, Mary is Eve). From there, one can add as many levels as one likes. For example, level two could be the Trojan War; level three could be a musical composition; level four could be the natural movements of birds and insects; and level five could be the biblical rise and downfall of man. The symbols are controlled by their allegorical level and the story it is telling, as opposed to the symbol being used to express its own natural sense of order. Instead of Nature being a dark, wild, inexplicably violent force, nature can be a setting described in such a way that it represents Eden, or 18th Century European society, or loss of innocence.

Allegorical techniques can become stifling from the modern editor's point of view in that the novels do not read as cleanly as a one level simple plot. If you do have the urge to write allegories, however, you can still get away with it to some extent by concentrating on science fiction.

Just as autobiographical writing has become a standard in the trade, primarily through the use of first person narrations (for the first novel, anyway), so has writing in the past tense become a standard. Using tenses in a sophisticated manner, such as to show time, mood or narrative shifts, is frowned upon by editors. The closest an editor will ever come to permitting an express shift in style is where *italics are inserted to show or emphasize shifts. For italics, like tense changes, were at one time played with to reveal a change in angles or point of view, as where a character's internal monologue was italicized.* To study tense shifts, you could look at the works of D.H. Lawrence, William Faulkner and James Joyce.

Time shifts are often represented by tense changes, the simplest example being the use of the present tense to denote the present, and the simple past or imperfect to express the past. But a time shift can also be drafted using a concept known as "devolution." There, the author remains in the same tense, but the chapter might begin with something which has already occurred, and then the rest of the chapter will relate the events leading up to that occurrence.

Internal monologue, or stream of consciousness, is another means of playing with time shifts. During the late sixties and seventies, partly because of some popularized French writing, it was thought that stream of consciousness meant primarily that: the author would sit down and let it all pour out. Analogous to that was the American writing done during the same time period where a writer on drugs would sit down and let it all pour out (sometimes onto the page and sometimes onto the floor or ceiling). But this form of writing is anything but hit and miss. A groundwork has to be laid for creating a respectable mind, in the sense that the thoughts, movements, needs and questions of the person being investigated have to fit together. Even where someone retarded or mentally unbalanced is being used as the vehicle, the internal thoughts have to yield an eventual consistency.

Word choice is also lacking from contemporary craft. There is the word choice where, for example, adjectives might be selected to so contrast with each other that they dramatize the noun being modified. Anatole France was a master at that. Word choice can also dramatize the character, in that the words selected appear to be beyond the normally expected ken of the character and thereby expand his dimensions, often into symbol or allegory. As Joyce did with Leopold Bloom.

But all of these quests, ranging from developing a facile knowledge of grammar to etymology, are frowned upon today unless you happen to be a South American who lives in a cave and is blind, but still intelligent enough to have a good PR man and one of the top agents in the world.

Scholarly Nonfiction

Scholarly nonfiction has publish or perish as its driving force, thereby yielding a number of sophisticated books and articles that no sane person would want to read unless an insomniac. This is not writing, but a political statement.

The main point about the trick of scholarly nonfiction is that the vast bulk of it has to do with the author analyzing a body of work left behind by someone else, or analyzing and responding to another academic's critique of that author's initial work on this dead person's body of work. Much as tax and trust and estates lawyers insistently lobby Congress to change the applicable codes so that they can generate additional income rewriting wills, trusts, and W-4 forms, academics lobby the publishing world to come out with the posthumous literary revisions of a Faulkner or Joyce.

Other than literary criticism, scholarly nonfiction has ups and downs based not upon what is needed in the world of knowledge, but what the marketers perceive as salable. If you attend college and take a course in physical anthropology, for example, and note that the copyright date of your text is 1950, there is a reason for that. Enrollment is down for physical anthropology, many universities are divesting themselves of the department, and so recent developments are relegated to the small run university press or the dry, scholarly, low circulation journals.

Trade Nonfiction

Non-scholarly scholarly nonfiction is nonfiction written by a supposed expert who actually has a Ph.D. or medical degree, although the book is probably not in the same field as the degree. The trick here is to convince the reader that he is actually learning something which is TRUE. In other words, the book is quotable at cocktail parties and, since it is TRUE, the citation can be used to put down someone you don't like in front of a lot of people who respected him until he could not refute the quote.

Since these books are only tricks, they can often lead to a deadly embarrassment if the contents are advisory. An example would be following the advice of a book on bettering one's marriage written by a social worker; another would be dieting in the manner prescribed by a doctor whose degree is in something like pediatrics.

Trade nonfiction uses the trick of convincing a reader that a non-expert is an expert. We are supposed to believe that a feminist can reconstruct the life of Marilyn Monroe more truthfully than a male chauvinist pig or the photographer who took her early or last photographs. And vice versa. Or that someone who has run for a couple of years knows about running (even if he drops dead after publication).

More, unlike fiction which incorporates a historical or public figure, these kinds of nonfiction are supposed to "accurately reconstruct" conversations for everyone from Adam and Eve to John Kennedy. On top of their words, we are told how they felt, what their bowel movements were like, and what their psychological hang-ups were.

Nonetheless, these forms of nonfiction are the easiest to get published. How-to books and biographies are particularly popular. However, a legal problem concerning biographies could well undercut some of that market; recent cases have fudged the issue of how much or what can be quoted from the personal correspondence of the person being written about. These cases have resulted in a number of biographies being completely rewritten prior to publication, with quotes from letters being slimmed down into the pablum of the paraphrase.

One other aspect of this kind of nonfiction is that it often lends itself to coffee table format. These are the big, weighty, heavily illustrated books which are renowned for being immediately discounted from the suggested retail price of $80 to a sale price of $25. The text, if any, in these books is usually ignored by the reader, who will instead study the illustrations, particularly if they are of Marilyn Monroe (who holds the record for coffee table books). The book can then be used to hold open doors.

Poetry

Poetry is brevity. Experimentation. Use of   Space. Ten cents a l i n e
or
rhythm
sometimes
and sometimes

not.

Poetry, like fiction, used to be a sophisticated art. Rhythm has been replaced with the use of redundancy, as in using the same word over and over again to create a sense of motion. Atmosphere is also established in a redundant manner. Poems, too, suffer from an inundation of sex. Dark tunnels; legs updown updown; nudes in the water; algae glistening in the moon. Still, poetry, because it is the poor man's art form, strives to retain a certain pretension that regular writing long ago lost.

A Safe Summary

A summary of this chapter comes down to this: to increase your chance of publication, write like everyone else who has published. As will be seen, editors do not like to be surprised. They do not like to be the first to publish in an area which has been ignored by other houses. They do not like having to *think* their way through a manuscript (or screenplay). Selecting the lowest common denominator of repetition is the key to success.

CHAPTER SIX

AGENTS

Classes Of Agents

The wonderful world of publishing (in the big times) is like every other wonderful world: you can't get there from here. You need contacts. If you don't have relatives in the business, or a great deal of money, or a perfect figure, or a con man's easy talk, then you need an Agent. An Agent is a person who has contacts and whom you pay for the privilege since you do not have contacts.

Agents are supposed to serve two purposes. One is to screen materials so that the appropriate proposal plus sample chapter, or the completed manuscript, reaches the editor or script editor who is at that moment desperately attempting to fill his list.

The second is to protect the house or studio from lawsuits premised on plagiarism or copyright infringement where the submission is rejected but appears two years later as a film or book -- by someone else.

There are four classes of agents. One class charges you for an initial reading by a staff member. Another class charges you for an initial reading accompanied by "editorial" comments.

What either of these activities for a fee has to do with being an agent is beyond me. The definition of an agent is "a person authorized by another to act for him." (Black's Law Dictionary.) The purpose of having an agency relationship is to promote a personal or business interest. Paying a fee to someone prior to entering into or as part of the agency relationship is absurd; these people are not agents, but freelance editors or yentas.

But if you want to follow that route, you deserve preliminary information from the agency. What is the exact fee, to the last digit? What exactly will you get for the fee? Who will be reading the manuscript? Is that fee refunded in the event the agency takes on the book? What is the placement success rate for the agency?

A third class does not charge for the initial read and may even take you on, although their efforts on your behalf will be somewhat hit-and-miss. This group is composed of those agents who are just starting out and who want to build a stable. They will take on unknowns in the hope that one of the unknowns will make the agent rich and famous. But these agents often have the wrong business address or a lack of funds which makes placement more difficult.

The last class is the established agency. These agencies do not accept unsolicited manuscripts and do not charge fees for reading; generally, they will not provide editorial comments. The manuscript is either taken on or returned.

Although most of these agencies are small, with from one to five agents and as many agent assistants, some are huge international corporations with the power to make a writer into a known author, commentator, tv personality and tap dancer.

Agency Listings

Most literary representatives (a euphemism if ever there were one) have offices in New York City and Washington, D.C. Most teleplay and screenplay agents have offices in Los Angeles/Hollywood/Culver City, California. By the way, if you can't figure out why that is so, perhaps you should cease writing immediately.

There is a society known as the Society of Authors' Representatives which publishes a list of member agents. The requirement for membership is simple: $250,000 annual property sales. A perk is that members get to fly to exotic places once a year for a "conference," much like doctors and lawyers. Other sources for finding agents are the *Literary Market Place*, published annually by R.R. Bowker and, like most of its publications, costing a small fortune. To be listed in the *LMP*, an agent must prove activity by providing Bowker with three names of editors. The annual *Writer's Market*, published by *Writer's Digest Books* (and why is the apostrophe before the s, instead of after it?), also lists agents.

Those two publications additionally list publishing houses, names of editors, and other pieces of data essential to being an author -- with one problem. A large percentage of the information is out-of-date by the time it reaches you. In this business, it seems that everyone moves at least six times a year.

On the film and television side, Celebrity Service, Inc., located in New York City, publishes an annual *Celebrity Contact Book* which includes a listing of agents for teleplays and screenplays.

Getting A Class IV Agent

Approaching a Class IV agent is much like approaching an employer for a freelance project or an editor for a major project. If you have no proper form of introduction, as in So and so suggested I write to you, then you have to generate interest in a letter or by a phone call.

Your best bet is to place a telephone call, one which you have perhaps practiced first on your dog or parakeet. You have to act and sound like a professional. And concentrate on only one project. Make sure it is marketable.

In the chapter on freelance writing, it was stated that ninety percent of your effort would be in selling yourself and your work, and not in writing. The same here. Agents handle the "big stuff"; you will not be promoting freelance material, university press material, short stories, or poems. You need to have the entire manuscript if you are unpublished in the trade market; a proposal and a sample chapter are sufficient if you have published. But you need an angle.

Staking Out A Market

Knowing a market means going to bookstores and seeing the arrangement of books; following advertisements for those books houses believe will sell well; following best seller lists; joining some book clubs to find out what they select as primary selections of the month; subscribing to weeklies such as *Variety* (for film) and *Publisher's Weekly* (for books); watching *Entertainment Tonight*, *Lifestyles of the Rich and Famous*, and *The Benny Hill Show*. You also have to take fads into account. For example, the early 1980's were not bad times for paperback humor publications, but 1984-1985 became a bad year because of the glut which developed from the prior, successful years. You would not have called up an agent in early 1985 declaring that you had just written the premier humor book.

There are two rules of thumb in the literary marketplace. The popular nonfiction market tends to be easier to break into, which means it is easier to attract the interest of an agent. The popular fiction market is easier to break into with 1) horror or mystery;* and 2) an autobiographical work where some of the characters are iden-tifiable to anyone reading *People* magazine.

In the motion picture/major studio marketplace, finding an agent means "remak-ing" classics from the 1940's by adding sex scenes; drafting sequels; writing a film which is exactly like a recently successful film (teens rebel in repressed town; monsters take over house; aliens invade planet); or writing about an event which will occur in about three years (such as a bicentennial of some event or famous person's birth or death). A screenplay written solely as a star vehicle usually requires that the star is available and has given an OK to the project.

Teleplays are almost impossible to place because production companies have in-house staff (all union), and a series is plotted out well in advance of shooting and airing. The only value of a teleplay is to convince the production company that you might be useful as an employee.

When you place your telephone call to the agency, you will have before you an outline and, in your mind, a pithy statement, including a brief hyperbolic biography.

---

* Sci. fi used to be a good market. Beginning in 1987, even sci. fi. editors started imposing the same Catch-22 used in other genres. Yes, we would love to see a sci. fi. manuscript, sci. fi. is a great market, send it along -- but only if it is by an author already published in the sci. fi. field. That rule holds true even where the author has published other, non-sci. fi. fiction.

The object is to persuade the receptionist that you need to get through to the agent specializing in the specific area you have selected, e.g., science fiction screenplay, trade American history, etc. Whether or not you get through to the agent, you need to have a name. Letters sent to an agency per se (or a house or studio) go into a slush pile much like unsolicited manuscripts, and are maintained in a damp corner until they turn into mulch used in the suburban gardens of the people you hoped to reach.

Packaging

Assuming you do get a name, the next step is the "package." As with anything from toothpaste to cars, writing is packaged when one wishes to sell it. Your cover letter should be brief and beautifully typed on rag content, water bonded, embossed stationery. Opening sentence: "Pursuant to [our conversation, my conversation with your office], I am enclosing [a proposal and sample chapter; an outline and complete manuscript; a synopsis or script treatment; a screenplay] for your consideration." New paragraph. Up to three sentences on the proposal. "X" -- always pick a tentative title -- "is a [nonfiction, fiction] work about [description]." One sentence on why it is exciting. A brief and extremely important paragraph on why it is marketable.

Since safety and marketability are synonymous, this paragraph should refer to works which have already been successfully marketed. *Never* say that your work is new, different, innovative, arty, literary or experimental. Always say that your work is *like*, or will *appeal to the same audience as*. You can look up facts and figures in *Publisher's Weekly* or *Variety* to add to the feeling of safety.

If you have the knowledge, you might embellish your marketing analysis with a production breakdown. This is particularly relevant to a house with regard to illustrated works, because four-color reproductions require a different press run and paper. In your case, you can "help" the agent in his decision by pointing out that most of the color illustrations could be done as black-and-white; or that it can be printed abroad where costs are lower, since most of the book is illustrated.

Screenplays are a somewhat more complicated budgeting matter. Agents and major studios are locked into working with high budget films. Every fifty million dollar fiasco generates yet another fifty million dollar fiasco; the average budget for a studio film is almost twenty million dollars. It's best to omit budget comments at the inquiry level.

The final paragraph should be no more than three sentences on yourself and your writing career. "After receiving my MA in writing from X University, I became a freelance writer and have over two hundred publications to my credit."

Go through every agent you can. Just remember that even as the years pass, you must state that the manuscript was recently completed. Never write: " ... a manuscript I completed three years ago (and which has been rejected by everyone else)."

Copyright Dilemma

The dilemma here is that if you have actually copyrighted the work, you are supposed to include the date of copyright. Even if you haven't officially copyrighted the work, the date the work was completed is the date when your copyright right vests. Writers therefore either omit the copyright date, or "update" it each year. Screenwriters usually ignore copyright altogether, relying on the supposed protection of registering a script with the Director's Guild (a route I do not advise; a copyright is still the best protection for any writing).

Submission

In the event an agent does want to see the manuscript, ensure that it is perfect. Presenting a manuscript means meeting trade format requirements. All manuscripts will have a title page; chapters must be clearly marked; pagination should be successive (the agent needs to know how many pages there are). The point size (the size of the type) should be 12 points for text, 14 for chapter headings beginning each chapter, and 10 for footnotes. Justified, double-spaced paragraphs are preferred over jagged, single-spaced paragraphs. For nonfiction, sample illustrations should be included, and a list of illustrations, charts and graphs placed after the table of contents. Nonfiction works should also have a bibliography and footnotes (although for trade nonfiction, footnotes should be kept to a minimum). Manuscripts intended for publication should be unbound; screenplays should be bound.

THERE SHOULD BE NO TIPOS NOR GRAMATICAL ERRERS!!! Typos and grammatical errors imply that the writer cannot write or cannot take the time to read over his own manuscript. Perhaps you have this intense belief that you can whip out something in one draft and that it *must* be perfect because it *feels* perfect. As Warner Wolf would say, Give me (and other agents) a break! If you can't face a manuscript right away, let it sit in a drawer for half a year. Then take it out and reread it, slowly. Mark it up. Don't send the marked up manuscript. Retype it. Let that draft sit for six months. Reread it. Don't send that one either.

And don't trust computer spell checkers. First, they don't proof for grammatical errors or style. Second, all they do is check recognized words. If you typed "more" intending "moor," the speller is not going to suggest that the word is out of context.

There are twenty million self-proclaimed writers out there, sending out hundreds of thousands of manuscripts a year into a marketplace which is more oligopolistic than competitive; the least you can do is send out something that looks clean. (Remember *A Hard Day's Night*, when Paul's father was always getting into trouble? The tag line was, "He's clean." Please, please be clean.)

If you are using a computer, inserting corrections is the easiest activity in the world and much more pleasant than spending holidays with in-laws. You can experiment with the various gimmicks your program might provide. You can have headers which state the title of the book on odd pages, and the chapter number and date of print-out on even pages. Page numbers can be centered on the bottom of the page. You will be able to select the point sizes mentioned previously (most typewriters will be unable to do that), and type families: bold, italic, normal, bold italic; and a font such as Times Roman. For nonfiction manuscripts, you can include line numbers (which would be for the editor's sake, not the agent's).

But don't abuse the freedom a computer might offer. Don't use only italics; don't use only helvetica (a stodgy, thick type face which looks like stifflegged troops marching to battle after a while); don't cram every piece of information you can into headers or footers; don't use bullets indiscriminately.

The most presentable print-out from a computer is by laser printer. If you use a dot matrix printer, double-strike and then have a copy xeroxed in the "darker" mode. (As will be seen later, agents and editors are usually fifteen years behind the time, and dot matrix submissions are frowned upon, if not utterly rejected). The title page

---

THINGS TO WATCH OUT FOR WITH AGENTS

1. Unexpected reading fees.
2. Unexpected editing fees.
3. Fees for expenses: postage, xeroxing, mailers, messengers.
4. Commission surcharges, such as for the placement of a book abroad or the exploitation of other ancillary rights.
5. The agent who sends out your book indiscriminately until every editor in the world blacklists you.
6. The agent who never sends out your book.
7. The agent who decides to become a writer by writing a book similar to the one he is handling for you, not sending yours out until his is placed and then telling you that yours has little chance of succeeding because there is too much competition in the market.
8. The agent who never returns your telephone calls.
9. The agent who never forwards accounting statements to you and who retains royalty checks for inordinate periods of time.
10. The agent who does not give you letters from editors concerning submissions of your work.
11. An agent who does not understand your field of expertise, particularly if it is computers.
12. An agent who keeps prodding you to write a mystery novel while blowing cigar smoke in your face.

---

should include the title, your name (or your a/k/a), a blurb (the one or two line description of the book placed within quotation marks), a copyright statement, and then your name, address and phone number.

Always mail your submissions by either UPS (which includes $100 in insurance for "free") or express delivery mail. For UPS, use a mailer with plastic bubbles inside since it will lend some protection to the manuscript and not shed paper fill when stripped open. Enclose a similar mailer with stamps already on it. Next-day-delivery

---

THINGS NOT TO DO WITH AN AGENT

1. Ask for money before anything has been placed.
2. Turn in unproofed manuscripts on yellowed paper.
3. Mail him everything you've written from age three on.
4. Call him at eleven o'clock Saturday night.
5. Call him at seven o'clock Sunday morning.
6. Refuse to follow standards of English grammar.
7. Hang around his office.
8. Threaten suicide, cry, remove your clothes, show up at lunch time, or make threats.
9. Start referring everyone in your neighborhood to him.
10. Claim that a nonfiction manuscript is fiction, or vice versa.

---

mail is more impressive, and this is a profession where impressions count for a great deal.

Do not make multiple submissions to name agents. Just as editors gossip freely, agents talk to each other at their annual meetings in Hawaii and if you inundate agencies you will end up blacklisted or at least in a doghouse. The only time you should use multiple submissions is where the agent understands it will be a multiple submission, but even that is not something you would do initially. Give the agent three months to review your proposal and/or manuscript and then in the follow-up letter or telephone call, state that if he has still not gotten to your work, perhaps you should submit it to others. The agent will state either that he will get to it within the month, or that you should go ahead and submit it to others.

You should be aware that agents, like editors, dwell with their own sense of humor on the people they rejected who later made it big. The fact is that agents (and editors) have absolutely no idea about what is good or bad, but do have a sense as to what they consider marketable.

Thus, the writer who has the acknowledged masterpiece he spends fifteen years trying to publish and who finally meets an agent who states, over the telephone, that he only handles "masterpieces," will rush over the manuscript. The agent reads the first and a few other pages, nods sagely, and says, "You know, you do have a masterpiece here. But we did not understand each other. What I mean by master-piece is 'best seller.' I thought you had written a good mainstream novel. Sorry."

In a similar vein, another writer got through the door to a high powered agency on the basis of his expertise in computers. He had with him outlines for sophisticated books on software development and use. The agency explained that it had thought he was one of those writers who could churn out computer manuals in weekly spurts that are based upon the user's guides accompanying systems and that include sample "programs" which are incompatible with the systems written about.

Another story involves the writer who was picked up by a famous agency based upon his literary work, which was never pushed. Five years later, the author asked the agent handling him why none of his material was ever sent out, and the agent said, "You see, we were hoping you would write a mystery novel in the meantime."

So here, too, as was pointed out in a prior chapter, you must hide any sophistication you have and speak to the lowest common denominator.

Agency Rejections

Before getting to an analysis of what happens should an agent accept you, consider what you should do if agents start rejecting you. The next chapter discusses editors, and you should certainly continue to send proposals to editors, using the guidelines established here for agents. A rejection by an agent should not discourage you. Like editors at houses and script editors at studios, agents have "lists." Most specialize and fulfill the needs of certain editors, who have their own "lists." Agents and editors have absolutely no concept of literature, nor are they intended to. They are movers, not intellects. They follow markets. Similarly, for you to succeed, first as a freelance writer, then as an author, you must understand market influences and distance your writing from the writing you can sell.

If you are rejected by everyone and everything, including your spouse, you might consider a Class I or II agent, consoling yourself with the thought that you are paying for the privilege of saying, "It's at my agent's," or you might investigate self-publishing, or subsidized or coop publishing; for screenplays, you could turn to the independent production houses (all of which will be discussed in later chapters). But take another look at your "market." Are you following the acceptable style? Have you selected a viable market? Is your cover letter precise and persuasive? Is your outline or proposal to the point? Do you replace spoiled pages with new pages?

MANUSCRIPT FORMAT

For all manuscripts:

1) Text -- 12 point Times Roman (if possible); justified, double-spaced paragraphs.

2) Footnotes -- 10 point; justified, single-spaced paragraphs; same page separated from text by a .5 or 1 point line of approximately 2.5 inches from left margin.

3) Outside margins -- 1 inch inside (left), .75 inch for remaining three margins.

4) Headers -- .5 inch from top, alternating pages with book title, then chapter number (and date of print-out optional).

5) Footers -- centered pagination at .5 inch from bottom, 4.25 inches from left.

6) Title on title page, chapter headings at start of each chapter -- 14 point bold (if possible); otherwise, all caps.

For nonfiction, add:

1) Table of Contents.

2) List of charts, graphs, illustrations.

3) Include sample charts, graphs, illustrations.

4) Sample bibliography and appendices.

For screenplays:

1) Follow format with regard to use of Continued, More, CUT TO, INT. (short for interior), EXT. (short for exterior), DAY, NIGHT, ANGLE (but do not get carried away with camera angles; that's left to the director and cameraman). For example, the header will be "Continued:" at the upper left; new scene may start: "INT., KITCHEN -- DAY -- NEW ANGLE"; then a line or two describing what is happening ("MARY hurriedly approaches TOM, who is leaning against the kitchen counter, eating a bagel."); then two blank lines to TOM centered, and beneath that, the left/right indented monologue (without quotation marks). If the monologue continues onto the next page, end page with MORE at lower right; otherwise, CONTIN-UED.

2) After title page, include Synopsis, List of Primary Characters, List of Secondary Characters with Speaking Roles, List of Non-Speaking Extras, and Settings.

Agency Acceptance

If by odd chance you are accepted by an agent (for reasons which you will never know for sure until years later), you must find out from the agent what he charges. An agent lives on commissions. Currently, commissions are at ten to fifteen percent for domestic sales and twelve percent and up for foreign sales. A fifteen percent average would be acceptable. Commissions should be straightened out before you commit yourself to an agent, or he to you. If the agent does not put the scale into a letter addressed to you, you should confirm the scale by telephone followed up by a letter to the agent stating the rates as you understand them and asking for a confirmation if the agent's understanding differs from yours. If the agent wants more than that, try to find another agent or continue sending letters to publishing houses on your own. Or, make sure that it is understood that you are placing only the one book with the agent (which will mean two, because the publishing agreement will contain an option on your next book), and if that does well, you will find it less difficult jumping to another agent. Never, never have a personal relationship with an agent unless he or she becomes a lover, or has placed more than two works for you.

You should also find out and have in writing, if possible, what the agent will do for you for that commission. Pay for xeroxing? Postage? Mailers? Editorial comments? Messenger service? Those four martini lunches with editors? Or do all those expenses get charged against your account -- and perhaps directly against you in the event a manuscript is not placed?

If the agent charges a low commission, he will probably require that you provide as many xerox copies as he needs, while he covers postage, mailers, taxis and lunches. But a number of writers have told me of this common experience: it was their understanding that there would be no charges, but once the book was placed, the agent sent a bill listing every cost imaginable, including telephone calls and legal fees (since he had consulted with an attorney). Since the agent received the advance, he took it upon himself to deduct his commission and all expenses prior to sending both the bill and an advance statement. Needless to say, these authors never saw a cent.

You may also not want the agent to handle all of your works. One example would be where you write both trade and scholarly works, and you want to place the latter yourself. Or you might want to divvy up your work between agents who specialize in certain areas, giving your high-tech material to one, and your general trade to another; or, similarly, having one agent handle books, and another screenplays.

Agents themselves generally do not like handling scholarly nonfiction, short stories, or poetry. The reasons are simple. The scholarly presses have scholarly editors, and agents cannot be bothered with knowledge. The short story and poetry market is severely limited; only a few magazines pay well, and the literary journals, which do not pay, impose severe constraints on when manuscripts can be submitted (such as between noon September 15 and 2 p.m. September 16). Of course, if you should end up making money from any of those avenues, the agent's interest will suddenly pique.

What you should have clear with the agent is just what the commission covers with regard to ancillary or subsidiary right sales. For example, are book club sales, paperback sales, and movie sales covered by the commission even if the publishing house handles all of those? With regard to movie sales, are subsidiary rights, such as rights to sell t-shirts bearing the name of a character, also rights covered by the commission structure? What about ancillary video or software sales? How does the commission change (upward) if the agent uses "sub-agents" for foreign translation sales?

Moreover, since the commission is supposed to cover the agent's job as your "accountant" in the sense that agents serve as conduits for royalty checks from the publishing house, does the commission rate change if you contract with the publisher so that the royalties are not sent directly to the agent? After all, there are some valid reasons for doing this. First, you get the float from the check, as opposed to the agent, who will hold onto the check until it clears and then send you your cut. Second, you might be afraid that your royalties will be in some manner attached if, when they are in the possession of the agent, the agent or another of his authors becomes a judgment debtor and the agent maintains only a general bank account. Third, you might be afraid that the agent will not account in an above-board fashion, a possibility that does occur from time to time in real life. Fourth, you save yourself the embarrassment of bursting into the crowded waiting room of your agency and announcing loudly that Ms. Agent has a check waiting for you, only to be told (also loudly), that Ms. Agent will not be back from lunch and no one knows where the check is.

Further, if the agent is acting as your collector of royalties, does that mean the agent will assume the responsibility of having an accounting performed at the publishing house in the event of discrepancies? And will the agent pay for that? Or you?

Another point is that most agents do not represent you in a legal capacity; they are merely people who know people who know people and who are supposed to get your manuscript read. They will not advise you on your legal rights or negotiate a contract for you -- and wait until you get that bill from a "recommended" attorney.

Some agents do state that they will negotiate a contract for you, but if they are not attorneys, I would not suggest that course. Oddly enough, certain agents have been permitted to negotiate contracts -- what they do is cross out lines and staple on xeroxes of pre-approved forms -- even though the practice of law by a non-lawyer is prohibited by state law (due to lobbying by the various bar associations). Why someone like Rosemary Furman, that Florida secretary who put out low cost legal forms, should be sentenced to jail for the illegal practice of law, while agencies openly practice the negotiation of contracts without prosecution is one of the mysteries of life.

One thing I can say from experience is that *most agents only care about the size of the advance, and that it should be paid as soon as possible -- to them.* They will twist arms, shout, cry, and throw tantrums to ensure that the advance is paid, at best, upfront, or, at worse, in two installments (half upfront, the rest upon acceptance of the final manuscript). The only clause which will lead to the same antics is the one declaring that the agent is agent for the Author (sometimes going so far as to declare that the agency relationship is perpetual and forever and cannot be ended until the universe explodes and is not recreated), and that all money is to be paid by the publisher directly to the agent.

Otherwise, agents scream "hoo-hah." You want to insert wording protecting your copyright pursuant to various international treaties and conventions? *Hoo-hah*, the publishers know what they are doing. You want to negotiate a different royalty schedule, or limit a distribution territory? *Hoo-hah*, the publishers will never go along with that. You want your book to be the lead book when released? *Hoo-hah*, whoever heard of such a thing. You only want to sell the hardcover trade rights, and not the trade or mass paperback rights? *Hoo-hah*, all publishers now take trade hardcover and paperback rights, and sometimes mass paperback rights. You want to ensure that your rights and accrued royalties are protected in the event the publisher is bought out or files for bankruptcy? *Hoo-hah*, don't bother with that, those things never happen. You want to provide that major revisions be done by you or someone of whom you approve, and that in any event your name will remain the name on the revised work? *Hoo-hah*, only an idiot would argue over something like that.

Agents, pushed to the wall on those changes, will sometimes go further and say either that further negotiation will result in a rejection, or that no such clauses exist.

You should get a written confirmation as to what occurs in the event you drop the agent or he drops you. The typical arrangement is that if an editor contacted by the agent picks up the book after your relationship with the agent is terminated, the agent will receive his fee. But that is for domestic house sales; you should retain the subsidiary rights.

Similarly, if you have placed the book with an editor prior to the time when the agent picks you up and that editor buys the manuscript, you should get all the domestic sales' fees, but you can offer the agent movie, paperback and foreign sales' commissions.

To repeat, it is important for these matters to be in writing -- either a writing from the agent to you and signed by the agent, or from you to the agent stating that it represents your agreement and if the agent feels differently he should write to you -- since agent/writer relationships are otherwise oral. In all cases, the agent/writer relationship should be terminable at the will of either party at any time.

Agency Action (?)

Of course, all of the above, once straightened out, does not mean that it will get you anywhere. You are still an "unknown" with regard to the big market, and the agent is not really going to pay that much attention to your work. As will be seen in the chapter on publishing, editors need to be wooed, prodded, tickled, wined and dined.

And agents need to be prodded and cajoled just as much as editors (after all, many agents are former editors). I could recite a hundred stories of top agents ignoring authors in their stables, not following up on submissions, letting books die, submitting manuscripts to houses where the editor had already said no over lunch, and not reading manuscripts in advance of submission thereby giving the wrong editor the wrong impression of the client.

Two of the worse cases involved direct competition and lack of knowledge. In the former instance, an author placed a how-to book with an agent and, as the months passed by, the author was told that the book was out but it didn't look promising. At the end of a year and a half, the agent promised to return the manuscript and the letters from editors to the author. Neither were forthcoming. Two and a half years from the date of acceptance of the work by the agent, the agent's own how-to book was published by a house that would have been a prime target for the author's similar manuscript. For some reason, the agent never was able to find the author's manuscript and all those letters from editors boiled down to one rejection letter from a house that had never carried a how-to book of that nature on its list.

An agent's lack of knowledge in an area is also something to worry about. Expertise is particularly necessary for topics such as technology. It is the agent who is the first presenter of a project, and if he garbles the topic completely, the editor, also lacking knowledge in the field, will merely tremble and shake his head until the awful thing is removed from his desk. Since the agent has to show the editor why that manuscript on some arcane machine or program is relevant and has an audience, he also has to know of what he speaks.

The point is that you have to assert your rights. The agent took you on and the agent must perform. Don't be afraid of alienating the agent and having him return all your manuscripts. He just wasn't doing the job to begin with. Moreover, just because the agent has your manuscript doesn't mean you should stop your market research. An example here is the author who handed over a nonfiction work which the agent lazily sent to three houses without prior investigation. Eight years later, the author withdrew the manuscript, submitted it to a house he had made contact with, and had the manuscript accepted within two weeks.

But you must also temper impatience with reasonableness. If the agent takes on one or two manuscripts, leave him alone for a few months. Do not start mailing everything you have in that green trunk to him. Overloading an agent or editor is the worse possible scenario. One thing at a time. And, in this business, everything takes time.*

A final point. If you do not have a large agency which will also handle your PR for you, hire a PR firm once a manuscript is accepted, whether or not the publishing house is going to provide some advertising. PR firms currently charge about one hundred dollars an hour, but the good ones can accomplish a lot in a short period of time. That means arranging for radio talk shows, television talk shows, and press releases in newspapers and magazines. Publicity means more for sales than anything else and it is an area requiring more expertise than being an agent or an editor. Which says something, one might surmise, about modern day life.

---

* At least, in this country it does. For example, a common timeframe from submission of a manuscript to its publication entails the passage of three or more years. But in England, the same process often occurs in six months!

CHAPTER SEVEN

EDITORS

From List To Stable

There are no great editors anymore; there are marketers.

In the old days, when a dime was a dime, editors existed who actually edited, took pride in their writers as individuals, and who followed through on a book from inception to release.

A writer today is part of an editor's "stable." He will often be labeled with a generalized stereotype: oh, he writes only pop fiction, or, she writes only restaurant guides by city.

Editors today do not want to discover anyone; they want to fill their seasonal list. If an editor can build up a stable which can output enough to fill the list, then the editor can concentrate on expanding both his stable and list. If the list does well, and if the stable is devoted, the editor can then threaten to leave his publishing house unless he is given a bigger office and cuter secretary. The threat is that he will take his stable with him.

Hi, ho Silver!

The writers an editor wants for his stable are people who have published before and are jumping ship from their stable. Second choice is famous people who have decided to tell all, as written by a hired freelancer. Third choice is anyone with yet more photographs of Marilyn Monroe. Fourth choice is those nonfiction writers who have not had trade publications, but who have published non-trade works which were given favorable reviews, and who can fill an open spot on a list. Fifth choice is a writer who has powerful contacts. At the bottom of the heap are fiction writers. Below that are poets.

Marketers

Today's editors are marketers. They want a list which makes money, and that means worrying about whether a book is marketable, whether the sales reps will push it, whether the bookstore chains will give it decent shelf space, and whether it will be successful in its price niche. The readability of the book is an issue for the design department. The impact of the book depends upon the jacket cover. The value of the book is purely economic. Commercial success is based on quantity, not quality.

As will be described below, this does not mean that editors never edit. But it does mean that responses from editors that go beyond a form letter invariably concentrate on the marketability of a work as opposed to its merit.

For example, one of the great editors was Hiram Haydn. One writer I know sent in a manuscript to Haydn when he was editor emeritus at Harcourt Brace. Haydn responded with a long single-spaced letter detailing the strengths and weaknesses of the manuscript and suggesting, quite civilly, that should the author believe that he, Haydn, had any insight into writing, perhaps the writer would consider revising the manuscript in a certain way. Haydn then went on with details and page references as to how the manuscript *could* be revised. As a closing, he said that if the writer agreed and made the revisions, he would be more than happy to consider it for publication.

The writer did make the revisions but, unfortunately, Hiram Haydn died the day the manuscript was finished. It was peremptorily rejected through a form letter from the Harcourt Brace "Editors" later on.

Obviously, editors will say that they are overwhelmed with work and that they cannot personally read or respond to every submission. But manuscripts do go through a winnowing process, and it seems odd that even for those few that do eventually get read by an editor, the most one can expect in response is a statement as to whether or not the book is considered commercial.

With some frequency, particularly with illustrated works, the decision is not even the editor's, but the production department's. The schizophrenia involved is astonishing. The editor, at first, will exhibit tremendous interest and excitement, and perhaps ask for numerous rewrites of the proposal. Then the editor will say the work is undergoing further review. Suddenly, the manuscript is returned with a note declaring that although the editor would love to do the book, production has pronounced the project too expensive.

I have also observed editors jump for joy when presented with a manuscript, declaring that they will give it their immediate attention and probably a favorable response, only to return it a month later with the comment that they thought the author was someone else, who was famous, and they had mistakenly confused the names.

In other instances, editors have held onto manuscripts for prolonged periods of time, always saying that they were still "struggling" over a decision. It turns out that the slippery decision involved whether the book would do better in a first hardcover or first paperback release. It seems that paperback houses ultimately decide that a work will do better as a first hardcover, while hardcover houses state that the book should be a first paperback.

Still, the final answer to most submissions hinges upon whether the work is perceived as "commercial." What that really means is, Has another house had success with this type of book? If everyone else is publishing how-to hammer books, then it is usually simple to place a how-to hammer book, until there is such a tremendous glut of those books that none of the books sells or is given shelf space. If no one is publishing books on the Ferbush Wars, then it will be almost impossible to place a book on the topic.

Technology books are a good example of how a market is suddenly recognized by trade publishers. Digital computers have been around since the late 1930's, but publications on what they were and did were left to the non-trade presses. In the early 1980's, micrcomputers made their appearance. Non-trade presses started to make money selling how-to books on the different computers.

Publishing houses are notorious for being behind the times. Most houses are not computerized, and no trade editor is an expert in technology. What many of these houses did to get onto the microcomputer bandwagon was to turn to so-called technology experts who were already in a stable, or published freelancers -- the kind of author who had previously been able to churn out simple how-to books, such as how-to tune an FM radio. The result was a slew of works which were supposed to detail how-to program on a variety of micro's. But almost none of those programs worked because the authors assumed that a programming language such as BASIC was the same for each micro, when it was not.

To make matters worse, some houses turned their attention to trying to monopolize the market for books on computers which had been announced by manufacturers but not yet released. As one example, a paperback house devoted a great deal of energy to getting out a book describing one home computer, even though it did not have access to the computer, could not test the programs, and industry experts felt that the system would probably not sell.

And the system did not sell, which meant that the book did not sell, and the house soured on trade computer books. As did many other houses, until something else was noticed -- MIT Press, which used to published only technical works, had begun to expand its list into the trade market. Technology books started to come back into favor.

A similar process evolved with regard to books for the homosexual market. Small, independent presses had been publishing gay and lesbian books for years, but their success had been hampered by restrictive distribution channels. Then everyone woke up one morning and discovered that even with poor sales' channels, the books had taken a ten percent chunk of the overall book market. Suddenly, editors from the large houses were raiding the stables of the small houses, homosexual lines were introduced, and editors started to come out of the closet.

Approaching an editor with general fiction by a non-trade published author is fruitless, since "marketing" has declared that people do not buy or read general fiction written by a non-trade published author. What that translates to is this: publishing houses have paid out such huge advances to known authors, there isn't much left in the kitty for unestablished writers, either for advances or promotion. The result, of course, is that the established writers, having a ton of money in the bank, either forget to write the contracted-for books, or turn in lousy books, much as a high-paid baseball player will suddenly start dropping balls and missing pitches. But an unestablished writer with contacts can still place his first novel for a huge advance.

Just as a large agency can make or break a writer, a publishing house can do the same. When those "unknowns" crop up with a book which is given an announced first printing of 150,000 or more, you know that the editorial marketing gears have been set into motion. There is no purported reliance on a marketing study here; the proof in the pudding is that houses can make the market. The large print run excites everyone in the business. The sales reps are excited because they get special incentives for ensuring that the book is given primary display space. The mass paperback houses and book clubs are excited because they know that with a first printing of that size, the hardcover house is going to push the book all the way. Since the size of the print run in itself is news, the media wants to interview the author right away. The major motion picture studio will want to pick up an option on producing the film.

In short, editors as marketers are the sound and fury requiring ear plugs. Some markets are based upon habit -- the housewife who picks up her potboiler, romance or gothic each week at the grocery store. Some markets are based upon what is currently newsworthy, whether it is a famous personality or a famous crime. And the rest can be created, whether it is a market for literary novels, literate nonfiction, or more pulp residue.

Specialty Editors And Excuses

If the above discourse has not disheartened you, it should have. Besides, none of the large houses will now accept a manuscript unless it is submitted by a reputable agency. The same goes for all major motion picture studios, most major videocassette distributors, and all major magazines. The exceptions are where you have contacts, or where you can create contacts (as by sending in the proposal letters discussed in the previous chapter). The alternative is to submit to literary magazines, independent motion picture companies or partnerships, the smaller, specialty presses, or to yourself (next chapter).

What is notable is that a writer might often discover that the specialty press is the *better* press. I like this kind of story: an author who was an expert in diabetes (published, on top of that), wrote another book on diabetes. It was hawked indiscriminately by one of the top agencies in the country. No response from the major houses. The agency ceased submitting. The book was brought to me. I had it rewritten, and then approached some of the majors myself. I pointed out that there were perhaps twenty million or more diabetics in this country alone, and many more worldwide. That it was a market which could be reached easily through the publications of the various diabetes foundations, and through direct mail. The response was, "But we have no experience marketing to diabetics." I then went to a specialty press, which picked up the book within the day. With that contract in hand, I started negotiating the licensing of ancillaries, again to distributors who had experience in the diabetes market. No complaints there.

But there are downsides, too. Some years ago, I sent a manuscript to a house specializing in lesbian publications. The author's pseudonym had been purposely selected to not give away his/her sex. The publisher called me a week later and waxed poetic about the book but, when I thought we were about to orally agree on a contract, she suddenly asked, "I assume the author is a woman, because we only publish women. Company policy." I explained that the name was a pseudonym and that I held the author's sex in confidence. The manuscript was returned.

If, in the case of fiction, the writing is exceptionally good, editors will often be averse to saying outright that the work is non-commercial; limiting the sex of the authors picked up for publication is one way, but a more common one is to classify the writing in a manner which declares it to be non-trade material. Editors will therefore say that a novel is "experimental," "overly allegorical," "overly satirical," "too dense," or "written too professionally."

Approaching An Editor

For those willing to try any route, listed below are some techniques which writers

---

THE VARIOUS ROUTES A MANUSCRIPT CAN TAKE

To the slush pile.

To a reader.

To an editor who turns it over to a reader who puts it on the slush pile.

To an editor who gives it to a reader who refers it to a new reader who loses it.

To inter-office mail where it ends up in the conference room being used as coasters.

To a reader who refers it back to the editor who gives it to another editor who refers it back to the original reader who refers it ...

To the slush pile.

To an editor who takes part of it home so that the manuscript can end up on two slush piles.

---

have conveyed to me as working a slight percentage of the time. Personally, I don't agree with many of them, which is a thought you could probably care less about.

Pseudonymous Agents. Using a pseudonym, you send a letter to a publishing house saying you are representing so-and-so (yourself under your writing pseudonym), you have this hot new property, but the author is currently traveling while working on the book, and the editor had better sign him up quickly before someone else gets him. You, as representative, state you are authorized to bind the writer to a contract, or that you are able to get the author's signature.

As a side note here, in many states, it is unlawful to conduct a business under a pseudonym without filing a certificate giving the pseudonym with a county clerk or some other official. But these laws generally have to do with conducting business in that county, and should not be applicable to doing business outside of your county and state. The underlying rationale for these statutes is to prevent someone using a pseudonym from becoming judgment proof, in the sense of stating you are XYZ Associates but, when the time comes for the unhappy party on the other side to sue you, it turns out XYZ Associates is not the real party in interest -- you are.

Writers, though, have always used pseudonyms and copyright forms have provisions for registering using a pseudonym. Banks will also generally permit the creation of accounts under an a/k/a, or also known as.

The conflicts among the above rights and liabilities is that the pseudonym statutes generally provide that you cannot use the name of a person unless it is your name. Thus, all the writers living in New York City, using pseudonyms that are personal names, and conducting business with New York City publishing houses, are arguably in violation of the New York State statute requiring registration -- but, they cannot register because they are using personal names that are not theirs.

If the PR tone of the letter is right and the subject sounds marketable, it is possible to get either a contract (although with a small advance, if any) or at least a nod from the editor saying send the work along when it is partially completed. This apparently succeeds once every two million tries, which is somewhat better odds than getting your first book published through normal channels.

Direct Outline. Another route is to provide an outline, or an outline and a sample chapter. As with agents, you should contact the publishing house first and get a name. But, again, precede this with a PR note of some sort and have a response. The purpose is to generate excitement and avoid having your work returned unopened or tossed onto a slush pile where it can disappear.

Ethnic Group. Ethnic groups come and go in terms of popularity with editors, so the third alternative is to state that you were climbing the mountains in some exotic South American country and came across an odd little fellow who had only a quill, ink and the rags on his back. This fellow lived in a cave and wrote marvelous stuff. You were able to enter into a contract with him to act as his representative and, since you are fluent in Spanish, you will also translate the work. However, you need a contract and an advance to permit you to finish the translation and to allow you to send some food to the impoverished writer in his cave.

Threatened Suicide. A common introductory letter is the suicide note. As one editor recalled, he was always being sent manuscripts to which the author had attached a razor and a note: "If you reject the enclosed, just send back the razor blade."

Literary Threat. A threat that positively will not work involves stating that if the editor does not read your work, you will toss all your work away. That is exactly what editors would like writers to do.

Coattails. The best letter has name dropping as its trade mark. "So-and-so [the recent Nobelist] suggested I write to you concerning my new work ..."

Impending Death. This sometimes works, as with R.G. Vliet, who, dying of cancer, obtained both an agent and a publishing contract, although he had apparently never published anything before in his life.

Actual Suicide. Suicide works if you have someone still alive with the devotion to the cause to pursue having your work published. This tactic once resulted in a Pulitzer Prize being awarded to an otherwise commonplace novel about hot dogs and passing gas. Unfortunately, an author can use this ruse only once (unless you are Shirley MacLaine).

Forged Letter of Recommendation. Curiously, this method was exposed with regard to a book entitled *Telling Right From Wrong*, written by a philosophy professor who wanted to be picked up by a large house as opposed to a university press. And the book was picked up, the fake letter exposed, the book rejected, and then picked up by another house because of the notoriety.

Famous Author Using Pseudonym Because of Flagging Sales. This was used successfully by Doris Lessing, who wrote two books under the name of Jane Somers. The reason given was to prove that unknown writers have difficulty being published and reviewed, but since Ms. Lessing's publishers apparently knew of the ruse and the escapade generated a tremendous amount of publicity, one might assume that the true rationale was to generate publicity and sales. On the other hand, some bestselling authors have used pseudonyms for the purpose of permitting two books to be published on the same list without eating into each other's sales. Stephen King does this, as one example.

Commit A Felony. A popular route to publication in the seventies and early eighties. The idea is to murder, rape or maim someone and then send thousands of letters out to writers, agents and editors. You are bound to find someone willing to adopt you as a protege. The problem is that the ruse has fallen into recent disrespect because all those published felons, released on parole, have then gone on to murder, rape or maim other people. Perhaps for the sake of a second volume.

Oddly enough, many of the prestige organizations that give writing awards now include a category for prisoner-writers. Unlike other writers, the prisoners can receive the stipend (usually $1,000 to $2,000), but for some reason miss out on the month-long stay at a writing camp.

Personality. The best chance for publication lies in being a personality, as opposed to being a writer. In this area, one would include the surrogate mother who "suddenly" changes her mind, the out-of-work model who has an affair with a politician, the politician who loses an election or has to withdraw because of an affair with an out-of-work model, the friend of the out-of-work model who happened to be at the trysts with a 35 mm camera, a video camera, a tape recorder and a stenographer, the evangelist caught with his pants down, or the Congressional staff member found with her clothes off or with her clothes on but stuffed with top secret papers.

Solicit the Editor. The safest, although the most expensive, route to publication. Agents and editors like to feel pampered, needed, sexually fulfilled and drunk. That is why they live in Los Angeles and New York, and not townships in states like South Dakota or Kansas. A working day is as follows: come into work at ten, putter about until noon, go out to lunch with a writer or agent, have a couple of drinks, become hilarious, chatter until three, stumble back to work at four, leave at five. During the summers, most houses shut down at four thirty Monday through Thursday, and are completely closed Friday. Of course, you can always pursue an editor to Fire Island, but you may not want to.

Again, regardless of the tack you take, downplay what you have written to a common denominator. You can also define the work so that it fits into an acceptable category, even though you know it is not in that category. For example, if your book has a murder in it, say it is a murder mystery. If there is a rape in it, say it is a potboiler. If there is a vision in it, specify that it is sci. fi. Never say that the book or story is an allegory, or is part of a trilogy.

The Desperate Wait

After a hundred ruses, phone calls and lunches, you may finally get a response. You send in a manuscript. Now is the time of waiting two to eighty thousand months. Unless you do want a posthumous publication, you have to follow up. You have to assume that you are a good writer, that there is a future for you somewhere, and the editor is, in a sense, someone working for you. After a month, call up the editor and say: "How are things? I wanted to make sure you had received my manuscript, "X." You have? Good. Read it yet? No? What's your timeframe?" And so on. If the editor becomes offended and sends back the manuscript by return mail that day, he had no intention of reading it to begin with. What is more likely to happen is that the editor will give it to a reader.

Now we have a new entity to contend with. If you believed that editors actually give manuscripts a first reading (where you are an unknown), you are wrong. There exists a class of people called "readers," although they will state to you that they are "editorial assistants." These people have BA's in English from relatively good schools and work for about five dollars an hour. Sometimes they are part of a publishing house's permanent staff, and sometimes they are freelancers. What they do is read a manuscript and fill out a one page form describing the book and stating what they do or do not like about it. It is that report that the editor reads.

If the book passes a reader and if the report passes the editor, the book will either go to a junior editor (i.e., a recently promoted reader) for a second read, and/or to marketing and production for analysis.

Another call to the editor is due after two months, at which point the manuscript should either be on its way back or on the junior editor's desk. This call is to find out what the initial reaction was. If the editor says it received a "favorable reaction," that means it has passed the reads.

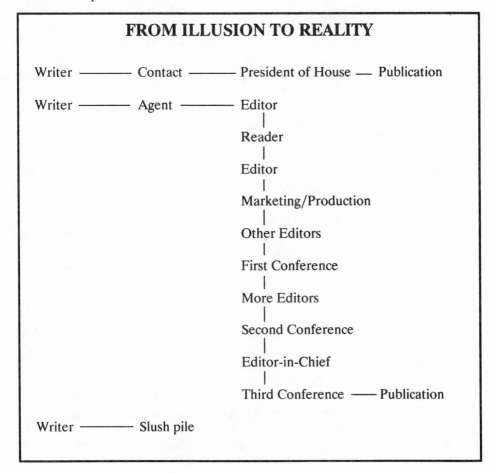

FROM ILLUSION TO REALITY

Writer ———— Contact ———— President of House — Publication

Writer ———— Agent ———— Editor
|
Reader
|
Editor
|
Marketing/Production
|
Other Editors
|
First Conference
|
More Editors
|
Second Conference
|
Editor-in-Chief
|
Third Conference ——— Publication

Writer ———— Slush pile

In the normal course, a manuscript's route will then be editor to marketing/ production, back to editor. If that report is positive, the editor will circulate the work to editors who owe him favors or seem predisposed toward the promoted project. Enough support at the first editorial conference will lead the editor to stick his neck out even further.

Editorial conferences on new submissions are held once a week. If feedback remains good by the second conference, the book might be referred yet again to production and marketing ("Can the market be expanded with little cost?" "What if we used that cheap glue on the binding?"). By the third conference, the senior vice president of the division, or the editor-in-chief will evince interest or lack of interest in the project either by staying awake during the final presentation, or falling asleep.

Editors at top-paying magazines are even more restrictive in their approach to a manuscript. Most magazines are overstocked with articles, short stories, poems and cartoons; those which pay are more than overstocked, they are basically impregnable. If the magazine not only pays but has its own stable, based upon following a defined style of writing (as *The New Yorker* once required), even the impregnable can't be wooed. Magazines, paying and "literary" (that is, non-paying and run by egomaniacs with visions), are so secure in their position that instead of sending form rejections to writers, they send subscription forms.

It is possible to break in with a new magazine, particularly in the nonfiction areas. The problem here is that to make a living, you will have to become a stringer for a number of magazines, writing travel articles for one, restaurant reviews for another, and the "Computer Tips" column for a third. These writers invariably start to burn out after a few years of scrambling and put their hopes into moving up to a decent magazine (unlikely), or in finishing their novel (which is unlikely to be placed).

Publication through a university press is usually an intensely political process. Although some of these presses have expanded their lists to include more trade-oriented works, the philosophy of these presses remains academic. Academia is a small world, and the presses even smaller.

What happens is that books are referred to readers, but these readers are supposed specialists in the field covered by a project. From one to five readers may be used for any field, and the odds are that the scholar submitting the work is despised by from one to three of them. Since the readers' comments are kept secret by the press, these professionals can solemnly stab whomever they want in the back. (The same situation occurs in academic and professional journals.)

This scenario means that a writer who researches and pens a scholarly work, but who is not a degreed entity, has very little if any chance of getting a work published by an academic press.

Perhaps worse than being mercilessly and secretly desecrated is that in many cases, certain readers will outright steal an author's findings. Then again, sometimes the author's findings are not his, but a graduate student's; there may be some inadvertent justice in the cycle.

Poetry, books of short stories, and some novels have historically fleshed out an academic press' list, but on the whole, it seems that these works were first published in the university's journals and magazines and, on the whole, it seems that the authors -- professors of writing and literature at the university -- are women and the editors-in-chief, men.

Screenplays and teleplays are also reviewed by readers, who refer works to script editors or story coordinators. Teleplays, as pointed out, are just about impossible to place because story lines are generated in advance of the season by in-house staff. Screenplays which pass the script editor are usually fielded out to one of the independent production companies which have a requirements' contract with the studio. Those are the independents formed by producers or directors who had some success on films while working directly for the studio, by studios and pay-cable companies which have formed joint ventures or limited partnerships, and by major stars. A screenplay will then go through the same procedure of reader to script editor and perhaps to director where, in most cases, the screenplay will be lost.

The Specialty Trade Reader

Like academic presses, trade houses will sometimes refer a manuscript to an outside reader who is a "trade professional" in the field, or who has his own imprint with a house. A book on mathematics which has trade possibilities will be referred to someone who supposedly knows about trade mathematics. A personality book (gossip) will be referred to a person who is also a personality. Science fiction books are inevitably fielded out for review, and most of the reviewers lend their names to the houses' line of sci. fi.

Although houses usually have only one reader per field, the reader's decision is the final one. If you know that your manuscript is the type to be sent to one of these readers, you should find out who the reader is and study his or her preferences, which means books that reflect the reader's philosophy of style and grace.

Acceptance

I have already discussed stables, lists, marketing and production in the context of rejections. The converse should therefore be that a manuscript is accepted because the editor has taken a liking to you and wants you as part of his stable (an unlikely rationale), the editor needs to fill his list and your book fits the marketing/

production bill, or corporate headquarters of the conglomerate has declared that some loss leaders are necessary for tax purposes, and your book has been selected to die.

There are times when a writer will never know why a book was accepted. A few years ago, a major house published a novel which had not even been contracted for -- the author discovered her good fortune by reading an advertisement for the book in a newspaper. But that is better than the book which is verbally accepted and then two or more years pass prior to its being returned. What has happened here is that an editor might have decided that the book fits his list, but the book was nixed at the final conference. He nonetheless continues fighting for the book. Or the editor is considering leaving the house and wants a backlog of acceptable books to take to a new house. Or the editor at the end of each season keeps coming across a book which is, to him, even more suitable to his lists than yours -- which he hangs onto anyway.

An author will never know whether his book has been selected as a loss leader until after publication, when the book vanishes from the sight and mind of the house. An author in this situation is left with his dozen free copies and the impression that the world is, indeed, an odd place for a writer.

Contractual Negotiations

But the time has come where you have finally received an offer in the mail. Magazines typically do not provide written contracts, relying instead on the industry practice of purchasing first serial rights. Editors always say, "If you want to reprint or excerpt from the work, just send a note to our Rights' Department and they'll mail a release." The requirement is that the reprint note that the work was first published in the magazine.

The absurdity is that, since the policy is to let rights return to the author, there is no reason to add the additional step(s) of having an author request an assignment. It would be a hell of a lot simpler to have a one page form setting forth the policy.

The reason for this assignment of rights, by the way, is because magazines usually insist on copyrighting everything appearing in an issue through the use of a single copyright notice.

Screeenplays are often optioned, which means that the production company pays a fee to have exclusive rights to consider producing the film during a defined period of time. If the option is exercised within that timeframe, a previously negotiated production agreement automatically goes into effect. Here, too, the author yields his copyright rights. Chapter Eleven discusses these issues further.

A publishing house contract is a neatly printed form which shouts out, "Don't touch!!" But take a close look at some of the rights you may be giving up, such as the copyright.

80

Copyright. Ownership of the copyright in the work means control over exploitation of the work, unless other arrangements are contracted for. After a rather long period of time has passed, and your death, your heirs can break that type of contract, but it involves an exchange of nasty letters and notices given to the Copyright Office and all the sorts of things your heirs don't want to be involved in.

The point is, there is no point in not owning the copyright in your name and then parsing out licenses as required. Most houses will now automatically register the copyright in the author's name, but just as automatically license back to themselves every right under the copyright.

Almost every nation has its own copyright procedures, which has led to the enactment of a variety of international treaties and conventions. The United States participates in some (such as the Universal Copyright Convention and the UCC revised), but not others. Strangely enough, many agents and editors are not aware of the international nature of copyright protection, even though foreign sales are a large enough portion of total sales to warrant some attention. The standard clause often states that a copyright will be taken out in the author's name, and nothing more. Adding that the copyright will be taken out pursuant to law and to applicable treaties and conventions shouldn't be a stumbling block.

Best efforts clause. This clause is usually not included in a first book contract, although you can always claim that it is implied in the contract. What it would say is that the publishing house will use its best efforts to promote the book. Stuff can be put in there in terms of what that means: full page ads in national newspapers; submission to writing contests and award competitions; arranging talk show appearances; display of the book in book stalls; pushing the book overseas. The list is endless.

The point is that publishing is a business and it is political. It is only infrequently that a book will create its own demand, and even that can be squelched by a publishing house if there are not enough books in print, not enough books inventoried, not enough books distributed. For example, one acquaintance had his first (and last) nonfiction work picked up by a house and it soon became apparent that his was a list filler also selected to be one of the season's money losers. No advertising and no distribution. The book was eventually placed in Japan where it became a best seller. But no effort was made to repackage it domestically.

Similarly, it is no accident that certain books are reviewed and that certain books win awards. Reviewers are regular people, like agents and editors, who do not like to be bothered. They have quirks. One famous writer, for example, used to live next door to a famous critic, who used to visit at the same time every weekend to use the writer's john. The critic would moan and groan and curse for an hour, then mumble his way out of the house. Yet a small investment in toilet paper can mean a great deal in the printed page.

If your publisher and/or your agent do not press getting you reviews, you will not be launched on the proper PR path. The sole purpose of a review is not what it says, but that it mentions you in print. From there, you can hire a PR person who will make sure print coverage maintains some steadiness over the years. He, moreso than most agents or publishers, will also book personal appearances for you in the electronic media and at book fairs and stores. The strategy is to build up a reputation of your name, a recognition that you exist, regardless of the literary value of your work.

To return for a moment to the comments made in the earlier chapter on Birth, this is the time for exploiting your enigmas. Note that no writer is ever described as living happily with the same wife, having well-adjusted children, and being otherwise sane and regular. Writers have "stormy" marriages, "stormy" affairs, psychotic and suicidal children, messy divorces, terrible car accidents. Writers live in "stormy" towers or bus terminals. Or, to be completely enigmatic, writers "disappear," never to be heard from again -- except when that new book comes out. Writers also keep journals which detail the horrible failures in their lives, primarily blamed on spouses.

This recognition is extremely important with regard to awards. The protege system helps here, too. As one of the Setinways told me, he and two other writers were serving as the judges for a particular prestige award. The first year, he forced his selection on the other two. The next year, another of the writers forced his selection. And so on. It was merely a matter of catching the other two off guard, which was not that hard since all three were drunk most of the time.

Final edit clause. Another no-no for first books, which means it is an important clause unless you don't give a damn about your reputation. What this clause says is that you, the author, gets the final edit of the manuscript before it goes to press. A subpart of this is the issue of use of name. For example, you can also contract that if you do not like the final product, you can have the publishing house print the book under one of your numerous pseudonyms. Or that you get the book back as is and get to retain the advance. A publishing house, if it does give in on this point, will probably request a reimbursement clause, i.e., for each change you make on a galley, you have to pay the publishing house a certain amount of money. This tactic is only a way of gutting a final edit clause, since at, say, a buck a change, there's no way you are going to make more than a few corrections. The publishing house should swallow the cost, particularly since typesetting is computerized and it does not cost that much to edit and reformat. The problem is in timing, since houses try to work at typesetting capacity. But that problem is the publishing house's, not yours.

An example as to why this clause is important: Author A spent three years carefully crafting a book. He then spent two more years getting it placed. Since he did not have a final edit clause, he did not even see the manuscript until it came out in book form. The editor had completely changed the book. The contrast was this: whereas Author A was a thoughtful, serious writer, the editor had recently arrived at the publishing house from a popular woman's magazine known for its breezy style and its constant references to sexual interactions. The book had been turned from an intelligent study to a long idiot article. Author A never told anyone about his major publication.

The author of a technical work also has to be extremely watchful. Editors edit on automatic shift. The usual pattern is that they spend their weeks soliciting and reviewing projects, then wake up one morning to discover that they are supposed to hand in an edited manuscript in three days. Picking up that illustrated manuscript on the biotechnology of Lower Ferbush white mice, the editor locks himself in an isolated room and whips his blue pencil back and forth across the pages. The result is often embarrassingly distorted science along with the wrong captions aligned with the wrong illustrations.

Advances. It is possible to make a decent living solely from advances. In the motion picture industry, there are screenwriters known for having the good life based on one script. The money paid for an option agreement is not returnable unless the film is produced. When an option expires, the screenwriter is free to option it to someone else.

A standard publishing clause insists that an advance be returned if a manuscript is rejected. The problem is that the agent will have taken his commission, and possibly more if he suddenly charges for postage, lunches and mouse traps. The Internal Revenue Service will have taken its share, too. Your ex-wife will have taken another part, the kids will have split to Europe with your credit card, and the copy shop across the street will have taken the rest.

So the first issue is to change that clause. At the least, you would want the advance returnable only if you place the *same* manuscript with another house for the *same or greater* advance. The best solution is to make the advance non-returnable; after all, the purpose of an advance is to permit you (and your creditors) to survive for another year, and it is being given you because what you have already shown the house has been found acceptable enough for the house to invest in you.

If the editor agrees to a non-returnable or returnable upon placement elsewhere change, he will then state that to get the top people to agree to the change, you will have to accept a dribble advance. A dribble advance is where fifteen thousand dollars is divided up into its smallest parts, and each part is dribbled out to you over the longest period possible, say, up to the publication date. The two standard trade-offs are to divide the advance in half (one half upon signing, the rest upon acceptance of the final draft), or to divide it into three parts (with that third portion sort of dangling).

You might actually find that a deferred or dribble advance is better for tax reasons. A house would be more than happy to go along with those choices; your agent, however, will kill you.

If your final draft is accepted by the house, the advance then becomes recoupable, which means that any income coming into the house from publication and the licensing of ancillary rights is retained by the house until the advance is paid back. Only then will an author begin to see royalty statements with more than a zero after the dollar sign.

Royalty schedules in general. These are never negotiable at the start, and are frequently described in the contract as an ever-changing list of percentages which is a tangled web of unknown import. Small houses sometimes give a percentage of gross income; some rely on gross profit; large houses have turned to a "freight pass-through" formula; all houses manipulate percentages for foreign sales and placement of ancillaries; *no house understands what it is doing*.

The same situation exists in the motion picture and television industry. I have a feeling that the economic tangle was purposely created by accountants and lawyers, for they are the only ones assured of making money. What happens is this: a book apparently sells well, a television series goes into syndication, a motion picture develops videocassette legs, and the shnook who started the ball rolling (i.e., the writer), continues to receive royalty statements which wouldn't buy a piece of chewing gum. The writer hires a lawyer, who files suit; the lawyer hires accountants; the opposing side hires a battery of lawyers and accountants; the lawsuit drags on for years; the writer dies.

Would it be so terrible to have a comprehensible royalty schedule? Houses declare that they have to fiddle around with rates because publishing and promotion are so costly. Hey, then what about setting a breakeven point? Small houses typically make back their money after sales of 1,000 copies; large houses, after 6,500. But even that rule of thumb is often high. A trade paperback costs approximately $1.98 per book in print runs of 1,000 or more, where the plates from the hardcover edition can be used and the book is no more than 300 pages. A trade hardcover costs approximately $2.98 a book, also at 300 or fewer pages -- but with gold ink used on the cover. The additional costs are associated with overhead (editing the book, sending out copies to critics), outside inventory control, commissions and incentives to sales' reps, bribes to bookstore chains, postage and wet bars. Moreover, if the advertising or method for sales are "out of the ordinary" -- which means direct mail -- the royalty rate decreases even if sales increase!

It's all beyond me. I remember listening to an editor going on and on about overhead, expenses and problems in reaching markets, and when I suggested some inexpensive alternatives -- trading ad space with target market magazines, or setting up a bulletin board service that the millions of computer users, including librarians, could access for book listings -- he merely continued his tirade. Another confusing point is that editors always forget that some books are chosen to be loss leaders, and that tax loss carryovers have been found beneficial to large companies.

Since royalty schedules are precious to the houses, the most one can usually negotiate is to up each percentage by half a point, and to lower the number of books which have to be sold by a dozen copies prior to a higher rate clicking in. But if you haggle too much, it's likely the editor will jump out the window.

Publication and licensing. Publishing houses also remain adamant about their cuts for the sale of licensing rights, which include mass paperback, serialization, book clubs, movies, television, videocassette, videodisc, radio, opera, operetta, and foreign sales in English and for translation purposes.

A lot of these rights can be stricken based upon absurdity. Most books are not going to be made into operas or radio shows.

Some of these rights should be renegotiated based upon what has already occurred. If the book has already been serialized in a magazine, or if arrangements have already been made with regard to film sales, then the house should receive either no cut, or a minimal one (five to ten percent).

Similarly, if some of those rights might be exercised by the author, such as film or videocassette production, the house should again accept an extremely low or no percentage.

Agents usually worry only about translation rights, striking that clause so that they have the right to place the book abroad.

Rights can also be limited by territory or time. An example of the former would be where the house has a list of licensing rights only in listed countries. An example of the latter is where the house has a right, but if a licensing agreement is not entered into within one to five years, then that particular right reverts to the author.

Reprints, revisions, new editions, sequels. A standard clause permits the house to reissue the book in its old or a new form. The concern here is with the new form. The clause will say that the author shall edit the book and it shall be reissued under the terms of the old agreement; if the author does not edit the book, the house shall contract with someone else to revise it. Newer clauses permit the house to have someone else write a sequel.

The clause would be fairer if the house retains an option to negotiate a new agreement with the author, including a new advance, to revise the work or draft a sequel. If the house is adamant (as it will be) about definitely retaining those rights, the clause should say that if the author is unable to revise or write a sequel, the author's name will nonetheless remain as the name on the revision or sequel, the writer will be hired subject to the approval of the original author, that writer will be paid separately from the author's original agreement, and the royalty rates in effect shall reflect cumulative sales of the original book and any revision or sequel.

But if the house gets to retain those rights, why shouldn't the author retain the right to have his original manuscript, as he wrote it and before it was mangled by editing and production, published later on?

Indemnification. One additional clause to watch out for puts all the liability of a possible lawsuit on you, even where it is the publishing house that defends the suit. If the publishing house insists on its large cuts for subsidiary sales, then the house can quite well absorb the losses from any lawsuit, plus the costs for carrying (and maintaining during the term of your contract) umbrella insurance. If the house is sole or lead counsel in defending a suit, it can take those losses. Optimally, you want the house to absorb all risks associated with hardcover sales. Houses have in-house counsel and outside counsel who can render opinion letters on potential suits; and they can also insure against these suits. In this litigious society, where everyone will sue everyone else at the drop of a blue back, the risk of frivolous suits is great and you are in no position to assume that burden.

Editing

You might have found it curious that a chapter on editors primarily involves non-editorial matters. And we're still not at the stage of an editor actually editing.

Who edits first at a major house? The insurance company, which covers the house for libel, and the outside libel attorney.

What do they edit out? Anything that even tenuously looks like trouble.

What if they end up editing out the entire manuscript? The book is not published.

What if they are unsure as to what to edit out, as where a book is a novel?

Then they insist that all tall people become short, all blonds become brunettes, and all psychiatrists be rewritten as veterinarians.

What happens when the gutted and revised manuscript again ends up on the editor's desk?

It sits there until the week before the editor's deadline. He then spends four days just looking at it, to see if it will go away. Then he spends three days furiously putting his favorite one-liners at the start of each chapter, his favorite literary quotes at the end of each chapter, while in the process moving the captions from beneath the right illustrations to the wrong ones.

Sometimes, an editor will actually do worse. The editor who has just come to a house from a magazine is the one to worry most about. He or she will feverishly rewrite everything so that it follows the style of the magazine.

More experienced editors use a tactic which is easier on them than on the writer. This is known as the push and stall technique. The editor pushes the writer for a completed draft, which the writer works on around-the-clock to produce. The first "deadline" is met. The editor says that he will get back to the author in two weeks. The author does not want to continue adding to or revising the manuscript in the meantime, since he thinks the editor might have his own ideas as to style or flow. Two weeks pass. A month passes -- that much closer to the contractual deadline for having a final draft in.

The writer decides that the editor has read the draft and hates it. He begins to think about rejection, being held in disdain by the editor and the house, not getting the rest of the advance while his creditors are breathing down his neck. He finally calls the editor. The editor says, "Oh, I haven't gotten to it yet. I'll get back to you in two weeks."

Two weeks pass. A month passes. The writer is not only on tenterhooks, but has approached the stage known as BLOCK. At this nervewracking point, one of two things happens.

The editor calls and says that he hasn't gotten to the manuscript yet, but how are the revisions going?

The writer calls and learns that his editor has moved to another house, and that the editor assigned to his book has not yet had a chance to review it.

But if the push and stall editor remains at the house, he might suddenly decide that it is time to get "involved." Editors meet one to three times a week to discuss how their lists are coming along. An editor will never say, "Everything is fine. The writing is wonderful so far. I won't even have to edit much." Instead, an editor will say, "I think I'm about ready to wrap up Fershlinger's book, and then I'll turn to Harmonica's." Harmonica, of course, has just delivered what he assumes to be the final draft of the manuscript. Suddenly, he receives a call from the editor, who says, "I skimmed this draft and don't like the voice." After recuperating from his heart attack, Harmonica asks, "What's wrong with the voice? I thought this was the voice we agreed to last year. And you never said anything about the voice before."

The editor sighs deeply and says, "Well, I do apologize for not having had the time to become involved before, but things have been pressured here. I'm able to get involved with your book now. I'd like you to start working on a new voice. In the meantime, I'll give this draft a thorough read and send you my comments. From now on, we'll have weekly telephone conferences."

After having no editorial conferences for a period of a year, Harmonica finds himself inundated with editorial criticism. The editor is suddenly using messengers or Federal Express on a daily basis to send Harmonica the critiques that are always one draft behind. The weekly telephone conference becomes a daily event. The editor then starts meeting Harmonica for working breakfasts, lunches, or sessions at bars. Since everything the editor says or writes seems to be extremely vague or inconsequential, Harmonica finds himself rewriting just for the sake of being able to send something new to the editor. He has no idea as to what the editor means by a new voice and is unable to pin the editor down to more than, "We're shaping things up here. Now we're on the move. Now we're involved. A few more months of this back and forth, and we'll have our book." After a pause, the editor adds: "By the way, all of my authors have either dedicated their books to me or given me really wonderful acknowledgements. I'm not one of those editors who just sits around. I work with my people until our books are the best they can be."

Wishing he had been assigned one of those editors who just sits around, Harmonica, completely dazed, revises the book for the nineteenth time. He hates the book and can't face re-reading it. He wonders how the original manuscript got accepted. He wonders if he has the knack for writing anymore, since nothing he sends seems to please this editor. The editor announces that he has pushed through an extension on the contractual deadline for a final draft. "Boy, things are going just great," he says. "I've got us another year. From now on, we'll talk at least three times a day. And have lunch twice a week."

The deadline extension means that Harmonica will not be paid the rest of his advance for another year, even though he had splurged and spent the expected money after submitting what he thought was the final draft. The editor has become so involved that Harmonica no longer has any free time left for writing. He starts submitting earlier drafts, working his way back in time until he is shipping over odds and ends he had written as a child.

Then one day, the editor calls and says, "I think we've got the voice down. Now we can concentrate on structure. I've got us another extension. We'll talk ten times a day and have all our meals together."

Years later, after being released from the sanitorium, Harmonica will realize that the editor was not editing. The editor had two goals. The first was to be able to tell the committee that he was involved, which means getting out of the office and having free meals. The second was to convince Harmonica to state in the book that the book had actually been written by the editor.

Most authors, by the way, toss out drafts returned with editorial comments without reading them and, when the editor who wants to be involved calls, they put the telephone receiver on the desk and continue to write. This procedure not only maintains the sanity of the writer, but now and then permits a decent piece of writing to slip through.

CHAPTER EIGHT

PUBLISHING YOURSELF

I Want To Paginate

Nineteen eighty-seven marked the year when writers could suddenly be more advanced than publishing houses. In that year, desktop publishing, which had been Apple's terrain since 1984, came to the IBM and compatible series. Everyone could now be in the business of publishing.

Even before the advent of desktop publishing, some writers and agents were trying to force publishing houses into the world of computers. Since many writers were using a microcomputer and a word processor, it seemed senseless not to take advantage of electronic publishing.

Some background information is necessary at this point. A word processor is a program that permits the input and manipulation of characters. You can set up how the document should look when printed out by controlling the margins, where the pages numbers go, where the page breaks are, how many inches the tabs should be, whether the paragraphs should be single or double spaced, and what kind of type face should be used. All of those elements together are known as the "format" of the document. Other parts of the program might permit a proof of the document for spelling errors, or automatic hyphenation.

Although the computer industry is not regulated by the government, there are organizations which establish some standards, while the major manufacturers, such as IBM, set other standards. One standard is called ASCII, which is an arrangement of code translated by computers into characters (the alphabet) and numbers.

But that is all ASCII covers; the format commands, the creation of symbols, and other odds and ends are not standardized. This explains why you cannot take a document inputted on one word processor and transfer it as is to another word processor, even though each word processor runs on the same type of computer using the same type of operating system. (The operating system, such as OS/2, DOS, or UNIX, is the program that controls your ability to communicate with the computer, and the computer's ability to perform and output tasks.)

To transfer the document, you would either have to convert it to run under the other word processor (and many word processors have conversion capabilities), or you would have to "strip" the non-standardized code from it, creating what is called an ASCII file.

The ASCII file can then be used by any word processor on any compatible computer; or can be transmitted over the phone lines using a modem and some programs that direct and control the transmission process. The transmitted file is picked up at the other end and saved onto a disk.

In the beginning, I would toddle over to a house and say, Since these clients are using word processors, why don't you accept one hardcopy print-out and one diskette for each draft? That way, you can read the hard copy, insert your comments or suggested changes on the diskette, and then send the diskette back to the author. As everyone becomes used to editing by computer, your overall productivity should increase.

But we can't, was the response. We aren't computerized. We can't afford computers. We're thinking about computers. It won't work.

I returned. Why, I would ask, is your accounting department computerized, but the editorial department isn't? The price of computers has gone down. The monitors are in color and have a higher resolution. Pretty pictures. The price of modems has gone down while the speed of transmission has gone up. Most writers now use computers.

The problem, they said, is that computers don't come in the right color yet.

Finally, they started to computerize. And perhaps the real reason came out: *Editors don't like using computers.*

At one house, no editor would touch a computer, so temps were hired. The problem with temps is that the agency will always say, Our girls are trained in word processing. And the temp who is sent over will sing psalms while completely screwing up the system. The results range from the creation of a thousand unidentified files to the deletion of identified and important documents. Since temps also don't know what editorial marks mean, they will type in "stet" and "^."

At another house, one anti-computer editor took it upon himself to undermine the system. He would pull the fuses, causing the computers to power off, thereby losing whatever was being worked on in volatile memory (RAM). He would go into files and change the printer ports from parallel to serial, which would mean that the computers could not communicate with the printers. He would go around at night inserting idiot phrases into documents.

But at least the houses were starting on the high-tech road. I again suggested the use of diskettes or modem transmission. Even knowing about ASCII files, the response was that it would be too much trouble. So I suggested this: purchase an extra copy of the word processor used in-house, and provide that to writers. Ipso facto, everyone would be working with the same format and symbol commands.

Nope.

Another factor was revealed: *Editors don't want writers encroaching on their domain.*

If everyone were exchanging diskettes, it would somehow mean that writers were participating in the editorial process.

SOME FACETS OF DESKTOP PUBLISHING

Your alternatives for self-publishing using computers include the following:

1. Scanning and conversion of written material to a format and word processor you can use. Problem: glitches in conversion, often resulting in the need to reformat an entire document. Possible solution: use of global commands.

2. Transmission of processed data to an electronic typsesetting, laser print-out house. You embed codes they provide to you for changing fonts and integrating graphics.

3. Typesetting and provision of typeset diskettes to laser or high-end photocompositing house. One example would be using Aldus PageMaker. This kind of program, which runs on microcomputers, can select fonts, integrate graphics, and permit the creation of dividers, boxes, gray-level shading and lines. You would select the target printer or photocompositor that would be used by the print house.

4. Printing out on a laser printer. Low-end printers tend to be built around either a Ricoh or Canon engine; only some use page description languages, such as Postscript. All print out at a resolution much lower than commonly used by publishing houses, although Canon-based printers can be pushed up using a raster buffer. Possible solution: print out pages at full-size (8.5" x 11"), using a large point size, and have the offset printhouse reduce the pages for a 6" x 9" book, while darkening the image. But low-end laser printers aren't worth it unless they can handle graphics and downloadable fonts, which means having at least two megabytes of RAM in the printer.

Typesetting

The phrase "desktop publishing" was coined by Paul Brainerd, the founder of Aldus, which set the standard with its PageMaker program.

The basic desktop set-up includes a computer, a laser printer, a mouse, and a typesetting program. The latter represents the final encroachment on the editorial domain, and has resulted in more bad feelings than when the invention of the wheel led to the first flat tire on a deserted road late at night.

The reason is because these typesetting programs can do every task a publishing house likes to control.

The program can pull in just about every type of word processed file, retaining even the format and some symbol codes.

The program permits editing.

The programs offer a wide range of screen fonts. That is, What You See Is What You Get (WYSIWIG). Instead of being limited to a basic screen font on a monitor which shows nothing more than that words exist, typesetting programs will show Times Roman 14 point bold, Helvetica 6 point normal, and just about everything else, in the right size and place.

The programs will integrate a wide variety of graphics and illustration directly into the text.

If something needs to be highlighted with a box, it can be.

Some of the programs permit an illustration to be divided up so that each portion can be printed in a different color -- an inexpensive method for color separation.

Most of the programs will now work with the same photocompositing and output devices favored by publishing houses, such as Compugraphic and Linotype.

In other words, the writer can now assert control not only over editing, but also over layout and artwork. The writer can now perform all of the functions of a publishing house, up to the point where the material is sent to the printhouse.

Still, when I go to a publishing house and say, This writer can not only provide you with word processed diskettes, but can also do the layout and design for you and provide you with a disk that can be run through your own printer's output devices, thereby saving you a ton of money, the invariable response is, *We don't want that!*

Even though it would save money and headaches. For example, captions would no longer be displaced during layout, because the captions would already be in place. Black and white illustrations, and some color illustrations, would be fixed on the appropriate page. Last minute editing would be simple because changes in the layout would be immediately visible. Fewer people would be needed in the production and art departments.

As of this writing, I know of three smaller houses, two of which started up only a few years ago, which work solely with the system I have just described. The money they save on regular typesetting and production (approximately $20,000 per book) is poured into advertising and public relations.

But by the time the large houses get around to desktop publishing, we won't even have hard copy books anymore. Take a look at Chapter Thirteen.

What Are We Talking About?

In Chapter Three, I pointed out that the education of a writer no longer includes a command of the English language. Not too oddly, the education of a writer also doesn't include a knowledge of what publishing is all about.

I have already mentioned a bunch of words in this chapter that should be common knowledge to a writer. A typeface is a family of fonts. The typefaces that are standard for typewriters are Courier, Pica and Elite. The typefaces used in publishing include Times Roman and Helvetica. The fonts within a typeface are that typeface in different sizes, measured in points, which are 1/72 of an inch, and how that typeface will appear -- bold, italic, normal or bold italic. A headline might then be Helvetica 14 point bold, while text might be Times Roman 12 point normal. In computers, there are screen typefaces and fonts, which is how the fonts are shown on the monitor, and print typefaces and fonts, which is how the fonts print out.

Fonts are either proportional or non-proportional. A non-proportional font is what you get with a typewriter: a certain number of characters fits into a certain space (an inch). That equation is called the pitch. In proportional fonts, the number of characters per inch will vary because the characters are designed to be different widths, creating a tighter fit. This varying fit between characters is called kerning. Kerning can be controlled by typesetting programs so that characters are either closer together or further apart.

With typewriters, you are limited to single, double or triple spaced paragraphs, which has to do with inserting blank lines between lines of type. In typesetting, the space between lines is called "leading," which is measured in points, and which can be controlled by the program.

A Page Description Language is a program that looks at each page of a typeset document as a separate entity, calculating the layout of the text and incorporated graphics as one unique picture. An example of a PDL is Adobe's Postscript.

A laser printer is a device which uses either a laser beam or light emitting diodes (LED's) to draw what's supposed to be on a page onto a belt which then picks up toner in the appropriate spots. The toner is then applied to a blank piece of paper, which runs through a heat element to fuse the toner to the paper, while the belt has the toner scraped off in preparation for the next page.

A scanner is a machine which reads the levels of white, gray and black from a page of text or a graphic. A beam of light is projected onto the page line by line; the intensity of the reflection from the page to a light sensitive device is converted into a code the computer understands. High-end scanners will also read color from a page.

Color separation is the process whereby an image is separated into the areas of its different colors. These colors are then matched with printer's ink (generally using a standard known as Pantone). A two-color run means running the same page through the press twice, once for each color.

You now know more than most editors.

PROCESSING PRODUCTION

Input: keyboard; scanner; modem transmission.

Editing capabilities: word processor. Placement and manipulation of text.

Editing/production capabilities: typesetting program. Selection of typeface and fonts; control over kerning and leading. Layout, including incorporation of graphs, charts, black and white illustrations, some illustrations to be color separated.

Output: low-end laser printer; Compugraphic; Linotype; selected high-end laser printers. Laser-generated or other high-end pages used as camera-ready copy to be shot at offset house for print run. Most color pages to be color separated into cyan, yellow, magenta (CYM) and black.

Offset output: print run at optimal price breaks (usually, 1,000 and 5,000 copies); binding with cover and jacket; optional packaging in mailers; inventory at home or use outside service which takes fee or commission for handling inventory, sales, mailing and receipts.

Advertising: space ads in newspapers and magazines which go to target market; direct mail through purchase of lists of people in target market, use of direct mail house for large mailings. Copy for ads written, typeset and outputted as above, for book. Note that some list houses will now transmit by modem, permitting you to save the lists on disk. As sales are generated, you can create your own lists of those who purchased and those who did not.

Costs and financing of your operation: rent or purchase least amount of equipment necessary, alone or with other writers; provide word processing and typesetting to other writers on an hourly basis; enter into subsidy agreements with other writers; joint ventures with other small publishing houses. Try to get large houses to acts as distributors (for example, Crown does this). Exploit ancillaries if sales are good --- sale of mass paperback rights is usual route. Remaindering: sell out inventory to direct mail book and video operations like Publisher's Central Bureau (part of Crown).

Foreign sales: research foreign houses and send copies.

Best way to operate: as a corporation, since the "Inc." lends credence to the enterprise.

Initial Options

If you have had no success placing your material or finding a decent agent, your options are to forget about writing, pay someone else to publish you, or publish yourself.

Vanity And Subsidy Presses

A vanity press means that you can be published for a fee. The press will offer editorial services, typesetting, layout, printing, binding, and some advertising support. The typical arrangement has the writer paying in three installments, the first upon "acceptance," the second upon "final draft," and the last on the publication date. Advertising is usually a space ad which lists a whole group of books, giving each two or three lines (title, author, blurb, cost). Books are sold by mail and not through bookstores.

A subsidy press can include a vanity press, and there are two types. In one, the subsidy goes from the press to the author, and is actually a loan repayable by the author to the press, with interest. The more common variety has the subsidy going from the writer to the press, with the press picking up some of the publishing costs. The subsidy is not a loan from the writer, but a payment which serves as an incentive for a house to publish the book.

In all cases, the cost to the writer can be negotiated if the writer can cut out some of the steps involved in publication. The primary example is where the writer only wants the press to handle the shooting, printing, binding and distribution of the book. In that case, the writer would be supplying the typeset and laid-out files created with a typesetting program.

What the press provides at the tail-end of publication should be carefully reviewed and negotiated. Some subsidy presses, for example, will do small runs of manuscripts set by hand and printed on antique hand presses. The intrigue is with the old-fashioned look, but unfortunately the old-fashioned look is frequently illegible. One writer I know paid five thousand dollars for two hundred fifty copies of a book of short stories. But many of the characters either did not come out at all, or appeared skewed, and some of the pages were printed at a slant. Although it was explained that the final look was just what it should have been -- old-fashioned in appearance -- I don't think the writer was very happy.

Whether the press is old-fashioned or modern, the author should become involved in selecting the paper stock, typeface, binding and cover, and all those terms should be put in the contract.

Other subsidy presses require that the author purchase all of the print run, as opposed to retaining some for distribution and the opportunity of making additional money. These buy-all runs are extremely popular among poets.

If the press is providing advertising and distribution, the writer should ask to see some sample ads, reports on how frequently ads are run, sales' rates for books of the same genre, and statements as to other distribution channels. The final agreement should again reflect what is going to be done.

Avoiding Equipment

Outside services are available which will word process and typeset manuscripts, with the final output being usable by the writer to either negotiate a lower fee at a vanity or subsidy house, or to move right into offset printing, binding and distribution himself. In the former situation, it obviously wouldn't make any sense to use a service if its charge is higher than the press'.

There are three types of input: computer to computer; hardcopy to be scanned; and hardcopy to be keyboarded or stroked.

In the first, the writer provides the service with the manuscript on diskette, already word processed. The service then typesets the document, either returning a diskette set to run the desired output device, or printing out the document on photographic, camera-ready paper.

In the second, the service scans the document and reads it into the computer, where it is then typeset.

In the third, the manuscript is inputted word by word. The services with the lowest price per page are the ones which send the manuscript to the Far East, where operators input what they see without understanding a single word. To prevent too many errors, these services provide for double keyboarding at a higher cost, where two operators input the same document, and then the documents are checked against each other by the computer, which flags inconsistencies. This service is solely for getting a document onto disk; the document still has to be brought into a typesetting program.

The costs for each type of service vary wildly. Keystroking (inputting from hardcopy) can range from a penny to five cents a word. Scanning can be seventy-five cents per page without conversion to a word processor, and from five to fifteen dollars a page with conversion. Typesetting can be four to fifty dollars a page.

The cost for camera-ready output also entails substantial ranges. Outputting on a low-end laser printer, for example, can be anywhere from one to four dollars a page. Outputting on a high-end laser printer means sending the diskettes or transmitting the data by phone to a service, which then mails back the printed copy.

But if you are lazy or plain anti-tech, the cost might be worth the lack of effort.

Renting Equipment

Unless you can track down a mom and pop rental store, renting is an extremely expensive alternative for an individual, whether the rental is for a single day or on a long-term basis with an option to purchase.

But renting does have some advantages over purchasing. You can time your rental for when you have the most work to do; the rental agency takes care of servicing the equipment; and you can rent different pieces of equipment to test things out prior to deciding upon a purchase.

As with purchasing a system, renting by an individual should involve sharing costs with other writers, friends, relatives or pets. That means selecting a place accessible to everyone based upon a written schedule. A joke about bedrooms comes to mind, but this isn't a humor section.

In some cities, writers' coops provide cubicles and rooms that can be rented cheaply. The system can be set up there.

Purchasing Equipment

Purchasing a low-end desktop system currently runs about six thousand dollars for a really clunky computer, a lousy monitor, a decent enough 300 dot per inch laser printer, and the appropriate programs. If you want to have fun while typesetting and laying out, you will have to spend another four thousand dollars for a fast computer, an additional memory board, and a high resolution monitor.

I won't get into the technical breakdown of computers and speed, or issues of bits, words, microprocessors, coprocessors and the other terms that litter the field. Simply put, what you are looking for is a system that operates as fast as you do.

Unlike word processors, which are generally text oriented, typesetters are graphically oriented, and anything graphically oriented consumes tons of storage (fixed drives, diskettes) and memory (RAM). If you can transfer the typesetting program from storage into RAM, then it will run more quickly. If you can also transfer your document into RAM, speed will increase even more (although you have to remember to copy the document back to fixed storage before turning off the computer; otherwise, you'll be in the uh-oh mode of having lost the revised document).

If you don't have the funds to purchase an entire system, you can start piecemeal, beginning with the computer and appropriate programs before thinking about laser printers or scanners. If you don't enough funds for much of anything, you should again turn to those friends, relatives and writers who might chip in for a share. Just don't insist upon being called President or Chairperson right away.

97

Now What?

Unless your only concern is to have something "in print," you might want to consider the business of production, marketing and distribution.

A completely one color, black and white book is no problem to produce. You either bring in your camera-ready laser print-out or your diskette prepped to output on the printer's machines, plates are made, the plates are put on offset presses, and your book ca-clunks out, ready to be bound.

Any book including color illustrations is a more complicated matter. You have to decide where the illustrations will be clumped. The usual arrangements are to have two bundles (actually, one, but after the book is folded and cut, it looks like two), with one bundle showing up approximately a third of the way through the book, and the other bundle appearing approximately two thirds of the way through the book; or to have one bundle in the middle of the book. In terms of numbers, you might have eight color pages, or sixteen, or twenty-four, and so on, the numbers evidencing the fact that a sheet of paper will be folded down once, then folded across and cut. Obviously, you can put as many pictures on each page as the type of picture will permit.

You also have to decide on the type of paper, since color remains more saturated if printed on a semi-gloss claycoated or litho finish.

Color reproductions require that the pictures be separated into their component colors, with each portion being shot and having its own plate. A four color separation using a laser beam tracing device costs about four hundred dollars an image. The print run itself will also increase in cost, since the color pages will have to run through the press as many times as needed to match the original illustration.

Under the current federal copyright law, domestic printers are given complete dibs on all publishing efforts with the exception of books containing more illustrations than written text. Art books, for example, are usually printed in Japan, France or Ifaly. Cheap illustrated books are printed in the Far East, where every color seems to end up red. To take advantage of the exception, you have to apply to the Copyright Office in Washington, D.C. for a custom's clearance and, even then, it is possible that your books will be held up at Customs for upwards of six months.

Otherwise, you are limited with regard to where and how you can the book printed. The statute covering this is Section 601 of the Copyright Act, which states in relevant part:

> (a) ... the importation into or public distribution in the United States of copies of a work consisting preponderantly of nondramatic literary material that is in the English language and is protected under this title is prohibited unless the portions consisting of such material have been manufactured in the United States or Canada ...

The exceptions include, among other things, limited editions (up to 2,000 copies, approved for Customs by the Copyright Office); or books which are printed from type or plates prepared in the United States or Canada.

Other Things You Can Produce In-House

A laser printer with a sturdy engine can churn out hundreds of pages a day. Since the quality is decent, the print-out itself can serve as, well, the print-out. This means you can print your own limited edition of a book, brochures, pamphlets, direct mail pieces, newsletters, and anything else you can imagine. There are programs available which will let you print out in any format available, even beyond what some of the typesetting programs provide.

If you are going to do a repeat performance publication, such as a newsletter, you should first set up a dummy. Typesetting programs permit you to do this, and some even come with a diskette of already laid-out dummies. The dummy file will contain the data and graphics that will be followed each week or month -- margins, typeface and font, masthead, copyright notice, columns, and so on. Then all you have to do is flow in the new text and illustrations.

Marketing

But the ease with which a publication can be produced should not hypnotize anyone into believing that everyone is already lined up to purchase the book or newsletter. To make a sale, you have to find a market.

Let me give an example of what not to do. A group of Russian emigres decided they *had* to put out a magazine for Russian women in the United States. Russians in this country seem to think that if they are passionate enough about something, and pound their breasts long and hard enough, then all the capitalist money available will seek them out. There was the thought that they should have something to show their seriousness, so, in between the poundings, they put together a magazine in Russian and had it printed by a Russian emigre printer who gave them credit. Then they threw a huge party for their capitalist friends, serving vodka and orange caviar. "What you think?" they kept asking. "You give us money now, get us ads, we put out next issue. Sixty million Russian female emigre read this magazine."

What's wrong with this picture? First, they were trying to get English-speaking people excited over a publication that was written in Russian. Second, they were passionate, and completely without knowledge as to their target market.

Who was the magazine for? How many of those people were around? How many magazines similar to theirs were already on the market, and how many had been on the market but failed? What would it cost to produce the magazine? Would they be able to fill each issue? Would they be able to offer subscriptions to readers? Would newsstands carry the magazine? Could advertisers be approached and sold on purchasing ad space? Which advertisers would be appropriate?

Of course, they never did any of that. Instead, they convinced a capitalist living in a loft to let them borrow the apartment "for but one evening for art show of famous Russian." This fellow agreed, the paintings were hung, and then the Russians insisted that he buy extra spot lights, champagne, glasses and caviar. "You get good commission for sale," they said. Those present at the opening night consisted of the loft's owner, the Russians, and the Russians' Russian friends, who drank the champagne, ate the caviar, and bought nothing.

The other side of the coin is where passion is put aside for the sake of business. The type of publication one can put out depends first on available and committed expertise. If everyone to be involved sits down and lists his or her topics, then the lists can be combined and the market research begun. The primary questions were given above; the remaining one involves what the target market would pay.

Magazines, for example, are priced relatively low, with subscription rates even lower because the more guaranteed readers a magazine has, the more it can ask for space ads. Specialty newsletters, on the other hand, are priced extremely high, not because they don't run space ads, but because certain markets consist of corporations and people who will just pay a lot for something they think they need.

Having defined the type of publication, its content, price and target market, the next step is to test the waters. This is usually done with a "charter subscription" mailing. Different lists are purchased, and different direct mail pieces are printed, so that not only segments of the market can be tested, but the marketing approach itself. The responses by piece and segment are then measured prior to another mailing, and so on until the market segments with the best response are sent the direct mail ads also getting the best response.

Direct mail can be used in conjunction with the placement of space ads, or the space ads can be used alone if a magazine or newspaper is a particularly appropriate method for reaching the target market (as in the placement of space ads in diabetes journals for the sale of a newsletter or book on diabetes). Again, different ads would be run in different publications to assess the best route.

Any type of ad can be jazzed up. Endorsements from known people give credibility to the publication. A "discount for limited period" captures those who are desperately concerned with saving a penny. Incentive packages are also used. There are places which sell items in bulk, such as calculators and watches. These can even be imprinted with your name. The average cost per item is two dollars. But that same person who automatically orders anything which is discounted will also promptly order something that includes something for free.

These techniques are the same ones used in the sale of books.

Distribution

Distribution of any publication will be primarily by mail, sent under special postal rates or, for bulk orders, by UPS. The actual process of inventory control, receipt of orders and mailing can be done by a drop-shipment house for a fee.

Coops here and abroad can also be approached. These are loose associations of small, independent presses which send out joint catalogs approximately once a year.

Specialty bookstores might carry books or magazines on a consignment basis, but forget about the large chains. If you have the money, you can rent a booth at any of a number of annual, domestic book fairs. If you have even more money, you can fly to the annual, foreign book fairs.

Distribution is the hardest nut to crack and many people end up losing their shirts. When times are hardest, just remember that you are upholding the First Amendment and that you now have the experience to become a computer typesetter at a law firm.

What Next?

If you survive, you should investigate incorporation. Incorporation is intended to ensure that liability (such as for copyright infringement) is limited to your corporate assets, as opposed to your own assets. The process of incorporation is not that difficult: articles of incorporation are filed with the Secretary of State (along with tons of fees, of course), by-laws are adopted at the organizational meeting of the incorporator(s), directors are elected, shares are issued. The main concern in incorporation: the shares cannot be sold to just anyone or you will run afoul of state blue sky laws and federal securities' laws. Start out with family members (the typical "closely-held" corporation, which often leads to internecine fights), or one or two business associates who have money and know exactly what you are up to. You will have to consult with an accountant about electing to become a Subchapter S (which makes the company more like a partnership under the tax codes), and how to handle arcane matters such as maintaining ledgers.

Overall, the cost of incorporating using an attorney should not be more than five hundred dollars, including filing fees, initial tax (for stock issue), and your corporate kit -- a three-ring notebook containing your articles of incorporation, by-laws, minutes, stock certificates, stock transfer ledger, and corporate seal.

But just because you are incorporated and feel that you are free from personal liability, don't rush out and start publishing up a storm of other peoples' work. Many new, small presses neglect to research whether a work they want to reprint is in the public domain, or they publish the works of friends without having contracts in place.

Another neglected chore is obtaining ISBN numbers. Those numbers, which help track publications, are issued for free by R.R. Bowker.

Developing a press is the same as developing a publication. You should define your market, whether it is general trade, specialty trade (yoga), technical, or reprint. With a year or two behind you, and a dozen books out, you can try for listings in the Literary Market Place and the Writer's Market. After another year or two, you can arrange to have your books hawked abroad by a book broker such as Feffer & Simon of New York. You might consider entering into a joint venture agreement or merging with another small house. Later, you could contact small, foreign houses and try for an affiliation.

If you are successful, you will suddenly realize that you started out with the incentive to publish your own books, and have instead become the stodgy, narrow-minded publisher who either doesn't have the time to write, or who rejects his own manuscripts as being non-commercial.

CHAPTER NINE

POST-PUBLICATION DEPRESSION

If You Can't Sing the Blues, Write Them

The most amazing sight in the world is that of an author after he or she has published. Suddenly, instead of being utterly obnoxious at parties about the meetings with editors and PR departments, the luncheons with agents, the sale of rights to a British house, the size of the first press run, this person hides in the bathroom with the door locked. Appearances occassion intense gloom and any mention of the beauty, grace and sensuality of being published yields a prolonged groan.

The initial problem is usually with the final edit of the book. The careful word choice, grammatical flow and twists of phrase are no longer in the printed version. Instead, there is indeed print between the covers, but its intent is beyond comprehension. One could be reading any other book, any other article, any other writing other than what the author had spent ten years of his life crafting.

As if that weren't enough, the author discovers that he is an unknown at the publishing house. In some instances this is due to the fact that editors and PR people often disappear and it is not unusual for an author to have three editors before the book comes out, and then no editor. But in most cases, since a book will not become a best seller by word of mouth, the lack of recognition at a house is based upon the fact that the book is out and no one wants to be bothered anymore. Besides, editors know that if an author wants to meet at this stage, it is usually for purposes of murder.

It is the distribution of the book that causes the author to call up the publisher. How many times has a writer announced the publication of his book, causing hordes of relatives to descend upon book stores only to be told that the book has never been heard of? Even worse is when the author triumphantly uncovers a copy of his book and discovers that it is stamped *Review Copy Not for Resale Half-Off Cover Price*.

Distribution also requires publicity. The publicity department that had promised loads of reviews, television and radio appearances, and autograph sessions at large stores is also suddenly bereft of personnel. In fact, the entire house takes on the aspect of a desert.

There is silence. Complete silence.

The author calls up his agent and asks with mustered indifference how the sale of ancillaries is going. Well, says the agent, there was the immediate sale to a British house. That money goes to the agent and the house, the latter starting on its road of recouping the advance. What about book clubs? Weren't galleys sent prior to the publication date? After some coughing, the agent announces that actually no galleys had been sent and in actuality if the writer wants the agent to pursue the matter, then the writer is going to have to buy copies of the book (at an author's discount, of course) to give to the agent to give (non-returnable) to the book clubs.

By the way, adds the agent suggestively, the first print run was eight thousand five hundred copies. I know that five thousand copies have been sold through normal channels. That leaves three thousand five hundred copies to be sold. That would force the house to a second printing and second printings are extremely important thresholds in this business.

The author, unshaven, unbathed, chattering to himself when he flashes awake from nightmares, sits in a corner of his room with a handheld calculator. He taps out the figures. Forty percent of this times a couple of thousand of that, with a dozen going to book clubs and ... what about awards?

He calls back his agent, who is not in. He or she is vacationing in Brazil on commissions from the book.

But it turns out that the award department of the house has decided against submitting the book for awards. The author, however, can take over that function. The author sends away for applications. Because the book was published in February, he has missed out on the current year's awards. He is, however, eligible for the next year's awards. Some organizations require a fee of $20; others, up to $2,000; all require tons of copies of the book.

Feverish, dreaming of auctions that never occurred, book club sales that never materialized, fourth and fifth printings that seem out of reach, the author feverishly whips out his calculator and decides to fork over the thirty thousand dollars that is supposed to force his book to a second printing. Carton upon carton arrives by UPS until his entire apartment is merely a warehouse. Using his own money, he applies for awards. He hawks his book on the street but is told that ten dollars (his cost) is too much since the Strand is selling it for forty-nine cents and Publisher's Central Bureau has a clearance on it for twenty cents. When he appears for the Thanksgiving gathering, his relatives talk over him as if he did not exist.

If anything, people are angry at him because they were not mentioned in the book. His wife is leaving him because the book was not dedicated to her, even though it had been written before the marriage. ("Ferbush dedicated all of his books to his wife, even before they met. It just means you don't love me.") People are enraged that he did not send them free autographed copies. It is pointed out that his eyes are crossed in the head shot reproduced on the jacket cover. Heavily edited passages are read at parties for their entertainment value.

But then the agent, having spent the commission, calls one day and says, "The house and I are interested in seeing your next project. Remember that the house has an option on it. Let's strike while the iron is hot. I noticed that the first edition has sold out."

This suggestion of being needed, that one is not completely forgotten, imparts some strength to the failing limbs and mental capability of the author. Sure, maybe he had had dreams of a best seller, of fast cars and beautiful women and film rights and sequels, and maybe those dreams haven't materialized, but it was a first book (or second, or third) and this next one will knock the socks off anyone who still wears socks.

He isolates himself for two months, drafting a proposal designed to disrobe the reader. That is sent to the agent. Calls aren't returned for three months when the agent finally rings up to announce that the new editor loved the idea but could the author make a few changes just here and there. He does so. Three more months pass. A similar call. Four more months, and a similar call.

The book awards are announced and he has won nothing. Comparing his work to the winners, the author cannot understand why his was apparently not even given serious consideration.

The cartons of books have taken on a life of their own and he realizes he will be carting them around with himself until they are tossed into the crematorium along with his corpse.

The agent calls back and declares happily that the project has been accepted. Here we go again, she says. For some inexplicable reason, the author starts to violently cry.

Prevention Is Better Than The Cure

The above is a description of the typical post-publication depression. There are steps you can take to prevent it. One, of course, is to insist on best efforts/publicity/ awards clauses in the contract. Another is to take the matter of pushing the book into your own hands. You could hire a PR agent, or you could put together your own press kit and mail that out to lists you create by researching places, organizations and people that would be interested in your book. You can also take the book to stores just to show the managers what you have and to promise to appear for autograph sessions should the store take a few copies on consignment. Some more specific examples are as follow.

Geographically-limited magazines, journals and cable television systems tend to highlight people who grew up or live in the state where their subscribers live.

A number of award organizations do not require the payment of a submission fee.

You must know someone who knows someone well-known who might be willing to give you a blurb endorsing the book.

Specialty magazines, newspapers and journals often have decent rates for placing two inch columnar space ads. Place some yourself instead of buying out the first edition.

Guest lecture, for free, at gatherings of people interested in the topic of your book. Bring copies of your book for resale. At the least, you will probably be given a wallet composed of manmade materials with your name misspelled in gold leaf on the cover. At the most, you will sell one copy and have a decent meal of lox and bagels.

Use the publication to become a writer-in-residence at an institution where no one else wants to reside.

Apply for a writing grant.

Propose your book as a documentary for production by the Corporation for Public Broadcasting.

Change careers for the sake of your sanity. The mountain of books can be cast in bronze for use as door stops.

Where's The Money?

Most writers don't understand that publication by a house usually means a monetary loss to the author. The average fifteen thousand dollar advance does not cover the expenses associated with writing a book -- food, rent, utilities, writing materials, xeroxing, postage, telephone and, for nonfiction works, travel, photographs, and illustrators. A writer either has to take on a regular job to add to the advance, or borrow from people he has not yet hit over the years.

If not changed by the time this book is completed,* another wrinkle is that our federal taxing authority has seen fit to tax an author's income in the year it is received, while not always permitting an author to deduct expenses the year they are incurred. Expenses are somehow supposed to be separated for each writing project (Let's see now, I bought this ream of paper for five dollars, and used two pages for the short story, two hundred for the novel, twenty for business correspondence ...) and then deducted only from those writing projects that are income-producing. The purpose of this new regulation is to ensure that writers devote their time to noting how much of a typewritter ribbon was used or how many envelopes were sent per project, instead of spending that time on the projects themselves. Since most writing is considered subversive, the result of the regulation will be to limit parodies of the president or Congressmen.

With the advance spent, indebtedness increased, and tax dollars on the current year owing, a writer's next surprise is yet another new tax regulation. This one

---

*It is April Fool's Day today, which is the holiday for writers preliminary to the ides. On the fifteenth, all the ratiocinations of the universe will not prevent the final filings for the previous tax year, and the first estimated payment for the current year. Congress, prior to adjourning for its Easter vacation (ever notice how Congress only does things prior to adjourning?), considered an amendment to the tax law to permit writers to return to the old standard of buy and deduct.

involves the payment of estimated taxes. Estimated payments now have to be paid pretty much in full by the end of the tax year, or the writer will have to pay a penalty. But even if the writer is due a refund at the end of the year, he can still be penalized if any of the quarterly payments required under the estimated tax rules was not as much as it should have been.

Since this is a discussion about taxes, there's no need to say, Huh? The tax regulations are written by editors fired from the large houses. What happens is this: the first estimated payment is due January 15. On January 10, the author is broke and in debt. The publishing house is not required to send him a royalty statement until March 15. The author has no idea as to whether he will receive any money and assumes he won't since his agent keeps pestering him to buy out the first printing so that the house will be forced to consider a second printing. The author pays no estimated tax.

On February 17, the author receives a royalty statement on a previous book which he had blocked out of his mind due to extreme embarrassment. If, by some odd twist of fate, that royalty is enough to put him into a tax bracket even without any additional income during the year, then he is already subject to a penalty going back to January 15 because somehow he should have known that he would be receiving that money. Suddenly, he finds himself praying that he won't receive any money on March 15 from the other book.

The taxing authorities may permit an author to plead variable income using the Annualized Income Installment Method, but other than the fact that relying on the method will result in audit of all of the writer's tax returns, the complexity of its calculations ensures that a large enough error will be made so that the author ends up being subject to an even greater penalty than if he had just paid in the normal fashion. In other words, this alternative method to a penalty is about as viable as trying to depreciate the copyright of a published book. The government is kind enough to say authors can depreciate their copyrights, but an error in how much is depreciated can mean even more penalties. To take advantage of this wonderful right without incurring penalties, the author has to follow certain clear and concise rules. First, what is the duration of the copyright? Under the Copyright Act, a copyright is valid for the life of the author plus fifty years. If an author decides he is good for another thirty years, he better be prepared to commit suicide in his thirty-first year.

Second, what is the economic value of the copyright? To figure that one out, an author has to know how the book is going to sell. But he just poured that fifteen thousand dollar advance back into buying out the first printing. What if the house doesn't go to a second printing? What if the book dies? What if the book is revived to tremendous success twenty years down the road? What if the book is already successful, but suddenly vanishes from the face of the universe?

Third, the author has to figure out which method of depreciation is applicable to the copyright. Assuming that the author decides for straight line, he then takes his accurate assessment of how long he has to live along with his accurate assessment as to how much money the book will produce and tosses all of those machinations into a hat to come up with the result that he can deduct about two dollars a year.

So far, the published author is broke and subject to potential tax penalties. His agent calls and excitedly declares that the book has been picked up by a book club. The author believes that the sale will solve his financial problems. To celebrate, he rushes out and eats his first cheeseburger in months.

What he will not know until his next royalty statement (not due for another year), is that unless a book is a best seller and has been auctioned to a book club, a sale to a book club typically realizes about twenty cents to an author. In most cases, a book club sale actually causes *lost* income to the author.

The twenty cents is based upon the standard 50-50 division of net proceeds to the publisher from the sale to the club. Some book clubs purchase the bound books directly from the publisher. But since the clubs immediately offer the book at a substantial discount to their members, they want to buy the book as close to cost to the publisher as possible. The ten cents a book going to the publisher is considered gross proceeds. Once overhead and expenses are deducted, the net proceeds per book come out to about a thousandth of a cent. That non-existent coin is then divided in half.

Other book clubs don't even pay for the books up-front. Instead, they take the books on consignment, which means that they pay their ten cents plus cost only for each book actually sold.

The lost income to the author is where the book club insists upon buying the book at cost and the publisher agrees (because it's a way of getting rid of inventory), or the book club releases the book at a substantial discount at the same time that the book reaches its retail market in the book stores. The fully-priced book is going to lose most of its market to the club's discounted book. To add insult to injury, the club will continue discounting as the months pass (while the blurb in the brochure becomes smaller and smaller until it is only one line), and will then threaten to remainder the book unless the publishing house buys it back at original cost. Remaindering -- selling book inventory at or below cost -- means that the retail market is completely cut out, since the jobbers and wholesalers will purchase from the club instead of the publishing house. An author receives no income from remaindering, which is the death knell of a book.

Since the exploitation of ancillary rights has the same trickle down effect, the typical author of the typically unpromoted, non-best selling book soon realizes that being published means facing personal bankruptcy and a long jail term for tax evasion.

CHAPTER TEN

CRITICS

That's No Critic I Never Heard Of

It goes without saying that critics are indeed the philosophical elite of society, maintaining an exacting lack of bias, a historical perspective, and the ability to write in six hundred word spurts. The fact that they are employed by newspapers, magazines and television stations that project a certain point of view would never affect their moralistic inquest into the those projects that they have somehow selected from the twenty or thirty thousand that crowd the field at any given moment. The fact that critics have been known to be fired for transgressions against their employers would never affect their realistic and objective determination of what to review and how to review it.

Nor would ratings. A critic is a serious arbiter of style, taste and substance. He would never consciously become a comedian just because that would affect his popularity. Or just because a popular critic is not only assured of his job but can freelance at industrial gatherings, lecture at universities and publish his own books edited from his previous statements. The life of a critic is beyond reproach. He would never, for example, use a grudge against an author to taint a review.

I Might, I Might Not

It is hard to critcize critics in a book unless one critcizes only the critics who are despised by the important critics. A despised critic is one who writes for a periodical that has a minuscule circulation. An important critic is one who writes for a periodical with a huge circulation. Despised critics tend to be thin, avuncular, nervous and astigmatic. Important critics tend to be fat, corpuscular, alcoholic and egomaniacal.

Then again, all critics are writers. Lest we forget. In other words, critics have to get a job as a writer and hold onto it until they develop a "personality" which might be stylistic or philosophical (not Kantian, just societal). Siskel and Ebert, for example, have parlayed a Laurel and Hardy routine of wit, sarcasm and sheer hatred for each other that lets them laugh all the way to the bank. What would happen, for God's sake, if they started agreeing with each other's reviews ninety percent of the time?

But that won't happen.

Instead, the successful style will be emulated by a dozen clone duos.

Then what of the philosopher critics? I don't know; that's them, not you or me. One might give a favorable to every film in which particularly buxom women appear under the guise of "strict feminist construction of post-production sequels." Another might pan every book by a certain author on the grounds of "the objective considerations of post-Joycean anagramatic behavior," until the author wins a Pulitzer, after which the author will be crowned as a "post-psychological industrial syndrome." And a third could very well pick every tenth word from the *Oxford English Dictionary* as his review, on the hypothesis that "random liturgy equals static etymology."

The philosopher critic wants to be king (or queen) through dense erudition; other critics want to rule through gossip; others through comedy routines. But is there any substance to what they write?

First of all, how do they select what to write about? Since there are about sixty thousand books published, two hundred plays and four hundred films released each year, how is that number narrowed down by the syndicated to fit into the half hour or six hundred words a week that they are permitted? The process of queuing seems to be this: friends of the publisher; friends of the critic; people represented by top PR agencies; photogenic women; nude women; anyone writing a "fad" book (diet, jogging, CIA, aerobics); anyone disparaging the opposite sex in fiction or nonfiction; enemies one is definitely going to pan.

Second step: how do they decide what to write? Sure, these critics have styles, piles of historical quotes, background files, and glossy photographs. But doesn't a review come down to how an author or film can be helped or hurt within the constraints of what the publisher will agree with?

One exemplary situation involved a critic who did rather well over a number of years for a prestigious newspaper. Then he wrote a review about a movie in which he declared it safe and fun for the entire family. The publisher therefore took his entire family to see the film. Apparently, the wife broke out in hives, the children discovered questions their hormones had not yet prompted them to ask, and the father fired the critic.

But within the confines of publishatorial censorship, the help/destroy syndrome is a more than shaggy head, sometimes lapping and sometimes barking. This dichotomy may very well have had its roots in our British ancestry, where wit was generally confused with the lampoon, and chivalry with the prospects of getting the favored person into bed.

The tip-off is frequently apparent in the first paragraph. If the critic starts out by discussing everything but the book or film, it is obvious he intends to draw the reader's attention away from the work, and therefore away from purchasing or seeing it. But if that first line is the hyperbolic poetry of "she's done it again," then we're in for a mixture of the author's, actress' or director's sterling life and career, dimensions, and the historical place the person/work has attained in the history of places.

Sometimes, however, it is the critic who decides that he himself is the historical place, regardless of what he is reviewing. This predilection is readily apparent in the nonfiction arena when the critic happens to also be an author in the same field. A wonderful example of this is the reviewer who pans any book which does not cite to each and every one of his own books. "This book is impossibly bad. It completely overlooks my research and comments on the very same topic in my books X, Y and Z. If the author had not been an idiot, he would have ..."

But a predisposed point of view is also apparent in fiction and film reviewers, as where one can latch onto the tiniest word in a work which is inflated into sexism, lack of sexism, conservatism, communism, and all the ism's which so cheerfully crowd the universe. Quoting a work completely out of context is the invented domain of the critic (while quoting a review completely of context so that it sounds like an endorsement is the domain of the publisher or studio).

What is an author or filmmaker to do? The belief that bad press is better than no press is not a bad one since, in most instances, people read the first line of a review and then move on to the next article. Since the first line is the name of the book or film, the author comes out ahead.

A writer can always send in a carefully crafted response. Who edits the response to fit into "available" space? The critic. Who gets to respond to the edited gibberish to make the writer appear even more doltish? The critic.

It is often best to leave well enough alone. If you become successful, you will eventually be asked to review books for prestigious publications. Then you can forget all your nightmares about how critics should be objective but aren't when it's your turn to review a collection of essays by *that* person.

Fight Fiction With Fiction

Because of the unsettled strabismus (is that the right word?) inherent to the realm of critics, I have decided to complete this chapter with a short story. What with the psychobabble of history books (George Washington walked down the street thinking to himself, What nasty weather we've been having. I think I'll foment a revolution), and the creation of novels based on history (George Washington walked down the street thinking to himself, What nasty weather we've been having. I would love to be in Mary's arms), I see no reason not to incorporate fiction into nonfiction.

111

THE CRITIC AND THE LADY

-- Only Joyce was permitted to avoid quotation marks, exclaimed Duffy Paddington to his advanced class of modern criticism. But of course, if he were writing today, no publishing house in its right mind and certainly most university presses would not touch his material with a velvet glove. He would be slashed to pieces and deservedly so. But the fact that we have an oddity of recent memory does provide for gracious work and topics of conversation.

He paced noisily back and forth since he was wearing galoshes even though it was a clear evening. That was the weatherman's fault, for the news had declared an impending, stormy night.

-- The Southern school, also, prevents us from placing our own authors in perspective, he continued. If Welty and Warren were not so enamored of a certain patois, we would be able to ignore Faulkner. Those long, twisted sentences. That attempt at pounding language so grotesquely inflated. Although I have to admit that by today's standards, the use of a corn cob as an outright sexual symbol does represent the markings for a potentially solid work, much in the way that contemporary authors of our own dwell on stickshifts in cars and the eating of hot dogs.

He sighed, gazing down the blouse of one of his better students.

-- In a way, I suppose, it's like saying that Dylan Thomas, because he was an alcoholic, had a valid excuse for dwelling on internal rhyme schemes.

The student crossed her legs, a shift which caused her skirt to ride a bit more up her legs. She was wearing nylons.

-- Similarly, one glance at the complete works of D.H. Lawrence reveals an excessive use of lakes, pools, rain and other sources of water as a sexually apocalyptic event. He also took liberties with the exchange of the imperfect past and the present tenses. The latter was not carried forward by Cheever. The former was, for you will note that many of his works favor the use of water, although with him it has the effect of cleansing away past sins and fears and yielding a sense of humanistic freedom to the protagonist.

-- Cheever's stylistic endeavors, however, were heavily influenced by Anatole France. The triad of adjectives, the surprise word, the genteel conversation. The charm and grace of a child's popsicle stick.

He was trembling in his attempt to fully express himself. The student seemed to be trembling, too, but he suspected it was an autonomic function of her well-filled body. He squished to behind his desk and sat down, clasping his hands together and peering over his fingertips.

-- Modern writing, of course, is much more straightforward. It does not attempt to be prosaic or florid. We are in the age of confessions and revelations. We no longer fear penises, nipples, thighs and natural body odors. We don't dive into lakes before

112

or after having sex. And our experimental writers are flexing the cultural tone of the technological revolution. To continue to bring up names such as the ones I just mentioned, except in a purely academic context, is absurd. For one thing, as I said, those people would never be published today except by the meanest of the literary rags.

Nonetheless, after the class, he beckoned the student to his desk and told her that he lived next door to Alan Adams, one of those old-timers with a bit of fame and not much else going for him.

-- I usually drop by there Saturday mornings for a croissant and Alan, Al is often kind enough to prepare coffee to go with it. If you'd like ...

She shrugged and prepared to take the train with him. As he purchased their tickets, he told himself for the hundredth time that he could just as easily pick up a student on his own charm as by dropping such miserable names. The girl carried a purple knapsack. He expected that she had in it a diaphragm, jelly, toothbrush, fresh underpants, and the assigned book on criticism written by himself.

-- I'll autograph my book for you, he suggested, pressing his shoulder against hers. She had been gazing thoughtfully out the window.

-- I don't have it with me, she said.

-- But I see a rectangular bulge in your knapsack and, unless you happen to keep a rather large diary, I assume it's the class book.

-- I never bought it, she said.

He was shocked and for a moment considered stranding her at the wrong station. But there was a bulge in her knapsack and it was in the shape of a book.

-- Well, what about letting me have a look-see? he asked.

She handed him the knapsack. He unzipped it with the curiosity, excitement and rage of an older man peering into the precious designs of the younger woman. Kleenex, of course; lipstick; a thick wallet which undoubtedly held credit cards and photographs -- that would be for later, after they had made love, for he did not like seeing the snapshots of the muscular blond surfers such women often dated; the diaphragm case (o modern freedom and love); not really enough jelly in the tube, but he would stop off at the drugstore on the way back, telling her he needed to pick up something for his stomach; notepad; pens; cigarettes; possibly a joint; and the book which, although it was the largest item in the sack, was the one he consciously investigated last. The new, revised, complete edition of Joyce's *Ulysses*.

-- Trash, he said, shoving the book into the sack and rezipping it. Boring trash. I assume it's for a term paper.

-- No, she said, still looking out the window. I picked it up for my own reading.

-- Well then, he said gruffly, I hope you are reading it with an open eye.

-- Kind of hard to do, she murmured, considering it is a somewhat complex work.

-- Complex? Complex? Let me tell you something, young lady, that is exactly why it would never be published today. We're too sophisticated nowadays. We see right through such posturing. Allegorical levels, mythological names, manipulations of time and space, no quotation marks, poor use of semi-colons and periods, anagrams in seven languages. Hogwash. About the only decent thing in the entire book is when Molly Bloom thinks of going down on a man. Now that makes sense and is straightforward. All the rest only points to the fact that he could not write a straightforward book.

-- *Portrait of an Artist* and *Dubliners* are relatively straightforward, she replied. She placed the knapsack between her legs.

-- Poop, sheer poop. They exhibit some craft, youthful and not yet tainted, but it's still poop.

He led her from the train to the stairs leading down to his car. It was a sports car with only two seats and he had strewn dozens of books, articles, reprints and newspapers throughout the passenger area. These were intended to impress and impose. She, however, cleared off her seat and then rested her feet before herself on a pile of works. He was half-tempted to not pick up the jelly or open a relatively decent bottle of wine, but he did both. He donned his chef's apron and began to prepare his special salad and dressing, acts which always served to endear him to women who leaned against the butcher block counter, sipping their wine, and breathing in the soothing aromas of his lifestyle.

But this one took her wine to the living room, clicked on a light and, as best as he could tell during his occasional glances from the kitchen doorway, proceeded to not only read her Joyce, but to underline phrases and words, cross-reference, and check meanings using his compact OED which he had never found the need to use and which he had purchased at a discount from a book club primarily for the value of the magnifying glass it came with. He called out some chatter while he worked, turned on his stereo to a love song station, refilled her wine glass, set the table, put out the cheese and bread, lit candles, dimmed the lighting, and still, she silently read until the hour had passed which was always a sufficient limit for him to thoroughly read one of the books he was about to critique.

-- So, he finally said to her, how many pages did you get through?

-- I guess three or four, she responded. She carefully marked her place and followed him to the dining room. He decided to avoid a literary discussion since she was obviously so on the outs with modern thought. He asked about her parents, siblings, career motives, and hobbies. She seemed to have none; she read. She read Faulkner and O'Neill; Shakespeare and France; Dickens and Horace; her appreciation of modern day writing was non-existent except for one or two writers who had been rediscovered and republished and rereviewed. One such was Alan Adams.

-- But I noticed in your last review, she said, that you missed the point of the book entirely. You did not pick up on any of the symbolism or on his word choice.

-- Those, my dear, are irrelevant except as they weigh down the flow of a work. And Alan, Al certainly has a way of doing that. That's why he never won more than the one Pulitzer, and that was years ago, decades ago.

-- When things were less political, she said.

-- Politics is writing. Writing is politics. To win awards, you have to politic. A writer who remains cooped up dwelling on word choice and allegory will never get anywhere. You have to entertain, travel to the cities, go on talk shows, radio shows, put together a comedy routine for the Carson show, emcee Saturday Night Live. You have to learn six words in every language, not to put in the books, but to use when you represent the United States abroad in a cultural exchange. You have to own a tuxedo and make sure it's cleaned before each party. You have to attend to discotheques, appear in the National Enquirer, and love dogs, quote from the Bible, be divorced two times, have an affair with a famous actress who is ten years older, and have a son who commits suicide, dies of a drug overdose, and becomes a writer himself.

-- What about the writing? she asked.

He did not like this at all and poured the last of the wine into his own glass.

-- Writing is an aspect of culture. It is not culture. You have to understand that. Who needs a book you have to think about, think with? A book should have one simple punchline, we should be guided toward that punchline, and it should take no longer than an hour for any of us to find the last page for a laugh or a cry.

-- But the last page of *Ulysses* leads us right back to the first page, she offered.

-- Another problem with it. No ending.

She did, at least, help with the dishes and during the washing and drying she did not protest when he kissed her lips. That was good enough for some brandies, but he did not heat the glasses for fear that she would return to her book. She was gazing out the living room window at the neighboring house.

-- That's where he lives, isn't it? she said.

-- Al? Yes. Actually, all of this used to be one vast estate but it's been slowly subdivided over the years. He bought in about the same time I did, but he's being a real rascal about things. A developer has offered to purchase the tract between us, one half his land, one half mine, because there's more than enough room to put up another house. And a damned good price, too. I know Adams needs the money. But he cares nothing for money and adamantly refuses to negotiate. He claims it would destroy the view. As if I want to stand here gazing at him while he goes over and over his writing making corrections which don't help it any. Both he and his writing are dense and should go to hell.

The effect of his speech was that she voiced some support for Adams rather than for him. Distressed, he poured more brandy, but from a bottle rather than his crystal decanter. He did not notice when she stopped drinking, for he continued until he reached a point where he felt she was his; the only issue was manipulating her to the upstairs bedroom, with its down quilt, satin sheets, and brass frame. He liked it as he had read it in some books he had favorably reviewed: the gentleman performing his ablutions undisturbed, donning his silk pajamas, relaxing in his comfortable bed with a good book before him. The woman then entering naked, pausing at the foot of the bed to sigh before climbing on top of him, clasping his cheeks with her hands and kissing him. That was the cue for rolling her onto her back. Habersham had written a book with a scene like that just recently and it had sold at paperback auction for half a million and at the movie auction for seven hundred and fifty thousand. If there was any objective way of proving literary worth, that was it.

Ah, but this girl might not understand such things, he thought.

-- Let's go upstairs, he said.

-- O yes, let's, she said. Tell you what, you go up first and do your things and I'll be up in a few minutes. You'd like that, wouldn't you?

He nodded and smiled excitedly and rushed up the stairs bearing his snifter. He brushed with tooth powder which he then hid beneath the sink, putting the tooth-paste tube on the counter. He plucked some hairs from his nose and the corners of his ears. He urged his bladder to function. He peeked into the hallway before prancing nude to his bedroom, where he jerked on his pajamas. He leapt onto the bed and pulled over the draft manuscript of his collected critical essays, volume IV.

But he felt he had forgotten something and he desperately searched his mind for a clue. His breath was passable. His deodorant was still fragrant. The bed was warming up from his heat. He had on but the one dim lamp. Then he remembered that he had left the jelly downstairs in its paper bag. He contemplated not getting it -- perhaps she did have enough, after all -- as against getting it -- he might end up being overly active. Deciding that it would definitely be the latter as long as she kept her mouth shut, he tiptoed to the door, noted that she was not in the bathroom, and then tiptoed down the stairs, rushing to the kitchen, retrieving the bag, and then tiptoeing toward the stairs. He paused to glance into the living room, for perhaps she had forgotten and become lost again in that dreadful book. But she was definitely not there, unless she was hiding somewhere as part of a game. That would have been Shouter's book. The older man unsure as to the sensual qualities of the younger woman.

-- I'll count to three, he said aloud. One, two, three.

He dove behind the couch, looked beneath tables, pulled back the fireplace grating, slammed open the den door, shouted out he was coming, and eventually ended up before his store of liquor. He poured himself brandy from the decanter. He could see the bathroom door from the base of the stairs and it was still ajar and the room dark. She could have snuck up during his chase, he decided, performed her ablutions and disrobed. She was undoubtedly waiting by the bed, sniffing the lingering scent of his domestic cologne while peeking at the manuscript.

-- Let her wait, he said. It will arouse her. That's what happened in Grovewell's book. But then the man died of a heart attack during intercourse. As he should have. But I eat roughage, jog, and have an annual check-up.

He wandered to the windows and gazed out toward his irascible neighbor. Adams' downstairs lights were on. Poor old fool, he thought. Night after night at his broken down table, working on drafts, alone. Believing himself to be an artist. One of these days to succumb to the urgent and pressing itch of suicide committed in a tragic and forgettable manner.

He was about to go upstairs when he noticed a shadow approaching Adams. Thinking it might be a robber the old fool would not hear until it was too late, Paddington pressed his face against the window. Look up, he commanded. Open your eyes. There is death and poverty awaiting you. But Adams remained intent upon his work. The shadow fell across the table and then reached up for Adams' face, enclosing it in a darkness which made Paddington shiver. Lord, didn't the man notice or at least have a gun? But then the source for the shadow came into view, and it was the most beautiful woman he had ever seen, voluptuous and blond and naked, and it took a moment for Paddington to associate certain facts until he realized that the woman was his date and that the lights were going out.

-- But you can't, you can't! he shouted, striking the windowframe. You don't understand anything about love, life or real estate! Your books are out of print!

An hour later, the frosted light from the upstairs bathroom went on. Paddington heard the faint drumming of the shower from across the way, and the passionate singing, and he cursed the casual nature of culture for betraying him on such a fine and contemporary night.

117

CHAPTER ELEVEN

TELEVISION, MOVIES AND GLAMOUR

The Lemming Approach

This chapter is not about the Lemming who won the Academy Award in 1960. Nor will Stanislavski's method of becoming a tree be discussed, or Marlon Brando's weight problem, or John Huston's last film (although that one is tempting, since it is based on a Joyce story).

I have mentioned television, motion pictures and videos in other chapters, but want to devote an entire chapter to this area of entertainment because it represents a dreamworld which is having a powerful effect on otherwise sane people.

To start with the old days, writing for a studio was considered an embarrassing form of prostitution. But writers went to Hollywood because the pay was good, they could act enigmatic and bed starlets, and they could drink themselves into oblivion. Writers back then, not having seen the films and television shows which would be prevalent forty years later, couldn't know that what they were writing would actually be in a classic mode, and that their plots and turns of phrase would be mercilessly appropriated.

There are reasons why the old films could become classics. The studios churned out a hundred times more films then than they do today. The deadlines for converting a story into a screenplay and then a film meant that there was less time for "development" sessions, which is a euphemism for taking anything decent and rewriting it into pulp.

The studios also held long-term contracts with charismatic actors. These actors and actresses were frequently paired in a series of films, so that individually, they had a unique presence, and together, they had the experience of a theater workshop. And they were not afraid to deliver five to ten minute long monologues, or conquer long scenes --- shot all at once! Films were crafted much more like plays, as was early (*live!*) television.

Today, most actors and actresses look like the same person. In fact, you'll never see any actors and actresses in the same room together. The guy is young and muscular. The girl is young and pretty. The guy grunts. The girl takes off her shirt. But it's as if these people can't even cope with a five minute physical scene -- scenes are shot like commercials, and even commercials are composed of a series of cuts.

Nor is television live anymore. The shows that declare an audience to be live is

119

distorting reality. The shows are video-ed in front of a live audience with a number of cameras shooting from different angles. Response shots (Bill Cosby close-up, scrunching his face into a bowl of jello) are often shot at another time. Each show is later edited.

Then why do people wake up envisioning a career in film or television? Money and glamour, the same syndrome that entranced the old timers.

When I said this was a dreamworld that had apparently become infectious, I meant it. Over the years, I have observed a Ph.D. in really archaic languages suddenly decide to pen a screenplay involving sex in a Catholic school; an Off-Off-Off Broadway director putting all of his money into hawking a film about a neo-surrealistic dream; a published author reneging on book contracts for the sake of a project concerning people with three fingers.

Their odds for success are approximately one in a trillion.

Film Schools

Film schools are just like writing schools. Students learn about formats: film formats; video formats; sound formats; screenplay and teleplay formats. They have the excitement of scripting, casting, directing and editing a project. It's impossible to walk the streets of New York without having to avoid groups of students screaming at each other over appropriate lighting, angles and facial expressions. Mentioning to yourself alone in the shower that you are working on a real film brings a thousand resumes from film school graduates. Most of them are terrible to work with, because they have *visions* that keep whispering, You have nothing to learn, you know it all, you are one of a kind.

The people who find value in attending film school are the ones who make contacts. The student film that stars an actual star, was shot in color on 35 mm film, and exhibits post-production special effects, was not the result of classes at the film school, but the pulling together of one's contacts, including financial contacts. Those are the students with the best shot of making it directly after graduation.

If they hang around long enough to graduate. Because the degree in itself will impress no one, although it might open a door or two for a look-see. An analogous situation involves a degree from a drama school. If you think writers are an enigmatic bunch, you should try hobnobbing with acting students at famous drama schools. They seem to believe that they are humankind's gift to God.

Once, when I was strolling across the campus at Yale, I noticed that the atmosphere itself was a deeper blue than it normally was. I glanced up and saw a man standing on a podium. He was perhaps two hundred yards away from me -- but the blue was from his eyes, which sparkled with an astonishing intensity. It was Paul Newman. As I recall, the Drama School was honoring him as a famous graduate that day, and he had taken the time to deliver an open speech in which he said he had been kicked out of the Drama School, which he considered the best thing to have ever happened to him, since it forced him to think about his career and his acting.

And that's the problem with film schools -- in teaching format, substance is overlooked. The graduates who do make it without contacts often get their jobs because they cling tenaciously to format. They can be like everyone else so that everything runs smoothly.

Film Seminars, Conferences And Institutes

Because most film school graduates don't make it, film seminars and conferences have become big business. For a couple of thousand dollars, an unemployed graduate can fly to California or Europe and spend a week commiserating with the other unemployed graduates while listening to lecturers with one film credit among them describing how easy it is to make it, all you have to do is not give up, keep knocking on those doors. The same old love yourself/make a million routine which has made fortunes for people lecturing on real estate, God and sex.

Institutes, on the other hand, are places set up by established (wealthy) directors or actors, who at first announce that they will be selecting the cream of the film crop and producing films that would otherwise not be produced and who, after three or four flops, announce that they will be selecting the cream of the film crop and producing films that would otherwise not be produced but which will end up being commercially successful anyway, and who, after two flops, announce that they will be selecting the cream of the film crop and producing the same kind of films which had originally made the actor or director wealthy, and who, after two successes, announce that the institute has entered into a multi-year requirements' agreement with a major studio.

Guilds

Entertainment people are members of guilds in entertainment states such as New York and California. Entertainment suppliers -- plumbers, truckers and electricians -- are unionized in those same states. If word gets out that you are shooting a film in New York City or Culver City and that you are not using union members, extremely muscular people will appear at your site and proceed to trash it while nimbly cracking a few of your bones for good measure. If you do shoot and release a film without using guild members and paying guild rates, then the film will not be considered for most domestic major awards. If you use both guild and union members, not only is the film budget suddenly large enough to fill a hundred pages in small print, but you will discover hordes of people on the set collecting pay for doing nothing.

Unions, being unions, can often be bought off. That usually means exchanging a thousand dollars in cash for the brick being held by the foreman. Guilds are not so easy to pay off. But there is a double Catch-22 involved here: actors and directors cannot join a guild unless they have met guild standards for admission by acting or assisting in direction. But they cannot get an acting or directing job until they are a member of the guild, unless they act or direct for a project being done in a non-union state. But if they act or direct for that kind of project, they are guild-breakers.

The guilds usually solve this roundabout by fudging on admission requirements so long as new members can pay them tons of money. As members of the guild, they can now apply for jobs open to guild members. But since most projects are shot in non-union states or require waiver of guild rates, they must either accept the job and hope no one finds out in the guild, or remain unemployed.

If a guild member does gain employment, then the contract has to be the standard guild contract and is reviewed by the guild to ensure that any changes meet its requirements. The requirement guilds seem to be most adamant about is the contribution to their pension funds.

There are guilds for television and motion pictures, for actors, directors and writers. Their true value comes only from the opportunity to make contacts. Conversely, when a guild goes on strike, non-guild people have the opportunity to have their work read and perhaps even produced.

Chapter Two discussed the importance of names in writing and entertainment. The Screen Actors Guild (SAG) has a rule stating that applicants to the guild must change their names if they are already in use by members. In 1987, the director John Waters (famous for the outrageous films he did with the recently deceased Divine) applied for membership in SAG because he had cast himself in a bit role in his film, *Hairspray*. He was informed by the name duplication committee that he could not use his name, since it was already in use. Waters protested that he had been in the film biz for twenty years, had scripted, produced and acted in numerous films, had written books and articles under his name, and was, in fact, known internationally by his name. In his letter to the guild, he stated, "I resent that I have to ask a union to be myself especially since I had to join to be in my own picture!"

As this book went to press, the executive committee of SAG confirmed the decision of the name duplication committee. John Waters can be by any name but his own.

Television

As I've already pointed out, having a teleplay accepted is almost impossible because series are plotted out by in-house staff well in advance of each year's airing.

Originating a series means actually producing a pilot, which is often a two hour mini-film for a "dramatic" series, and a half hour or hour for a sitcom. Unlike motion pictures which, as will be seen, have a greater likelihood of distribution, television time set aside for series is limited, so even if you could raise the two hundred thousand to one million necessary for scripting and producing a pilot, the chance of getting the project picked up by a network or pay cable station is slim.

Not only are writers at the bottom of the television hierarchy, the purpose they might serve is often circumvented by market studies and the executive producer. The essence of television is the rating point, and those points establish advertising revenues. If a show maintains a high rating, a number of things happens: revenues go up; network promotion of the show goes up; and show content stabilizes. Viewers get what they have declared they like, and they're going to get it week after week until the ratings start to go down. Then content will shift until the ratings go up, at which point the content will again stabilize. It is important that the ratings be maintained for three or more years, because then the show can be syndicated and make a bundle. That's why many series are still produced even where the cost per show is higher than revenues. The net from syndication can be in a range of thirty million to one billion dollars.

And that's also why so many shows are the same. Nothing within a series is sacred, and nothing in a successful series is beyond appropriation. If one show receives a high rating because all of its cast is apparently shot off in a cliffhanger, then all the other shows which are just like it will also shoot off all of their casts. Cast members will be juggled and replaced if they grow too old, sag or demand too much money. It is the formula content which is perceived as impacting on ratings and longevity.

So writers are not essential. An in-house writer wants to be the story editor, who wants to be the producer, who wants to be the executive producer, who is probably also the creator of the series. If creativity were the issue, one would say those desires are because the writer's story is going to be edited by the story editor, whose version is going to changed by the producer, whose product will be tossed out by one of the producers or creators, who will insist on his own script. But the reality is that the writer may be making about twenty thousand a show, while the story editor brings in double that, the producer double that, and the executive producer or creator so much that they have to hire an entire accounting firm.

The Studios

Major motion picture studios decided that they would emulate publishing houses and become parts of conglomerates which could then have their products used as props in every film made by their divisions. Screenwriting in large part therefore involves ensuring that each scene has at least one person or animal eating or drinking.

The studios went even further in their emulation and agreed that pouring all of one's money into a potential best seller made more sense than trying to maintain budget control so that others, perhaps even those with talent, might get a break. A best seller generally means doing a film exactly like a film that was a best seller.

A screenwriter is an above-the-line cost in a movie budget. Above-the-line includes him, the producers, the director, and the paid actors. Everything else is below-the-line, which includes extras, production staff, set design, construction, and grips. The schedule is divided into pre-production, production and post-production. Shoots are supervised by first unit, second unit and other lower units, with the first unit containing the name director and cameraman, who will be doing the major scenes and any scene involving nudity. The other units do minor scenes and special effects (such as underwater shots; computer-generated effects will be done where the computers are, either during production or post-production).

From writing to production involves demolition of the original idea. A writer submits a script treatment or screenplay to an agent (studios only accept works from agents). If the agent places the work, the studio either buys it outright or options it. An option agreement is usually an irrevocable option to purchase the motion picture rights to the screenplay for a certain period of time, such as a year. Annexed to the option agreement is the production agreement, which defines the rights that will vest among the parties in the event the option is exercised.

A "low/high" is where the price for the option is low, either because the option period is short or because the value of the property is uncertain, and the price for exercising the option, vesting the production agreement, is high.

A "high/low" is where the price for the option is high and the price for exercising it is low.

What studios look for are the proper format and length (discussed in a previous chapter), safe content, and a large budget. As in a publishing house, a screenplay will go first to a reader for review and comment, then to the script editor. The screenplay, if it passes those people, will then be looked at for marketing potential. Thereafter, it will either be passed up the ladder in-house, or sent out to one of the "independent" production companies that has agreed to produce films for the studio to distribute.

Unlike a publishing house, a screenplay will then be ripped to shreds by a number of different people. There will be a number of project "development" meetings, at which the in-house writers and script editors will argue with the marketing people who will smirk at the director who will rage at the producer who will call in the executive producer. The screenwriter himself will often be ignored, although if he has contracted for dibs on the initial rewrites, he will have the chance to rewrite his work in accordance with the guidelines now laid down by others.

But in most cases, the screenwriter won't even have rewrite rights. The screenplay will be redone by in-house staff, studio freelancers or a blood relation of the director or producer. This situation sometimes leads to strange lawsuits, where the screenwriter is either suing to have his name reinstated as a credit (after he had insisted it be taken off, believing the film would be terrible), or to have his name deleted (even though he knew it was no longer his concept when he let his name be used, believing the film would be a success).

When a screenplay is finalized, it then ends up with the director and production staff for revision into a shooting script. The director draws up a storyboard which sketches out how a scene should look when shot, while production clumps together those scenes that can be shot one after the other. During production, scenes might be rewritten; during post-production, scenes will be edited out and edited in. New scenes might be shot. A new post-production director might be brought in. The film will be screened and, if audience reaction is bad, additional editing will be done. If it is decided that nothing can be done with the film, it will be put in the can, either to waste away or to be released years later when the market is perceived as having changed.

But in no event will the original screenplay ever end up as the film upon which it is supposed to be based.

Why do screenwriters put up with it? Because they want to be story editors, and story editors want to be producers, and producers want to be executive producers. Why? Because screenwriters make fifty to two hundred thousand dollars a produced script, while story editors make double that, and producers and executive producers take a percentage right off the top. (It is this skimming which promotes big budget films, and also explains part of the reason why a studio will use a director known for huge cost overruns. The other reason is the safety factor in a known quantity.)

Films fill studio lists much the same as books fill house lists. One sci. fi., one romance, one mystery, that sort of thing. Most films are released domestically with an R-rating, because most people want to see tits and ass, hear curse words, and observe blood gushing. Of those, many are triple shot, with harder scenes replacing softer ones for foreign release, pay cable and videocassette, and softer, shorter scenes being edited in for commercial television.

The basic formula is establish hero; establish heroine; ten minutes to have them meet; twenty to thirty minutes of their dancing about each other and the plot line (aliens, murderers, interfering parents); preliminary kissing and fondling scenes; the nude sex scene sixty-five to seventy minutes through the film; the first resolution; the second resolution; loud music.

The establishing part can be eliminated entirely if the film is a remake or sequel. For a remake, you take a known actor and actress, plop them into the period piece, have them overact, and wherever the original film called for a train tunnel or ocean wave, you have the actors do a nude scene accompanied by heavy breathing. What is interesting is that we are now seeing sixth and seventh remakes of the same film, but even odder was a film released in 1986 that was a remake of a film which had come out in 1984 -- where each version was produced and distributed by the same group!*

Sequels are remakes of original, successful films, where whatever is perceived as having made the first film fly is put into every scene, instead of just a few. If the first film ended with a rousing fight or battle, the sequel will start out with a fight or battle, and then have one every few minutes. If the first film had one horrible monster in it, the sequel will have a hundred billion horrible monsters (compare *Alien* and *Aliens*).

Of course, the great advance of the 1980's was a process that enabled studios to circumvent screenwriters, story editors, producers and directors; a process so wonderful it completely eliminated the need for anyone to think or be creative; a process that even gets rid of guilds and unions. For what could be better than colorization, where you let a computer add color to a black and white classic that is already selling well in the videocassette market? And nothing could be safer.

Independents

Perhaps eighty percent or more of all films are produced by independents. Of those, around ninety percent are immediately released as videocassettes and fill for pay/cable television. The remaining ten percent start out as first theatrical releases, but usually in a limited territory (translation: shown at one theater in one city). Of those, ninety-five percent are not really produced by independents at all, although the companies call themselves independents. Those companies are the ones which were either spun off from the studios, entering into requirements' contracts, or from the major videocassette or pay television companies.

Although independents will always espouse their philosophical premise as being "creative control," in actuality they are people who could not make it at the majors. It is easy to get a production company going. All those film school graduates are hanging around on street corners, some of them owning their own equipment. All those drama school graduates are hanging around between jobs as waiters and waitresses. Assistant and second unit directors pant heavily at the possibility of being *the* director. Every sort of screenplay imaginable is there for the asking.

In short, breathing the word "film" will promptly provide the ideas and personnel for doing a film. The problem is money.

---

*The original film was *The Ambassador* (1984); the remake was *52 Pick-Up* (1986). Each was produced by Golan-Globus and distributed by their Cannon Films. In a similar vein, studios, instead of releasing a dubbed version of a successful foreign film, will spend millions remaking it with an American cast. An example is *Three Men And A Baby* (Touchstone, 1987), which is a remake of *Trois Hommes et Un Couffin* (Flach, et al., 1985).

INDEPENDENT GUIDELINES

Obtaining a property: option screenplays; write own screenplays.

Initial feelers: letters of commitment from actors, director, cameraman, soundman, owners of selected sites and props, possibly city officials.

Initial budgeting: draw up best budget and bottomline budget.

Approach: parents, relatives and friends for money.

Second budgeting: draw up next best budget and bottomline budget.

Second feelers: oral agreements from actors, director, cameraman, soundman and everyone else that they will work on a deferred compensation basis.

Attempting deals: approach cable, pay television, theater owners, videocassette distributors to see if will put money up-front, which they won't until they see the finished product.

Approach: parents, relatives and friends for more money.

Create credibility: form a limited partnership or corporation for purpose of producing the one film; limited offering of interests or shares to a select few parents, relatives and friends.

First stab: shoot all the nude and/or violent scenes.

Second attempt at deals: take rough footage to cable, pay television and videocassette distributors, because one is bound to become excited. He, however, will demand complete control over the film, including a reshooting of the nude scenes, during which he will be present with his Instamatic.

Completion: submit for awards; release in one theater if lucky; otherwise, go immediately to cable, pay television and videocassette.

Plan next project: getting out of bankruptcy.

Before discussing how money is raised, such as by selling your roommate's possessions, one of the intriguing aspects of the film business is the ease with which people's lives can be manipulated. It is not difficult to convince actresses to disrobe during a pre-casting call. It is simple to have actors perform like utter fools. And it is easy to persuade a writer to devote one or two years to writing and rewriting screenplays on the promise of eventual production.

Mr. X is someone who lives glamorously, appears to have a great deal of money, talks movie talk on a first name basis, and thinks you are the cat's meow. Sometimes, Mr. X actually does, or, rather, did, have a film experience, something he fell into years before and that resulted in a substantial return on his investment. What you won't know at first is that, although Mr. X truly and really is desirous of finding a new investment property, he wants to make his return based upon the smallest initial cost possible.

This scheme of things will create a few months of glory and hard work. Mr. X will say that you are his one hope in life. He will take you out to lunch and dinner (all deducted by him as business expenses) and perhaps give you little gifts: radios, batteries, blank cassettes (also all deductible). He will invite you to his parties, where catered food is served by delicate, mini-skirted women, and half the guests have foreign accents and the other half are all tangentially involved in films.

In the meantime, you will work on your screenplay. After you give him the screenplay, he will let you dangle for months on the excuse that he is very, very busy and always in preparation for business trips.

Then, one day, you get the phone call. Mr. X is absolutely enthralled with the screenplay. He has you come over right away, where he pours two glasses of Scotch and states: "This is the beginning of a great relationship. A year from now, you'll have so much money, you won't know how to handle it." Giddy, you drink while heady plans are tossed into your ears, about how Mr. X has already lined up a famous, foreign, non-English speaking director (typically a Russian), and the most beautiful actress whom he knows personally. He reveals that he owns a chain of theaters and has already opened the schedule for the release of the film. He asks how you are doing for money and, although you are deeply in debt to everyone you know, you coolly answer that everything is fine. You leave believing that the world is about to become your oyster.

And you never hear from him again. This Mr. X comes in many different guises, and his primary purpose is to generate screenplays at no cost. He can be a wealthy person, as described above, or someone who is renting office space from an actual studio but who gives the impression that he is a big honcho at the studio itself. The variation on Mr. X is the person who declares that he or she has already lined up financing for an idea, and would you be so kind as to spend a year writing the screenplay.

These people will even enter into option agreements, but at most they will pay a hundred dollars, and the rest of the time they will put in a figure without paying it, while gracing the production agreement with a stunning amount due to be yours if the option is exercised. Which it never is.

I don't know if any horror story is sufficient to kill the entertainment bug. Slave relations are prevalent in this business. People will do anything for free in the hope of that screen credit.

If you want to avoid enslaved poverty, you can either ask Mr. X for money up-front, or you can produce your own film.

Packaging

Packaging a film has a number of components premised on making the enterprise appear to be professional. The screenplay still has to be written in the required format and to the required length. Copies of it should be nicely bound along with descriptions of the primary characters, the settings (and actual locations, if scouting sites has already been done), the proposed production schedule, and the optimal budget. Actors desired for leading roles can be included as a pre-casting suggestion. You don't have to go to a pre-casting agent, who will sometimes charge a thousand dollars a week, and sometimes defer the charge until production is started. Instead, you can go directly to the theatrical agencies and request head shots and resumes.

The next step is to incorporate or form a limited partnership. To save money, independents will write out a first draft using forms available in law books. The form is then reviewed for free either by a local arts' group that has signed up lawyers to provide *pro bono* services, or by a young lawyer who also has the entertainment bug. The only out-of-pocket expense will involve filing fees.

At this point, for very little money, you will have all the makings of a film, ranging from the screenplay to the actors and director who will work on a deferred compensation basis, to legal documents. Some independents then take the route of trying to interest pay and cable companies, majors and videocassette distributors in a pre-production buy of rights. The response is invariably, "Come back when you've got it in the can."

That leaves the next route: parents, friends, friends of friends. Anyone with money. After a half year of begging, pleading, sobbing, bowing, cajoling and spieling, you will come up with perhaps a hundred thousand dollars. But your bottomline budget is four hundred thousand. So you try convincing suppliers to give you a break; you go to the post-production house, the equipment rental house, the truckers, and beg, plead, sob and froth. Of course, they don't listen; as a matter of fact, you'll probably have to take a number and wait your turn behind all the other independents trying the same tactic.

So you go back to your parents, friends, and friends of friends, thinking, *Woody*

Allen and Ingmar Bergman never suffered like this. And you raise another twenty-five dollars.

With your one hundred thousand twenty-five dollars in hand, you then go to the entertainment division of a bank. If the bank makes an offer, it will be a loan of five thousand dollars secured by the film itself. That means one default by one second will give the film to the bank to do with as it pleases.

At this stage, you either take the money and run, or you go into production. Costs can be cut substantially by switching from 35 mm to 16 mm or video. The hope there is to squeak by and complete the project; if money later comes in from the licensing of ancillaries, the film can be transferred up (although it will become grainy). The alternative is to shoot as much as possible before the money runs out, praying that companies will be astonished enough by the rough cut to put up the money for completion.

There are an awful lot of half-finished films floating around, available for a song. Flirting with them is the ubiquitous Mr. X.

Videocassette

Developing and marketing videocassettes as an independent is much like self-publishing. Two lucrative markets are the how-to video and Sunday porn.* The difference between the former and the latter is the dress of the participants, since both are typically shot with one set, one camera, one microphone, and one light. Personnel will be used on a deferred compensation basis, so the only real expense will be renting the camera, purchasing broadcast or better quality tape, and renting out a post-production room for a day. Music will be composed on a synthesizer.

The duping and packaging of videocassettes is not costly. A run of a thousand or more copies at a time costs about a dollar ninety-eight per unit, which includes the cassette, the printed cardboard package, and shrink wrapping.

As with self-published books, distribution relies primarily upon direct mail, space ads, and joining video distribution coops. Specialty video stores (such as Facets Video in Chicago) will sometimes carry the products of an independent, but a growing outlet happens to be grocery stores.

You can imagine how impressed your family and friends will be when they find your videocassette on *How To Self-Publish* ($9.98) next to your ghostwritten potboiler right there in the aisle stocking spam, baked beans and toilet bowl cleaner.

---

*Until about 1985, most "adult" films were shot with film. Budgets averaged $250,000, with a third or more being fronted by the major "adult" video distributors. (Remember that from the advent of consumer VCRs until recently, hard core was the primary video market.) In 1985, the wide availability of home video cameras led to everyone suddenly shooting porn, but directly on video at budgets averaging $10,000. The adult directors, to remain in film, shifted to R-rated productions.

CHAPTER TWELVE

SOFTWARE PUBLISHING

Trying To Define Something When It Doesn't Want To Be

Software publishing is one of those phrases that has an absurd ring to it. Does it really mean publishing software? Can software be published (as opposed to being duped)? Is software software? Who knows? The publishing houses certainly don't.

As could be expected from the arbiters of good linguistic taste, software publishing does not mean publishing software and it is not the converse of hardware publishing. You do not, for example, go into a store and request a book composed of screwdrivers, although I recall Time-Life running some advertisements where screwdrivers and hammers miraculously sprouted from books. Asking for a software would seem to represent a similar obstacle; one expects to be given something that will melt in one's hands.

Thus the question: what is software publishing? Originally, it was devised to mean those items published by a house that were not really books. Videocassettes were the prime example. Audiotapes another. Not included in the original definition, of all things, was computer software.

This game of words has had a number of specialty agents howling over the years because the worse thing in the world is to see the ancillaries of a work remain unexploited because a publishing house won't cooperate. And the house won't cooperate because the terminology means what the house wants it to mean, which is, we will exploit what we have always exploited and otherwise do no more than stab a toe into the water to see if it is warm or cold.

Safe Ancillaries, Ignored Ancillaries

Earlier, it was pointed out how difficult it is to get a book published and how easy it is to let a published book die. For those expecting burial in the great remainder house of the sky, located outside of Newark, New Jersey, the fact that the ancillaries have also been buried adds nothing to the sense of pessimism.

But one always wonders why publishing houses put in a contractual list of ancillary rights, ranging from database transmission to operas composed for radio, and then fight tooth and nail over their deletion, when they have little or no intention of exploiting those rights in great part because they don't understand what those rights mean.

For example, if one is lucky, a house will exercise its right to first serialization, which means lopping off part of a book and sending it to some magazines. Magazines are like tiny books, so editors can understand that ancillary. Magazines will also pay a fee to the house for the first serial right -- a fee that can be applied to recouping the advance prior to the book being published. Moreover, magazines go to people who read, and publishers feel safe knowing that their product is going to an established market.

The problem, as we all know and have known for fifteen years, is that more and more people are not reading. We can all wail at the fact that this represents one of the great plagues of our time, known as illiteracy, and that a study done some years ago discovered that a large percentage of Americans, having been forced through our school systems, could still not write a check or, for that matter, write anything legibly or in a language approaching English.

I'm sure that somewhere, when that report came out, the education divisions of some publishing houses must have called meetings to determine the market possibilities of a text book on writing checks.

But there were other forces at work. The one that has been a threadlike theme here is that most printed material has become homogeneous. This deja vu syndrome or safety factor means that, just as houses do not like to be the first to publish in a new area, they also don't like to be the first to exploit ancillaries in ways never before done by another house.

Where do Americans find their different kicks? Radio, television, films, stereos, rotating chandeliers, Robin Leach, illustrated magazines, and four-color advertisements for Calvin Klein underwear. In short, input that changes or can be changed almost at will. Input that, if viewed for a prolonged period of time, will become homogeneous, but that remains entertaining because it never is viewed over a prolonged period of time. Ten seconds is about enough except for certain fold-outs.

Certainly, one would think, these are areas in which publishers must have a great deal of interest. But publishers don't. If a book is to be made into a film, then a studio has to option the book and go to production. Studios are in the business of making films. The fact that the major studios tend to go over budget, cast actors because they are names rather than suitable talent, and then squabble over final edit rights, does not detract from the fact that studios are in the film business and publishers are in the publishing business.

In the software area, house are more comfortable having matters evolve in reverse. Many houses have film/book development departments. The studio makes the film and the house hires a freelancer to transform the screenplay into a book. The film is released along with the book and, on the cover of the book, we discover that the main characters happen to look exactly like Robert Redford and Kathleen

Turner, and in the middle of the book we see frames from the film. These are comic books for grown-ups with little sense of writing style because there is no need for anyone to sweat over details. The reader already knows what the characters look like, what the scenery looks like, and how the film and book end. The only difference is that the book does not have rolling credits.

Video Tie-Ins

A few years ago, when only a third of the households in this country owned VCR's (and just about everyone in Europe and Japan owned a machine), no publisher would be the first house to put out a videocassette. Videos were not the written word. They were edited by people who did not have degrees in English from Smith or Barnard. They were rolls of brownish tape stuck in a black case squished into a plastic or cardboard cover. Book stores (at the time) did not carry videos. Forget about producing a video, how could one market it?

That type of response was often enough to drive some agents to nervous breakdowns. Because if looked at closely, it is obvious that there is just about no difference between a videocassette and a book except that one goes into the slot of a machine and the other goes into the mirrored cradle kept in the bathroom. Advance costs are about equal: $15,000 advance to the author for a book, $15,000 in production money. Production costs come out about the same: $2.00 for hardcover, $1.00 for mass paperback; $1.50 to $1.98 per video, including duping and packaging. Mark-ups are about the same: retail the hardcover for $20.00 and the paperback for $9.00; retail the video for $19.95 to $29.95.

All right, fine, a house might say, but we have no experience in production. That's all right, one can hire people to put together the package. Then the hemming and hawing and the declaration that there is no way to market the video.

One returns to the fact that publishing houses really don't know how to market their own products. They prefer jobbers and wholesalers and book store outlets and book clubs because those are the ways marketing has always been done. Since book stores and book clubs, at that time, did not carry videocassettes, there was no way a house was going to include that product in its line.

But what, one could have asked at the time, was so wonderful about the system of distribution for books? The great problem with books and book stores has always been returns. Why are there tons of returns? Because most books are not marketed to their appropriate market. Why not? Because that means additional effort. That's why publishing houses could say to me that they could not market a diabetes book or a bridge book. Even though there are millions of diabetics and bridge players in the world, easily reached through organizations, specialty magazines and journals, and direct mail, houses do not see it that way. What they see is that books on diabetes and bridge do not sell well through book stores.

How much worse, then, is the idea of marketing a videocassette? Sure, how-to books do very well in book stores, but where would one place the videocassette? Next to the book? In a separate, video area? And video hasn't caught on yet. And in video the how-to aspect of something intricate will flash by, whereas with the book one can keep the appropriate page open while banging one's thumb with the hammer.

In the usual manner of product shifts within publishing houses, the houses finally realized, once almost everyone in the universe owned a VCR, that videocassettes might be here to stay and might be a good tie-in market. Oddly enough, some independents had produced how-to videos which turned out to be best sellers. By God, the houses were never in the dark ages, they were going to become involved in videocassettes .... as soon as the book stores decided to open up shelf space.

You might have observed this transition yourself. The book store I frequent down the block seems typical. Two floors of books. Paperbacks, hardbound and magazines in neatly separated areas. Those areas neatly broken up by topic. New Fiction. Science Fiction. History. Philosophy (on half a shelf covered with dust and out of reach).

Then in 1985, one section toward the rear of the second floor was cordoned off while men sawed and hammered. It reopened as a videocassette section. There were only two cases, primarily showing videos of motion pictures, but one shelf toward the bottom contained How-To's.

Six months after that, more scaffolding went up and when it came down, the video space had been expanded to four times its original size.

The book store I go to has now devoted one half of its first floor to videocassettes. About two-thirds of the videos are of motion pictures, but the rest are from publishing houses. How To Cook. How To Diet. How To Eat. How To Hammer. Art At The Louvre. How To Get Published. And there are huge television monitors showing product around the clock.

By the way, you can purchase the videocassette of this book at your local store. I even wear a purple Danskin in it.

Computers

A sub-heading generally means we are now entering a topic that doesn't quite fit into the main topic of the chapter, but there was no other place to put it that seemed to make sense and it is late at night anyway. And that about sums up what publishing houses think of computers.

I pointed out previously that most publishing houses are not computerized. I have sometimes thought that the manufacturers of red and blue pencils must send out anonymous letters to editors describing the horrors of word processing and desktop publishing. Typesetters also have a lot at stake. After all, they charge by the keystroke, both for initial input and corrections.

If publishing houses are not computerized, but are a prime market for the use of those machines, then it should not be difficult to comprehend the astonishing fact that publishing houses have put up a huge fuss over both computer books and computer software. The former has been covered elsewhere. What about the latter?

Software is not considered part of software publishing. Software is considered foreign territory. People who write software are aliens. Book stores do not sell software. How does one market software? Computers, like VCR's, must be a passing fad. Besides, there are too many technical words to learn and standards change with astonishing frequency.

Let's get back to production costs again. Fifteen thousand dollars to the author as an advance on the book. Fifteen thousand dollars to a programmer for a program (broken up into development cycles, tests, and options on revisions). Two dollars per hardcover book manufactured, one dollar for mass paperback; seventy-five cents to a dollar per diskette duped, serialized, verified and labeled. The manual for the diskette can be included in the diskette -- let the end-user print it out. Otherwise, toss in another dollar. We know the retail pricing for the books; a diskette can be sold for upwards of $70.00. Computer owners seem to like spending through the nose for a few lines of code.

But there's something more here than meets an eye usually bloodshot from squinting at a computer monitor: programs can be updated, enhanced, revised and otherwise modified to great financial advantage. If the first version is marketed at $70, then over the next year, one can market upgrades for $10 or up a pop, and then spring version 2.01 on the end-user for another $70. Another year of upgrades and boom, version 3.01. And the upgrades can be for the simplest program module: new drivers for new printers; the ability to export and import data; an interface with another program; or the ability to change the color palette of the monitor.

Oh, but the book stores and the book clubs and the ... not printed word ... whole new area ... don't know how to market ... harumph.

Actually, this reaction is more understandable than the one involving VCR's. Videocassettes are rather simple products. You take a how-to cook book, have the author/chef stand in a kitchen, and film the person cooking. Close-up of chef's hat, close-up of chef's smiling face, close-up of chef's hands chopping up string beans. The package for the cassette is similar to the jacket for the book. The cassette is about the same size as a paperback. There are currently three signal standards to cope with - - NTSC for the United States, and PAL and SECAM for other areas of the world - - with Super-VHS and high definition video slowly catching on.

But computers are not like that, as publishers discovered when they tried publishing computer books that made no sense. One has to worry about syntax, architecture, formatting, disk size, operating systems, monitor and graphic card types.

135

Or does one?

Marketing and common sense could have cleared the air. Houses started to evince interest in computers by concentrating on the low end -- producing useless books written by freelancers relying on advance copies of computer manuals. These books had a general success even though the programs contained in them typically presented the wrong syntax for the specified computer. By concentrating on the low end, the houses forgot to keep track of what was really happening in the market: increasing sales to homes of IBM's and compatibles, and Apples. Rapidly falling prices. Astonishing shifts in technology, permitting more RAM, more storage space, quicker operations, better colors, and graphic print-outs. This blindness resulted in one house gearing most of its energy into producing a book explaining a system that was "assured" of revolutionizing home computers: the Adam. The who?

Sure, there are changes, but the changes overlap and yield sufficient lead times. For example, 32-bit microcomputers hit the scene in early 1987 and became official by mid-1987. But that doesn't mean the end of the 16-bit machines. It means having two markets. And, yes, there have been changes in operating systems and diskette sizes, but that too is not the end of the world as we know it. It means a few changes in the program and the use of a smaller diskette.

But the book stores. It is true that most book stores have not put up scaffolding to create shelf space for programs. Book stores are, however, branching out to sell blank diskettes and computer paper.

Besides, targeting a computer end-user market is again as simple as finding a diabetic or a bridge player. There are specialty magazines, specialty mailing lists, and even magazines and computer-animated advertising on diskette.

Still, other than converting dictionaries, thesauruses and a few diet books to diskette, publishers remain in the dark ages.

So I won't even mention database exploitation or CD-ROM's. Those can wait for the tenth edition of this book, which will be marketed on optical disk.

CHAPTER THIRTEEN

JEWS, APES AND COMPUTERS

This section is not about Jews, apes or computers, but the title is one I have been attempting to use for years. There was also no need to mention Playboy in this chapter, but hopefully the reference will increase chances of serializing at least this part.

THEY'VE DIGITIZED THE PLAYMATES. That's something my daughter said to me when she loaded the public domain disk. It cost $3.50 and of course came from California. Everytime I go to California on film or computer business, I'm amazed at how blond everyone is. But the more than shapely image on my RGB monitor was not blond; she was black and white and could be printed out at 300 dots per inch.

I could make her blond if I wanted. The disk came with a simple paint program. Reverse; invert; solarize; tint; that sort of thing. The kind of options one gets for a thousand dollars (retail) on VCR's hyped as being "digital." I've already complained to the manufacturers that they made a terrible mistake. Digitizing a single frame for the purpose of solarizing it doesn't make much sense for a thousand dollars. For a few dollars extra, wholesale, they could have added enough memory to digitize a couple of minutes; and for a few dollars more, they could have included an output jack so that I could transmit the images to my computer.

But since they haven't done that yet, one is left with diskettes that promise pin-ups, already digitized and ready for manipulation. I was immediately interested because of the price (any object associated with computers and selling for less than two thousand dollars attracts my attention) and because the use of computers in entertainment is one of my specialities.

Most people still don't understand computers and even fewer understand what the impact of the technology really is. That's why I purchased the diskette. A diskette is a round object sprayed with a magnetic medium; by changing the polarity of the medium, one can declare that something is plus or minus, 0 or 1. Each of those is called a bit. There are stop bits and data bits and tag bits, but all those terms mean is that something is 0 or 1, on or off, starting or finished, and the reason they mean those things is because engineers have said so. So on the one hand we have the binary system and on the other we have the understanding that a certain kind of impulse, representing the binary system, is to be translated into a mechanical response.

But how did that image get squished into bits? That's the question the answer to which means that entertainment as we know it has entered a new period of cross-fertilization. In the past, one would receive his or her issue of *Playboy* (unless it was a special issue, in which case the postman would usually intercept it), read the articles, unfurl the fold-out, study the other snapshots, and then either toss it or file it away for resale at a flea market. Whoever put together the diskette I purchased decided that was not good enough. What he or she did was purchase an inexpensive device that was then attached to his inexpensive printer. The fold-out or photograph was then carefully fed into the printer. A program directed the peripheral to move itself so that the picture was read for gray levels. Minutes passed by as the printer slowly moved the photograph up line by line and just as slowly the Playmate started to appear on the monitor. First the hair, then the face, the torso, until boom! there was an image composed of dots (pixels or pels in technical terms) on the monitor.

What's the difference between that and taping a television show on a VCR? When you tape using a VCR, you are recording analog signals. As you should realize by now, analog signals tend to be messy -- that's why the music industry is shifting toward CD's and DAT's. It's also why some high-end consumer VCR's are offering the capability of digitizing an analog image, using an ADC board (analog to digital converter). Right now, those VCR's will digitize one frame for you, but when you call up that one frame you finally realize what you've been missing on your television set: a decent picture.

Another difference is the ability to manipulate the image. If you hook up your VCR to another VCR and start to re-record because you want to put together an edited tape of favorite scenes, you quickly discover two facts of consumer life: even expensive home video equipment is pretty useless when it comes to editing a videotape and what does end up on the second tape has worse quality than what was on the first tape which was pretty bad to begin with.

Digital information is not only purer and more stable, the equipment available for processing it has gone down dramatically in price. The device used for inputting the images is called a scanner, and those range in price from $150 to $10,000. But you could also purchase your own ADC board to put in your computer and that would only set you back about $250 along with the cost of the RCA jack for hooking your board to your VCR or video camera.

The entertainment part comes in because once you have your images stored, you can play with them. That requires another set of programs, most of which will be paint programs. With some paint programs, I can pull in the image and actually reshape it and put back the color lost in the digitizing process. With a simple animation program, I can link together my new string of images into a film that I can play back on my monitor. Or, with the purchase of a DAC board, I can reconvert my digital film into an NTSC-analog one, transmit it to my VCR and have my own home movie of Playmates. I just saved myself $19.95 on the purchase of *Playboy*'s own Playmate videocassette.

But that in itself could be rather boring. It might be more interesting, for example, to include myself and selected friends in an animated special starring the Playmate of my choice. Simple enough -- I digitize all of us and incorporate us into the film. On the other hand, it might be more intriguing to see whether the Playmate's body might not go better with Sally's, and Sally's head with my body, and my head on the dog's tail. While I'm at it, maybe I'll digitize the Bill Cosby Show and put his head on the Playmate's body.

If you haven't caught on yet, what this technological revolution means is that the consumer can create his or her own entertainment. You can create the Bill Flushenagle Show, or the *Playboy* Homemate of the Month. You can use a typesetting program to incorporate your images with text and compose your own Playboy magazine, each and every month.

The uprushing reality of the combined analog/digital home entertainment center is that pretty soon, no one will be the prisoner of publishing houses, studios, videocassette distributors, television, radio, spouses, children, in-laws or even dogs. Just about everything we buy now has some hole, socket or pin waiting for when it can hooked up to a computer. Unless the marketing people in the standard entertainment industry catch on, they are going to lose us to the electronics industry. And what we are going to do is develop a new form of couch potatoism, where we can control the timing of what we want to see, hear and believe, the intensity of it, its color, its depth, and its quality. Since what we will be leaving behind will be the same old homogeneous book, film, sitcom or soap, we will soon forget what those things are. And if we believe that what we have is good, we can zap it over to a bulletin board service and let others pull it up.

A nice aside is that this technological era should put an end, once and for all, to those who want everyone else to believe and act as they do. I know that sounds like the entertainment industry, but I am talking only about a subset of it -- evangelists and their hordes. Since books, films, magazines, videos, artwork, maps, descriptions of the world as being round, crossword puzzles and all the rest can be put on various storage devices (optical disks can now hold 200 to 600 megabytes of data quite easily; that translates into a bunch of books and their film versions and the remakes), and even a child cannot see anything except a shiny disc, then there can be no more outrage over the visibility of an offending object. If you can't be sure of the contents from the title, you can program your computer to act as a censor. This combination of graphics' code means an areola, so don't show that film. Don't bring up any book with these words in it. Freed from the biblical worries over the First Amendment, these people can then start marketing their censorship programs, while leaving the rest of the world alone to explore humanity, love, beauty and the exploitation of electronic ancillaries.

CHAPTER FOURTEEN

OUT-TAKES ET CETERAS

Out-Takes

One of the more intriguing aspects of present-day culture is that we are desperate to rediscover, recycle and reformat. It is no longer a question of sitting down in front of the television set and, having watched a new show for five minutes, shout out, "I've seen that before!" This horrible sense of reliving one's cultural heritage over and over also infects movies ("My God, but this is the sixteenth remake of that film and it wasn't good when it came out the first time"), Broadway musicals (the reviewer: "Although first produced in 1897, the jokes do not appear at all outdated"), art, inflatable furniture and, of course, books.

One of the more interesting aspects of publishing is that not only is it difficult to get a book contract in the first place, it is even more difficult to get all of the work published. For an editor, there is nothing more satisfying than slashing. Sometimes, that slashing has its benefits; other times, it is merely an exercise in using up the pencil inventory of the publishing house.

The net result is this: an author accumulates fragments, chapters and entire manuscripts through editing, rejection and revision. If the books evince no interest and eventually go out of print, one might suppose no harm has been done (although a writer might always wonder whether the books might not have done better if the climactic chapter had been left in). Where the books achieve a relative success or win awards, then the grand creature known as the Revisionist Editor rears its ignominious head and hand and declares -- well after the author's death -- that the true works are yet to be rediscovered, recycled and reformated.

This is good news for doctoral candidates in English. Imagine being told in 1985 that your dissertation on Joyce's *Ulysses* would not be accepted because there were already two million such dissertations in the stacks. What luck that the following year the definitive edition (by personal account, the nineteenth definitive edition) should be published containing the correction of 5,000 errors.

This kind of event has been occurring with dramatic frequency. The discovery of bits of Thomas Wolfe, hidden manuscripts by Hemingway, even the completion of manuscripts left incomplete due to the demise of the author. Besides Joyce, "authorial discovery" has been applied to William Faulkner, Mark Twain, Stephen Crane, Theodore Dreiser and Thomas Hardy. And once all the errors, fragments and cocktail napkins have been put into print, one then turns to correspondence. First, correspondence from the author to famous people. Then from the author to unknown people. From famous people to the author. Unknown people to the author. Famous people to other famous people about the author. Unknown people to neighbors about the weather and the author. Once all that is cleared away, one can turn to the serious business of writing a satire about the author: "Faulkner as he would have written *Leave it to Beaver.*"

In the motion picture world, this wringing out of the last dime from another person's creation is achieved through remakes and colorization. Television was always years ahead with the invention of the syndicated re-run. But the subset of the entertainment industry that has had the longest success with revising, revamping, reissuing and re-running the living dead consists of politicians.

ET CETERAS

The following consists of quizzes, checklists and similar devices to see if you actually read this book.

1. In book publishing, titles are as important as R-rated scenes in motion picture remakes and sequels. If you have an agent, the agent will spend more time discussing titles with you than anything else other than commissions. After you have spent a solid week coming up with a title, the agent will start submitting your work.

Assume your work is accepted by a publishing house. What happens next?

a. The editor loves the title.

b. The editor suggests you come up with another title.

c. You come with another title and the book is published with that title.

d. You come up with another title and the book is published with a title selected by a member of the marketing department who has never read the book.

2. Name thirty published writers without looking at your book shelf.

3. Name one screenwriter.

4. Name the first or last name of any teleplay writer.

5. Give the initials of a radio scripter.

6. List five publishing houses that are not owned by conglomerates.

7. If your book is published and you die, what is the worse thing that can happen to you?
   a. The book is revised based upon "authorial intent."
   b. The book is abridged.
   c. The book goes out of print.
   d. The book suddenly becomes a best seller.
   e. All of the above.

8. You spend half of your life writing a novel and it is accepted by a major publishing house. You and your agent neglect to insert a final edit clause. When the book comes out, you discover that your editor, who has completely rewritten it, was a former employee of a magazine you particularly despise. What you do is:
   a. Buy the first print run and burn it.
   b. Tell people you've decided to "go popular."
   c. Change your name (for the tenth time).
   d. Hope that the translation into Japanese restores some of your literary conventions.

9. You've spent half of your life writing a screenplay and it is finally optioned. The producer exercises the option and turns the screenplay over to his niece, who has no film experience and is seventeen years old. Your contract contains no rewrite clause and no name clause. Your main character is changed from a man to a woman; the lover is changed from a woman to a goldfish; the child is transformed into a dog with cute ears. The niece is listed as executive producer and producer; you are listed as screenwriter. Your next step is to:
   a. Leak that you had an affair with the niece, which will explain everything.
   b. Change your name (for the eighteenth time).
   c. Show up at the Academy awards wearing a pink tux jacket and jeans.
   d. Start training goldfish.

10. You are ninety-five years old and have a green trunk filled with twenty novels, fifteen nonfiction trade books, sixty-two screenplays, one hundred teleplays, six thousand radio scripts, and the score to an opera. You should:
   a. _____ .
   b. _____ .
   c. _____ .
   d. _____ .
   e. __ .

11. Of the sixty thousand books published annually around the world:
    a. Ten thousand are worthy of publication.
    b. One thousand are worthy of publication.
    c. Two hundred are worthy of publication.
    d. Eight thousand seem to say the same thing.
    e. The same sixty thousand should be published the following year in abridged, revised and definitive volumes.

12. If you were the son or daughter of a famous actor, actress, writer or executive producer, you would:
    a. Change your name and not tell anyone of your relationship.
    b. Change your name but have your publicity manager leak out your relationship.
    c. Not change your name but deny any relationship.
    d. Not change your name and tell people it was harder for you to get to where you are than someone not burdened with that name.
    e. Change your son's or daughter's name.

13. In the event you run out of ideas, you should:
    a. Stand in a crowded shopping mall and eavesdrop.
    b. Hire an idea person.
    c. Age some photographs of Marilyn Monroe in your oven and claim that they are the last, last, last, last photographs of the actress taken at her very, very, very last sitting.
    d. Get a regular job and be happy for the rest of your life.

14. The epithet given a book that has made it to the top ten in sales is spelled:
    a. bestseller
    b. best seller
    c. best-seller
    d. Peter Sellers
    e. none of the above

CHAPTER FIFTEEN

ART BY NUMBERS

Continuing The Theme

It seems that most writers also doodle, draw or paint. Thankfully, many don't take their output seriously until they become famous authors, at which point they usually have the contacts for arranging a gallery show.

But the art world is very similar to publishing and movies. A handful of powerful people controls what gets seen, reviewed and bought. An artist's relationship with a gallery is often a form of slavery. In this country, until the laws are changed, artists will usually never see any profit from the resale of a work or its ancillary exploitation.

Yet it is also startling to observe that a lot of contemporary art is just as homogeneous as what the rest of the entertainment industry gives us. "Decorative" art seems to be the key word, because people who can afford art are apparently always decorating. They need an endless supply of colorful images. "Appropriation" art is an up-and-coming area for those people who can no longer afford the original Van Gogh. Instead, they can buy a Picasso, Rembrandt, Titian or Dali which has been painted by someone who has projected a slide of the work onto the canvas, and then airbrushed in the colors. The National Endowment for the Arts even gave a grant once for the pursuit of this technique.

For the sake of parity, and because so many writers dream of being artists (and vice versa), I am including this short story.

THE MUSEUM

The first curator would be a Rhinelander, six feet tall with blue eyes and black hair and a three hundred acre estate upstate, part of which was used for breeding horses. His family would not build the Museum, or even contribute any money to its founding. That type of family didn't; they had old money and therefore knew how to invest other people's new money in projects dear to their own hearts. A Rhinelander wife would coordinate the fundraising, a Rhinelander banker would be the accountant, a nephew would control the publicity ("The Rhinelander Foundation announced today that ..."). It was called "lending a name in support of a worthy cause."

Rhinelander Senior stepped into the role of curator lustily, traveling the world for everything modern to place into the newly established Museum of Art. That had been the idea, the philosophy -- enough with those stodgy museums filled with the old classics, what was needed was a museum dedicated to fledgling art, cutting edge art. The concept created a carefully orchestrated uproar in the cultured circles. The Museum was condemned as a frivolous pursuit. Critics laughed that no one in their right mind could ever rationally suppose that enough modern "art" existed to fill even one small wall of one small room in the Museum. Even architects tossed in their paragraphs of outrage, commenting that the Museum, being made of steel and glass instead of the beautiful, thick granite blocks every other museum was carved from, was doomed to collapse during the first rain.

Rhinelander Senior thrived on the opposition and knew, besides, that bad press was nonetheless press and it was better for the public to know that the Museum existed than to not know at all. He also knew that he would be able to fill the Museum, its basement and a few warehouses, for nothing was simpler in life than picking up articles from starving artists for the cost of the canvas and paint. He did not have to be discriminating, either -- he himself preferred marble fountains of naked women in the classical mode -- since no one knew what modern art was and, therefore, anything could fit the bill.

Opening night was *una grande festa, un gran fete, ein grosser Ding*. Guests, bearing engraved invitations, made their way between rows of fluorescent lightbulbs which sizzled and were declared pestilential and bad for the eyes. The chirruping lights cast their glow upon what would be termed the following day in all newspapers of repute, "the grotesque, the outrageous, the childish, the absurd." Some paintings were made up of pinpoints. Some were splashes of color. Some had women with both eyes to one side of elongated noses, and breasts which stretched into hands and legs. The sculpture seemed shapeless. Even so, the crowd did not disperse until the crystal punch bowls had been drained and the silver ladles stolen.

Rhinelander knew he had a success when people kept saying, "But is it art?" as

146

opposed to "It's pure trash," for as long as people had a questionmark in their minds -- and the cultured tended to, since they had been proven wrong so many times before and didn't want to get caught yet again -- a cultural shift could occur. He charged a dime for admission and the first rains came and went.

In five years, the Museum was a remarkable success. Rhinelander brought in Rhinelander Junior and his college roommate, Amsterdam, to be, respectively, curators of painting and sculpture. Rhinelander Senior retained the role of curator of administration and special events. But now they didn't have to scour the world, for the world came to them, a world of one-eyed, one-eared, one-legged, astigmatic, tortured, tormented, wild people bearing banjos they had jumped on, books they had partly burned, canvases they had rolled over while naked, dogs they had stuffed and then painted. One artist even brought his wife sitting on an uncomfortable chair with a placard hung across her naked chest reading *Do Not Feed*. He had signed his sculpture in a place Rhinelander Senior found distasteful but which Junior and Amsterdam found hilariously fitting. Senior won out by commenting they could not possibly store her in a crate in the basement when the show was changed.

But by now courses were being given in modern art at the best universities. Students traipsed through the Museum with their notepads, art pads and conte crayons. Jones had to be brought in to coordinate education programs. That led to Myers taking over special events, Cranston handling floor arrangements, Wilentz looking into watercolors and Killebrew becoming involved with mixed media. Rhinelander Senior died, leading to the first battle.

"His body falls under sculpture and that's my domain," claimed Amsterdam.

"Once it starts decaying, it's mixed media," put in Killebrew.

"I think every rational art historian and curator would acknowledge that death is a special event," said Myers.

"Regardless of what you decide, where the body goes is up to me," declared Cranston.

"And what we say about it has to pass through my office," said Jones.

Rhinelander Junior claimed the prerogative of blood relation which was hooted down as being irrelevant. So he threw his vote in with Amsterdam and Wilentz, which was not enough to prevent Myers, Jones, Cranston and Killebrew from having the body stuffed, dipped in acrylic and stored in a crate in the basement. But the defeat did cause the three losers to meet secretly in a coffee shop in the Village where they discussed strategy.

"I say we break off and form our own museum of post-modern art," suggested Amsterdam.

"I'm not leaving a museum my father founded and is now buried in," said Rhinelander Junior.

"What about galleries?" said Wilentz. "We can set up art galleries and buy certain artists at the same time we buy up the same artists with our Museum budgets. Then we pick a year to make an artist famous, bring him out in our wings of the Museum ... and in our galleries. That way, we become famous as curators and make tons of money on the side."

The conspirators slapped their foreheads at the foolishness which had kept them from devising the idea years before. The next day, three galleries opened: The Artists' Gallery, the Gallery of Art and The Art. The first specialized in paintings, the second in sculpture and the third in watercolors. And they all had large basements which, in a year, were filled with modern, post-modern, impressionist, cubist, post-cubist, pre-nouvelle and mid-strata art.

In an ensuing December, the three curators invited Cranston to a party where they got him drunk and into bed with an inexpensive woman. Afterward, he signed the papers permitting the construction crews to come in and change around the three wings. Jones, Myers and Killebrew, finding themselves outflanked, met in a bistro on the upper Eastside.

"What do you think they're up to?" asked Jones.

"They're pulling a coup, obviously," said Myers. "To me, what they're doing comes under special events. And I don't like having my toes stepped on."

"Well, I think we better come up with something or those three will think they can get away with anything from now on." Killebrew pushed his beer glass back and forth. "My brother, for example, has been doing some exciting things in mixed media. I had meant to bring this up at the last meeting."

"If your brother is good enough to get into the Museum, then my sister should, too," said Jones. "She's doing amazing things with hair, paper and glue."

"I can dig up some relatives, too," said Myers. "Let's get Cranston to sign the work papers."

The next night, Cranston was embracing two voluptuous women and one expensive bottle of whiskey.

The Museum was entirely closed down during renovations which had the world of culture buzzing with suspense and curiosity. By now, the Museum was post-establishment and the artists who exhibited in it had thick, four-color books written about them and were invited to the cheekiest parties. The curators were themselves sought after, although those in the know knew which ones could be positioned in the same room. Closing down the Museum turned out to be a boon for the party business in a whirlwind attempt to wear down the curators, artists, friends and families who might know what was under foot.

The first leak, however, came from the galleries. The Artists' Gallery was suddenly hanging only Shlemiel's canvases, large, stark paintings, some of them all white with a black dot, some of them all black with a white dot, and one daring statement having a blue dot and a yellow dot impressed over orange. But it was a brilliant orange.

The Gallery of Art contemporaneously announced the presence of Varksteck, whose sculpture was almost unbelievable in its simple yet overbearing complexity.

A rubber tire with a screwdriver sticking out of it; a mannikin with areolae painted on; an Edsel (just an Edsel, but signed under one seat by the artist); and plaster casts of various members of the artist's family wearing their own, original, unwashed clothes.

Students, art historians, reporters and buyers rushed over to The Art and gasped at the work of Wasserman. Never had watercolors been so varied or suffused with a sense of "something" (the technical word would come later, in a doctoral dissertation). For example, there was the piece of paper that had been soaked in water until it had wrinkled. It was sold on the spot for one thousand dollars. Not to mention the watercolor entitled, "Five Men on Horses in the Middle of a Deserted Street on a Hot Day in some Italian Town the name of which is unknown Having a Conversation over some good Espresso and Mentioning Women they had *Known*," which was part of a series, actually, but unfortunately the titles took up most of the spatial elements and one had to struggle to find the horses.

After the new finds had sold out, the remaining question involved the other half of the Museum. Jones, Myers and Killebrew, who had at first been chagrined by the maneuvering of their opposing curators, realized on opening day that they had the upper hand when everyone rushed to their wings. Killebrew's brother came through with flying colors. One entire room was devoted to his mixed media "Ball point pen which has been peed on for three hundred sixty-six days." Jones' sister was well represented with a collage of pubic hair. Even Myers had found some nieces and nephews who made profound statements with mechanical objects. One which went on to great fame and was the leading piece in the first cultural exchange with China was an electric fan blowing on a light bulb entitled, "Socrates in Deep Discussion Prior to Death."

Thus began the Second Battle. Only this time, it was each curator for himself.

Rhinelander Junior and the Artists' Gallery cornered the market on fruit glued to canvas. Amsterdam bought up post-destruction art, including a number of artists who cut off parts of their bodies and signed them until they had no fingers left. Wilentz honed in on watercolors painted without water. Killebrew's brother sped up his output by being force fed seltzer. Myer's nieces and nephews entered a phase of neo-incestuous iconoclasm and clap. Jones' sister, having run out of her own pubic hair, turned to animals until the ASPCA got onto her, and then concentrated on synthetic hair. Cranston became fat, indolent and impotent, ran for mayor, and lost.

But what could the curators come up with next? The Museum ... its avant-garde attitudes, its flamboyance, its taste, its intelligence. It could not possibly remain static for more than a few moments. It was a shrine, an arbiter, a godhead. People literally died to get into it (Rhinelander Senior, coated with dust and forgotten in a damp corner, might have had a laugh over that). What next? cried the world of art and culture. Who next? The galleries and the Museum had already made and then kicked out dozens of artists and relatives. The curators were wracking their brains for another major leap forward. Blank canvases had been done; canvases with dots had been done; naked female bodies were always good for a month or two, but then what?

The curators, exhibiting an almost mystical collective unconscious, singly arrived at the same conclusion. Cranston was repeatedly filled to the brim with whiskey and signed the required papers. The Museum was closed down, only the second time in its history. The world hummed with expectation. The Museum which had brought forth spaghetti *al dente* to crawl in, pubism, neo- and post-self-destruction, was undoubtedly about to create a new new new post post post pre pre pre.

On opening day, no one was disappointed for no one could possibly say "But what is it? What does it mean?" In one marvelous wing was a pocket calculator. In another, a saw blade. A box of matches, unspent, on a white pedestal. A lawn mower, a coffee pot, a saddle, a helicopter (what grace! what brilliance! a green helicopter!), a talking robot of Abraham Lincoln, a propeller, a razor blade, a bicycle chain (and theft-proof lock). It was endless, a wonderful display of the new and the best in art and all of it available for purchase at Harvey's Hardware Store (formerly the Artists' Gallery), Amsterdam's Gallery of Tools and The Sculpture Garden, subject to local tax. The other curators, not to be outdone, started mail order businesses which carried tasteful, thermographed Christmas cards and nudie calendars. Art and man, as one commentator gracefully put it, had finally been brought together in an embrace of common, industrious devotion.

APPENDIX

SAMPLE REJECTION LETTERS

The rejection letter that means your manuscript was never read and was probably used as a placemat is usually xeroxed on a small sheet of paper and reads as follows:

Dear Writer:
The material enclosed has been given careful consideration and is not suitable for use in our publication at this time. Due to the volume of submissions received, we regret that we cannot offer individual criticisms.

All submissions should be accompanied by a stamped, self-addressed envelope, if their return is desired.

Your interest in [X publication] is most warmly appreciated.

The Editors

The above letter does not mean that you should resubmit the manuscript when the Zodiacal signs are more favorable. Loosely translated, the letter means this:

Dear Writer,
Why are you bothering us? We have our own stable of writers. And, boy, the gall of sending us something without a return envelope. The only reason we are sending it back to you and including this form letter is that you might end up being famous or, more likely than not, you are the type of idiot who purchases magazines [or books] to see what we are publishing and we do not want to lose your money.

If you send us anymore items, however, we might be inclined to cancel your subscription and refund your money.

Yours,

The fed up secretary who has to rip open the manuscripts, type out return labels, put on postage, and clip on this stupid rejection letter.

The following is a typical real letter written to someone who is just starting out.

━━━━━━━━━━

Dear So-and-so:
Enclosed is the manuscript you were so kind to send to me. I have given it a careful reading and have come to the unfortunate conclusion that you would have a better chance placing it elsewhere.

Sincerely,

━━━━━━━━━━

Loosely translated, this letter is a step above a form rejection letter. It means:

━━━━━━━━━━

Dear So-and-so:
Thanks for sending the time-waster that not even our reader could stomach. But the reader did feel you had potential and I want to make sure you send me your best seller.

━━━━━━━━━━

The Joyce letter goes as follows:

━━━━━━━━━━

Dear So-and-so:
Your book, entitled "X," is certainly a masterpiece. We have never seen a book like this and feel deeply that it deserves to be published. Our house, however, does not publish this type of book anymore. It can only be termed "experimental," and that is an area we are not involved with. I wish I knew who to tell you to send it to, but I do not.

Best of luck.

━━━━━━━━━━

Translated, the letter means:

━━━━━━━━━━

Dear So-and-so:
Your book is a masterpiece. Unfortunately, a publishing house can no longer take the risk of publishing a masterpiece. If only you wrote a number of "popular" pieces that we could put out, we might be able to sneak it onto our list. As for other places,

there are none.

Best ...

━━━━━━━━━━━━━━━

Sometimes, an editor who takes a personal interest in your work, will decide that he is also the arbiter of good taste. As in the following:

━━━━━━━━━━━━━━━

Dear So-and-so:

I have read your manuscript entitled "X" and find that it is not particularly appealing. I do not understand why you would write such a piece. You obviously have talent, but you have misused it in this instance.

Sincerely yours,

━━━━━━━━━━━━━━━

A variation on the above:

━━━━━━━━━━━━━━━

Dear So-and-so:
I have read your manuscript entitled "X" and, although I find it well written, I have strong feelings about the ending. You do not have the ending I would have thought would have followed from what came before. Whereas you have the heroine dying, I envisaged her happily coming together again with her former lover who betrayed her so many times. An upbeat ending is what I saw.

Best wishes and sincerely yours,

━━━━━━━━━━━━━━━

Loosely translated, the above two letters mean:

━━━━━━━━━━━━━━━

Dear So-and-so:
Although you were able to keep my attention throughout, I want a book written the way I see how books should be written. That means plot, including endings. Until you can read my mind, you can forget getting something published through me.

As for why I don't offer you a contract subject to you rewriting the book to fit my needs, I know that you are an upright writer who would never condescend to rewriting a book according to my dictates. You don't really want to publish something until

153

you write it the way I want it to begin with.

Sincerely,

═══════════════

Now that you have an idea as to how rejection letters should be interpreted, I am going to toss a bunch of form and personalized notes at you so that you can test yourself. For those of you who have already accumulated a stout pile of your own letters, you might compare phrasing. I am keeping the original misspellings, misstatements and other idiocies that editors are supposed to be expert in excising from a writer's manuscript.

═══════════════

Dear   ,

We are sorry to tell you that your proposed manuscript doesn't seem ritgh for our list. We are grateful to you for thinking of us at thise time and wish you the best of luck in finding a publisher for your work.

Editorial Staff

═══════════════

Dear Ms/Mr.   ,

Thank you very much for your query concerning "X." Although the subject is indeed timely, we just feel that such a book is for us.

Sincerely,

Assistrnt to the Editor

═══════════════

Dear   ,

You are quite right that in this Bicentennial Year everyone is working on a show that deals with some aspect of American history. Our production company is no exception. Ours is a kind of documentary on the inside story of the battle of Little Big Horn. Which is why, after encouraging you to submit ideas, I must reject the first one you send, on American in the international scene.

Your proposal is really journalistic or news-oriented. You might have better luck submitting it to the news department of one of the stations or networks.

Sincerely,

Dear   ,

Thank you for sending your two novellas which we have read with interest. I am sorry to say we don't feel they are good possibilities for our program here at the present time, but I am grateful to you for considering us and wish you the best of success with the novellas elsewhere. I am returning the manuscript material to you separately.

Sincerely,

*

*Dictated by [editor] and signed in his absence.

Dear   ,

I am sending back your two articles, not at all because of any defects in them but quite simply because the backlog at [the magazine] would not enable me to print them for more than two years, surely far too long for you to wait.

Cordially,

·

Dear   ,

I am returning here your manuscript "X." I have to confess that I found it hard to find the "comic" in this novel. Nor did it seem truly tragic.

Thanks,

Dear   ,

Sorry. No.

                Yours,

Dear   ,

It was good of you to remember me for your novel "X" which I have now had the chance to consider. It is too narcissistic. But as you know, editorial judgments are necessarily subjective and perhaps someone else will react with more enthusiastically.

                Best,

Dear   ,

Thank you for sending us the two stories which we have read with interest. Despite their merits, we are sorry to report that they do not seem right for our list.

                Sincerely,

Dear   ,

We don't like this one, but thanks for the look.

                Yours,

Dear   ,

We have now had a chance to give thoughtful consideration to the two children's books. Although we enjoyed reading them, I am sorry to have to report that we don't feel they would be right for our juvenile list. They are better suited to publication as a part of a language arts program developed by the school division of a publisher.

                Sincerely yours,

Dear   ,

We have now had a chance to give thoughtful consideration to the two children's books you sent. Although we enjoyed reading them, I am sorry to report that are not really suited for our language arts program. They would probably be right for a general juvenile list.

Yours sincerely,

═══════════════════

Dear   ,

Thank you for sending us the four stories. We enjoyed reading them tremendously. I'm sorry to say that we can't do anything for you with respect to stories but if, however, you have something longer, such as a novel, we would be happy to consider it.

Good luck,

═══════════════════

Dear   ,

We have now had the time to read and consider "X" and regret to say that we will not be making a publishing offer for it. This decision is based on our judgement of its sales potential.

Best,

═══════════════════

Dear   ,

Sensible, but dogged and unoccasioned. Thanks for the look.

Sincerely,

═══════════════════

Dear   ,

We have read your manuscript with interest and admiration. It will not do for us;

fiction is in a very bad way right now, ad we are taking on almost none.

Thanks,

━━━━━━━

Dear   ,

We have read your manuscript with interest and admiration. It will not do for us; nonfiction is in a very bad way right now, especially the type you write. If you do, however, write a How To book, please send it along.

Cordially,

*

*Dictated and signed in absence of [editor].

━━━━━━━

Dear   ,

Please excuse the long delay in replying. Four years may seem inexcusable, but I spent one of those years tracking you down. I tossed and turned with the other editors over this story. Although we are not taking it, I want you to know that we admired it and would like to see other stories of yours. Just remember to send us a change of address form now and then.

Best and good wishes,

━━━━━━━

Dear   ,

I want to thank you for giving us the chance to consider your manuscript "X" but I must tell you that we will not be making an offer to publish. The fiction market is so very tight these days that we are taking on only those works to which the department feels very strongly committed. Judgements of fiction are lamentably subjective, though, and you may well find another publisher more receiptive; I urge you to try elsewhere.

Sincerely,

========

Dear   ,

I appreciated the opportunity to read your nonfiction manuscript "X." You have certainly done your homework. However, the manuscript deserves publication in a scholarly journal -- which, of course, is a compliment to you. We are keen on accuracy and objectivity, but our manuscripts must have some drama.

I regret the bad news.

Sincerely,

========

Dear   ,

I appreciated the chance to read your nonfiction manuscript "X." You have certainly done a great deal of research, almost all of it new and startling. But I'm afraid the manuscript is too dramatic for our type of audience, which is more scholarly. I think you would have a better chance with a popular publishing house, as opposed to an academic one.

Best wishes --

========

Dear   ,

Thank you for sending me your novel "X," but I am sorry to say that my publishing schedule for the very small list which I handle personally is over commited and I cannot consider any new projects at this time or for the foreseeeable future.

Sincerely,

*

*Typed and signed in the absence of [editor]

========

159

Dear   ,

Thank you ever so much for permitting us to consider "X." I'm afraid, however, the the two of us here who have looked at it, while appreciating its intelligence, are not 'quite enthusiastic enough about it to think we could have any real financial success with it. I know how hard it is waiting for a decision and I hope the one year delay did not distress you.

Yours, with kindest affection,

*

*Composed, typed and signed in [editor's] absence.

═══════════════

Dear   ,

Our editors have now read "X" and I am sorry to report that they do not feel it is suitable for our list.

While our policy does not permit us to release editorial reports, let me quote a portion which you may find helpful: "The problem here is that the author is so set on writing an allegory that the story suffers. Instead of writing a good, solid story involving love, death and perhaps a tint of mystery, he digresses into symbols and imagery that only serve to bore the reader who wants a quick read. There is no doubt that the author possesses the style and intelligence to draft a masterpiece, but until he understands that allegories are passe, he will have difficulties coming to terms with contemporary publishing life."

Yours,

═══════════════

Dear   ,

Many thanks for sending in "X" for our consideration. We greatly appreciated reading it but, unfortunately, we feel the story relies too heavily on symbols, image

160

and allgory and not enough on action.

Hope you have a happy New Year --

Dear   ,

Thank you for sending me the manuscript "X" which I have now read. Although I took pleasure in the writing, I found the idea puzzling. Why would I want to read a satire? It strikes me, in short, as an undertaking quite unlikely to appeal to many readers. Who reads satires anymore? I wonder why you don't just tell the story straight.

It seems to me that there is perfectly good writing here put to peculiar use.

Yours truly,

Dear   ,

Thank you for having had given us the opputrunity to consider your manuscript entitled "X." We have it read it with great interest. It contains some very good writing. Our generly feeling, however, as that its was relentlessly grim. Relentless grimness is not something that we felt would fit onto our list.

Yours,

Dear   ,

Enclosed herewith is your manuscript "X." A number of us reviewed it and no one was enthusiastic. There is no doubt that your are a sophisticated writer but your choice of material just doesn't work in today's market. I hope you find someone mmuch more enthusiastic than us.

Yours,

Dear   ,

Thank you for sending you manuscript "X." Our Literary Department thanks you for showing it to us but they tell me that in their opinion it is not in form appropriate for a trade book. When you have it in form appropriate for a trade book, please send it back to me and I weill again refer it to our Literary Department.

sincerely,

Dear   ,

Frankly, I can't remember the manuscript you sent me seven years ago, but if you really want to give it another try, I'd be happy to consider it again if you like.

Best,

Dear   ,

I'm returning "X." I am sorry I held on to this for so long but it took me a while to get to it and once I read it I spent the rest of the time, quite a while, trying to decide what it is and how to handle it and now I have decided that although I thinks it's really lovely and I really like it I think that it would be too difficult to publish appropriately.

The story is after all quite bizarre, although strangely appealing but I think the whole thing would come out as too complicated and expensive a package and it would be hard to market it effectively.

I don't really have a clue as to who else would want to chance reading this.

Sincerely,

Dear   ,

Thank you for giving us the opprotunity to consider "X" which I found quite literate and sophisticate while conveying very nicely a sense of time and place but, alas, it is

162

the wrong time and place for us. Perhaps another editor will have a better sense of committment since, after all, publishing is based on a sense of committment.

Cordially,

Dear　　　,

Thank you for letting us have a look at "X." Unfortunately, it is too literary for release as an original paperback. Get yourself an agent who can steer you to the right hardcover publisher. If your book becomes a commercial succees and it is reviewed by prominant reviewers so that the more educated reader would get turned on to it, then definitely please do send it back to us. In paperback first, however, the book would die.

Yours turly,

Dear　　　,

Thank you for submitting "X." I have just finished reviewing the material which you sent to me and I find it to be high quality work. Although I sincerely feel that your novel is worthy of publication, I regret to inform you that we will be unable to participate in bringing it to press. Thanks anyway.

Best,

Dear　　　,

Nope. Sorry.

Yours,

Dear　　　,

Thank you for your inquiry. We are no longer set up to read unsolicited manuscripts and it would be virtually impossible to separate your submission from the 80+ or so that we receive daily. Your only chance would be if you could convince your agent to represent you in your short fiction, although we understand that agents generally

163

do not do that.

Thanks for your interest anyway and we hope you enjoy your subscription to our magazine. Enclosed is a renewal form.

Sincrerly,

———————————

Dear   ,

Unfortunately, although we liked the story "X," we cannot consider it while it has a tragic ending. We doubt that any woman's magazine would take the story with a tragic ending.

Best,

———————————

Dear   ,

I regret to say we are not going to make a publishing offer on "X." I think it conveys a marvelously sharp sense of time and place and the setting is well chosen, but it is not suited to the popular press as we know it. The manuscript will be returned to you herewith.

Sincerely,

———————————

Dear   ,

Yes, we did receive your manuscript and please accept our apologies for not ac-knowleding it sooner but things have been in a clerical mess here after the small office fire.

Best,

———————————

Dear   ,

Thank you for writingmea bout your story "X." At the present time, however, our finction bank is well-filled.

Sincerely,

━━━━━━━━━━━━━━

Dear   ,

Thank you for letting us see "X" but I'm afraid it's just not what we're looking for. It's very difficult, we find, for men to write a women's romance with the proper sensibilities. For example, the rape scene is just too male oriented.

Sincerely,

━━━━━━━━━━━━━━

Dear   ,

We are returning forwthith the children's stories you were kind enough to send to us. Although we felt here that they were well written and, at times, beautiful, we found that they were too moralistic to fit into our list. Children, we find, do not like moralistic tales anymore and we hope that if you write a more contemporary tale, about divorce or AIDS, for example, you will send it on to us.

Best wishes for these Holiday Seasons --

━━━━━━━━━━━━━━

Enough for letters. You get the drift, for certainly these letters, collected from an assemblage of writers over the years, create a drift in themselves. What about membership in one of the great societies of authors? One friend, having published over three hundred works in national publications and for national television, applied and was sent the following letter from one such society:

Dear   ,

The Membreship Committee did not feel that the publication record in your application would qualify you for membership in our society.

As you know, our society is highly regarded internationaly and our list contains some of the most famous writers currently living. Once you have achieved a greater measure of success, please do reapply, at which time, if accepted, you will be able to attend our luncheons and receive advise from us with regard to your contract negotiations.

Sincerely,

PUBLISHING CONTRACTS

In the event you strike gold and receive a letter stating you are to appear at the offices of the Editor to pick up a copy of your contract, you might want to go in with some idea of what you will be handed. Obviously, not all publishing contracts are the same, and what follows is an example of a contract executed by a well known author. After each clause, I will give some comments in brackets as to the meaning of the clause and how it could be renegotiated, if necessary. These comments are not meant as legal advice. They are only to be construed as fiction.

If you want real legal advice, go to a lawyer who will charge you an arm, a leg and a copyright. But if you do go to a lawyer, remember the following: 1) shop around, making sure that your initial consultation is free; 2) get a lawyer who has done publishing contracts before; 3) get an estimate of the fee (this is your first contract and the negotiations will be rather one-sided, favoring the publisher); and 4) request an itemized bill. An itemized bill does not mean a bill stating: "For services rendered: reading documents, negotiating new contract, drafting new contract 40 hours .... $5,000.00." An itemized bill means: "For services rendered: by associate X, reading of documents, which he has never done before, z hours at $[money]; by associate Y, researching possible clauses, which he has never done before, z hours at $[money]; by me, the partner, making a phone call, passing the bull with the publishing house's lawyer, and not getting anywhere, z hours at $[money]; lunch for all of us at your expense, $[money]; fling with prostitutes for all of us at your expense, $[money] .... TOTAL .... $[your advance]."

Remember: don't get your hopes up. Editors are used to two events. First, the contract signed without a peep. Second, the contract to which the agent appends some xeroxed clauses, primarily involving the nature of the agency and the agent's address, to which accounting statements and royalty checks are to be mailed.

But even where an editor, having crawled back down from the ceiling, agrees to negotiate, the process is a strange one because all changes have to fit on the house's form contract. A series of changes results in cross-outs, lines leading to typed-in clauses, white-outs, landscape and portrait insertions, until the contract looks like the diagram for a microprocessor.

One of the more interesting reactions is evoked when the author is incorporated. Some houses have a lot of experience here, in that many of those series in the potboiler, romance and mystery genres are provided to a house by a corporation that fields out the writing to freelancers. But where a house has not confronted an author/corporation before, the struggle to have the contract phrased appropriately is often prolonged and bloody. One might finally get in the name of the corporation and, lower down, the fact that the corporation will be providing a manuscript written by the author himself, but the house will inevitably white-out a sign-off by the corporation and re-insert the name of the author. The house wants the author to be individually liable on the agreement which, of course, obviates the entire reason for having an author incorporate.

AGREEMENT entered into on the ___ day of _____ , 19__ between X Publishing Co., a New York corporation ("X"), and Y, residing at _____ ("Author").

[This contract omits the preamble of "Whereas" and "Therefore" clauses that establish what the contract is about and that it is entered into for valid consideration.]

WITNESSETH:

1. GRANT OF RIGHTS. The Author hereby grants and assigns to X with respect to Author's literary work provisionally entitled "Z" (the "Book"), which title may only be changed by mutual consent, the exclusive right to publish and authorize others to publish the Book in the English language in book form throughout the world (the "Territory").

[The above is an overly general grant and assignment, somewhat defined in the subparagraphs that follow. Some small problems are: 1) change of title should be in a separate clause. A mechanism and a time period for exercising a right to change of title should be described. For example, a publication date can be established and the author or publisher will then be given six months prior to such date to notify the other of a suggested title change, and the other party will then have ten days thereafter to accept or reject the title change. An author could, of course, contract that the publisher will be able to suggest title changes, but the author has the final say. Publishers are notorious for changing perfectly good titles to absolutely dreadful ones on the basis of "market studies."]

["Authorize others to publish" is much too broad. Those terms need to be defined and limited. For example, "others" could be defined to mean other prestige publishing houses on a par with X.

[Since the paragraph is embellished by what follows, I will not comment on the remaining generalities.]

Without limiting the generality of the foregoing, such rights shall include the following exclusive rights throughout the Territory:

(a) The right to print, publish and sell and to authorize others to print, publish and sell the Book in the English language in paperback form, which term "paperback form" shall include "mass-market," "quality paperback" or other paperbound editions.

[Who are these "others"? Paperback form is vaguely defined, and one can state that it and mass market and quality paperback are terms that already have a certain meaning in the publishing industry. But what if this other publisher, or X, decide to have the book typeset in 6 point type, printed with bad ink on a bad press so that the ink runs, and bound using cheap glue? Won't that cut down on sales? And won't that also mean that the publisher can set an extremely low price, and won't that lower the net or gross on which the royalties are based?

[One way to prevent those situations here and below, is to actually specify the book's physical form. Everything involving size, type size, jacket design, biographical blurbs, quality and stock of paper, and so on can be specified in a spec sheet annexed to the contract and incorporated into it by a reference in the main body of the contract. A spec sheet can be drawn up for each type of book, since hard covers and mass market paperbacks are typically cut to different outside measurements. X would then be granted the contractual right to have "others" publish the book pursuant to those spec sheets; any variation from the spec sheets would require the approval of the Author in a signed writing.

[Most houses will not agree to spec sheets, even for art books, which still leaves the alternatives of generally stating that every edition of the book will be of equal or superior quality to other such books, and/or that the publishers of the other editions will be prestige publishers in the trade.]

(b) The right to print, publish and sell and to authorize others to print, publish and sell the Book in the English language in hardcover form.

(c) The right to authorize others to translate the English language version of the Book into one or more foreign languages and to publish and sell, or to authorize others to publish and sell, such translations in paperback or hardcover form ("foreign translation rights").

[Sub-clause (c) is usually deleted to retain translation rights. But where it is retained, you might want to have a say in who the translator is. Publishers object that foreign houses generally refuse to permit interference in the selection of translators.]

169

(d) The right to license first serial, second serial, book club edition, book selection, periodical selection, excerpt, abridgement, condensation, digest, textbook, microfilm, transcription, tape, cassette, syndication, anthology, and all other publishing rights not specifically enumerated herein, whether now in existence or hereafter coming into existence.

━━━━━━━━━━━━━━━

[Too broad, needing a good pruning with some good definitions and clarification of rights. For example, who excerpts, abridges, condenses or digests your work? Why not you? At an additional fee? Or, you might not want your work put into an anthology -- you might end up being associated with other authors you don't particularly want to share a bed with. Never give up all rights from the time the world was created until the time someone uses the Bomb. A publisher can always take out an option on obtaining such new rights from you. But those new rights might very well end up being extremely valuable, and you don't want to shed yourself of them before you know what they are worth to you. For example, is a "publishing right" a right including software creation and distribution?

[Note that the rights being discussed in this subparagraph and the others in this section involve rights your agent may be handling for you. Someone will not do their job, because it makes no sense for two entities to be competing with the same list of rights for sale. But both parties will be claiming their percentages unless that is clarified; in many instances, neither party pursues the rights. Alternatives include a time limit by which the publisher must have placed certain rights, or those rights revert automatically to the author.]

━━━━━━━━━━━━━━━

(e) The right to publish or broadcast and to permit others to publish or broadcast by radio or television, without charge, such selections from the Book for publicity purposes as may benefit its sale.

X shall have the right to utilize and authorize others to utilize the name and likeness of the Author on the covers and generally in connection with the advertising and promotion of the Book.

━━━━━━━━━━━━━━━

[PR redux. By covers, X apparently means book jacket covers. X should say so. But who has the final choice as to the photographs or other likeness? You can always submit a selection of likenesses to X, from which X can select one or two. If X doesn't like any of them, X can pick up the tab to have your likeness refashioned. Same with advertising and other promotion.

[But PR is always a sticky point with houses. They will orally say that their PR group will click in a few months prior to the publication date, but in most cases that means nothing more than using the same list as always for mailing out a limited number of review copies. Promises will be made with regard to book store promotions, space ads, interviews and perhaps direct mail campaigns, but only in a few surprising instances will those ever result.]

The exclusive rights granted to X hereunder shall remain in effect during the full term that the copyright to the Book subsists (including any renewal, extension or reversionary terms thereof) in any country in the world, except as provided for in paragraph 25 hereunder.

[The rights should exist only as long as the agreement exists.]

In addition to the exclusive rights set forth above, X shall have the exclusive right, throughout the world, to use, or to authorize others to use, the Book, title, plot, episodes, events, scenes and or characters depicted therein, in whole or in part, for the purpose of:

(i) writing a dramatic version thereof and performing same on the spoken stage with actors appearing in person in the immediate presence of the audience and the right to cause the broadcasting, telecasting, recording or photographing of such performance ("dramatic rights").

[Why shouldn't you have first dibs at writing the play? Even if your book is *1,001 Ways to Use a Ballpeen Hammer.*]

(ii) writing screenplays, treatments and other plans, specifications and designs for motion pictures and the right to cause the production, distribution and exhibition of such motion pictures in all mediums ("motion picture rights").

[Or maybe you want to write the screenplay.]

(iii) writing teleplays, treatments, storyboards and other plans, specifications and designs for television programs and the right to cause the production, distribution and exhibition of such television programs in all mediums ("television rights").

171

[Ditto.]

—————

(iv) performing the Book, or an adaptation thereof, on radio ("radio rights").

—————

[Unlikely, but why not you as the adapter?]

—————

(v) writing and composing musical compositions, including both words and music, and the right to cause such musical compositions to be produced on sound recordings and to distribute and sell such sound recordings or sheet music thereof ("music rights").

—————

[Unlikely, but with another ditto. If you can hold a tune.]

—————

(vi) causing the manufacturing, selling, furnishing, supplying and distributing of products, by-products, services, facilities, merchandise and commodities of every nature and description, including, but not limited to, still photographs, drawings, posters, artwork, toys, games, items of wearing apparel, foods, beverages and similar items, which make reference to or are based upon or adapted from the Book or any part thereof ("commercial rights").

—————

["Causing the manufacturing" presumably means licensing others to manufacture, as opposed to waving a magic wand on a mountain top. "By-products," on the other hand, must mean the guts and organs of cows and pigs, intended for sale either to Leopold Bloom or dog food companies. The clause does not mention use of trade or service marks, or names, use of character names, use of title, and so on. Moreover, does this, too, cover software rights?]

—————

(vii) advertising and exploiting the rights set forth in (i) through (v) above, to condense or to authorize others to condense the Book, or any screenplay, teleplay or treatment based thereon into not more than 10,000 words.

—————

[The infamous Campbell's soup clause. One hopes that it means copywriting.]

—————

Author shall, when requested by X, execute all documents which may be necessary or appropriate to enable X to exercise or deal with any rights granted hereunder. In the event of the failure of Author to execute and deliver or cause to be executed and delivered to X all instruments required in accordance with the provisions of this agreement, Author hereby appoints X as Author's irrevocable attorney-in-fact, in Author's name and on Author's behalf to execute and deliver all such instruments for the purposes aforesaid.

[If you have retained certain rights but permit X to serve as a pseudo-agent in their placement, such as movie rights, the clause should be mutual in terms of X also being obligated to execute documents you might need signed by X. I would also be wary of any relatively general "irrevocable attorney-in-fact" requirement. Is that something you would grant to your spouse, child or cat?]

2. DELIVERY OF MANUSCRIPT: The Author agrees to deliver to X a complete, final, edited, typewritten manuscript of approximately   to words in length (in duplicate) not later than   (months, year) after the signing of this agreement. If the Author fails to deliver the manuscript within the time referred to above, X may, at any time thereafter, at its option, terminate this agreement by giving written notice to Author and thereupon shall be entitled to repayment of all amounts which may have been paid hereunder. Author further agrees to deliver with the manuscript, at his expense, all photographs, illustrations, drawings, charts, indexes and other material necessary to the completion of the manuscript, provided that if Author shall fail to do so, X shall have the right to supply such material and charge the cost thereof against any sums accruing to Author pursuant to this agreement.

[Complete, final, typed, edited, duplicates, drawings, charts -- tell me about it. And if you don't get all that in place in time, you have to give back that glorious advance -- that hasn't even been mentioned yet. How about a manuscript of z words in length on 8 1/2 by 11 inch paper, white in color, either typed or printed out by a double-strike dot matrix or letter quality printer, but in any event in legible form? Even better, what about diskettes of a certain size and format with the book processed using a program loaned to the author by the publisher? And how about a little leeway in there with regard to time? In the event the Author cannot meet the deadline, the Author shall notify X in writing as to when he feels he can meet such deadline and give his excuse therefor. You can agree in advance as to those excuses that will automatically be considered valid by X, such as illness/hospitalization. After

173

all, publishers always list excuses for not meeting publication dates, thereby maintaining rights under the agreement. Also, a mechanism should be described here as
to the manner of repayment, if you do eventually contract that the advance is recoupable by X as opposed to being a bonus for signing.]

3. ACCEPTANCE OF MANUSCRIPT: The payment to Author of any or all
portions of the advance due pursuant to paragraph 7 shall not constitute acceptance
of the manuscript or any part thereof. If any installment or the entire manuscript shall
not, in the sole opinion of X, be suitable for publication, X shall have the right to
terminate this agreement by notice in writing to the Author given within ninety (90)
days after such delivery and, in such an event, neither party shall have any further
rights or obligations hereunder, provided that any amounts actually paid to the
Author prior to the delivery of the rejected manuscript shall be repaid to X, but only
in the event the manuscript is subsequently placed with another publisher and only
to the extent of any sums paid by such publisher with respect thereto.

[There is some case law brewing to the extent that an author may have some claim
to editorial comments and a chance to follow those comments prior to an outright
rejection. This clause is an outright rejection clause. You should try for a couple of
changes. X, for example, could have a limited period of time to read the submitted
manuscript and either accept it or accept it conditioned upon certain changes being
made within a certain time period. Let's say the clause provides that you have two
bites at the apple and, even after that, X has some valid editorial reasons for not
accepting the manuscript. Maybe you should have the right to call in a mutually
selected ghostwriter and pay that fellow from your advance. The bottomline
difficulty, of course, is that editorial judgments can be fudged and/or purely subjective or can change because the editor who loved you has left X and been replaced by
an editor who hates you with a passion. But if you have valid reasons as to why the
manuscript meets the editorial critique and X cannot rationally counter, you should
at least be able to retain the entire advance, regardless of any subsequent publishing contracts with other houses.]

4. PRINTER'S PROOFS: Author agrees to read, revise and correct, without
material changes in, additions to, or eliminations from, the manuscript accepted by
X, all galley proofs or proof sheets of the Book. Author agrees to return such
corrected proofs to X within thirty (30) days of the receipt thereof by Author. The
cost of alterations in the galley or page proofs required by Author, other than
corrections of printer's errors, in excess of ten (10%) percent of the original cost of

composition, shall be charged against the earnings of Author hereunder or shall, at the option of X, be paid by Author in cash; provided, however, that in either case, X shall, upon request, promptly furnish to Author an itemized statement of such additional expenses, and shall make available at X's office the corrected proof for inspection by Author.

═══════════

[Back in the old days, meticulous writers used to edit and rewrite up to the last moment -- i.e., when the editor finally caved in, climbed onto the windowsill, and threatened to leap unless the writer finalized the project. The pay-if-you-change policy was partly in reaction to that, and partly just a way of getting additional costs of publication from the Author. But what if the overhaul is good for the book? Certainly, if the changes are valid and agreed to by the editor, X should absorb the costs. Otherwise, the charge for substantial changes should only kick in on the second go around. With everything computerized, changes are not that terrifying. Moreover, if X uses or has a typesetter that happens to work from diskettes and on an operating system and in an application program that fits your computer, there should be no fee at all with regard to changes. You can take dupes home, fiddle around there, and transmit changes with embedded typesetting code directly to the typesetter.]

═══════════

5. PUBLICATION OF THE BOOK: X agrees to publish, or cause to be published, the Book in book form in such style and manner and at such prices as X may deem best suited for the sale of the Book, not later than   (months) after the delivery of the final manuscript.

═══════════

[The deem best suited clause does not involve shopping at Bloomingdale's. To one house, it could mean newspaper stock and plastic-based glue; to another, acid free paper and machine stitching.]

═══════════

Should X be unable to print, publish, and/or sell the Book for reasons beyond X's control, including, by way of example, governmental restrictions, strikes, war, invasion, civil riot, breakdown of market distribution facilities, or shortages of labor or material, this agreement shall remain valid and the rights and obligations it sets forth shall be resumed when X shall again be able to print, publish and/or sell.

═══════════

[This is a broad force majeure clause. It does not really make that much sense in a publishing contract since there is nothing unique about publishing. The plates will fit anyone's offset presses. Besides, the houses don't give the author a similar clause. If an author is struck by lightning or a union, he has to plead for an extension.]

6. COPYRIGHT: X agrees, upon the first publication of the Book, to copyright it in the name of _____ in the United States of America, in compliance with the Universal Copyright Convention. If X shall add illustrations, charts, diagrams or any other material to the Book, the copyright in such added material shall be effected in the name of X.

[X must ensure that the manner of protection is valid in all countries by convention, treaty, pact or statute. Compliance with the U.C.C. is too limiting, as is limiting registration to the United States. The manner of registration or compliance is particularly relevant since just about all houses retain worldwide English edition rights. The clause should be broad.

[Second, whoever has copyright rights in the illustrations, charts, and whatever, retains their rights, as noticed in the book. But X here is not warranting or representing that such new material has been released to it and that it has clear rights to the use of such material. That last sentence is also broad enough to imply that X has the outright right to add any materials it wants to the book -- you might not be happy with a fold-out of Ella Snodgrass in the middle of your book on tribal relations in upper Nigeria. Third, X must agree that it is responsible for ensuring that all copies of the Book, in whatever form, will bear the appropriate and valid copyright markings and, if any such copy or copies are lacking such markings, X shall bear the cost of either calling back all such copies for marking or of fulfilling any and all other statutory requirements for bringing such copies back under the ambit of a protected work.]

Subject to paragraph 18, this agreement shall be binding upon and inure to the benefit of the parties hereto and their respective heirs, executors, administrators, successors and assigns. Without limiting the generality of the foregoing, this paragraph 6 shall be binding upon the person(s) entitled to any renewal, extension or revision of the copyright to the extent permissible under present or future law.

[I tend to doubt that X, a corporation, is going to have any heirs, executors or administrators.]

7. ADVANCE: X shall pay to Author as an advance against all of the Author's earnings under this agreement the sum of _____ Dollars, payable as follows:

    (a) $_____ thereof on execution hereof;

    (b) $_____ on X's acceptance of the outline;

    (c) $_____ on X's acceptance of the complete manuscript;

    (d) $_____ on X's publication of the Book.

[Was "outline" ever mentioned before? Usually, an outline is worked out prior to signing the agreement and is often appended for reference and incorporation. This section should also list all rights with regard to the advance, rather than having those rights and liabilities spread out throughout the agreement.]

---

8. PAPERBACK AND HARDCOVER ROYALTIES: X shall pay to Author the following:

(a) On all copies of the English language mass-market paperback editions of the Book published by X, royalties shall be payable on copies shipped, less returns, at the following rates:

(i) For copies sold in the United States, its territories, possessions, and dependencies and Puerto Rico ("United States"):

    ___ % of the _____ price on the first _____ copies sold and,

    ___ % of the _____ price on all copies sold thereafter.

(ii) Two thirds (2/3) of the royalty rate as set forth in subdivision (i) above on all copies sold outside the United States.

(iii) An amount equal to five (5%) percent of the net amount actually received by X on all copies sold on a non-returnable basis at a special discount of fifty (50%) percent or more off the cover price.

(iv) An amount equal to five (5%) percent of the net amount actually received by X on all book club sales.

(v) An amount equal to five (5%) percent of the net amount actually received by X on all premium, mail order or remainder sales.

(b) On all copies of the English language quality paperback editions published by X, if any, royalties shall be payable on copies shipped, less returns, at the following rates:

(i) For copies sold in the United States:

    ___ % of the _____ price on the first _____ copies sold and,

    ___ % of the _____ price on all copies of each sold thereafter.

(ii) Two-third (2/3) of the royalty rate as set forth in subdivision (i) above on all copies sold outside the United States.

(iii) An amount equal to four (4%) percent of the net amount actually received by X on all copies sold on a non-returnable basis at a special discount of fifty (50%) percent or more off the cover price.

(iv) An amount equal to five (5%) percent of the net amount actually received by X on all book club sales.

(v) An amount equal to five (5%) percent of the net amount actually received by X on all premium, mail order or remainder sales.

(c) On all copies of the English language hardcover edition of the Book published by X, if any, royalties shall be payable on copies shipped, less returns, at the following rates:

(i) For copies sold in the United States:

_____ % of the _____ price on the first _____ copies of each book sold;

_____ % of the _____ price on the next _____ copies of each book sold; and

_____ % of the _____ price on all copies of each sold thereafter.

(ii) Two-third (2/3) of the royalty rate as set forth in subdivision (i) above on all copies sold outside the United States.

(iii) An amount equal to ten (10%) percent of the net amount actually received by X on all book club, mail order, premium or remainder sales or on sales of copies sold at a discount of fifty (50%) percent or more off the cover price.

(d) Should X find itself with an overstock of the Book on hand, when, in its judgment, the demand for the Book would not deplete this stock in a reasonable time, or should X find itself with a stock of damaged copies of the Book, X shall have the right to sell such copies at the best price it can secure, subject to the payments of royalties as set forth in subdivisions 8(a)(v), 8(b)(v) and 8(c)(iii) above.

(e) No royalties shall be payable to Author on copies of the Book destroyed, distributed for review, advertising, publicity, sample or like purposes, or any copies sold at cost or less than cost, or copies sold to Author pursuant to paragraph 15 hereof.

[Wouldn't the world be wonderful if royalties could be on a sliding scale across the board based upon profits? But then houses would have to provide an accounting of costs and sales, there might be arguments about defining overhead, and the author might actually end up receiving annual payments.

[Reality, of course, makes the royalty schedule the most arcane in a society of MBA's. Years ago, the rate was based on the retail price or gross revenues. Then publishers retreated to net before devising the "invoice list price" as part of a "freight pass-through" supposedly due to a postal rate increase. But even that never yields a definable figure, because the schedule is replete with loopholes, exceptions and markdowns. Often, for example, a house will drastically reduce the royalty on a book that is marketed "by direct mail," or "to non-book stores," or "by means outside of the normal course." Another ploy is to increase the number of units that have to be sold before a rate kicks in: " ... shall be 5% of the rate given herein payable after the first 10,000 books have been sold without return."

[It should come as no surprise that, in the usual instance, an author never receives royalties.]

━━━━━━━

9. LICENSING AND PERFORMING REVENUE: (a) All net revenue (as the term "net revenue" is herein defined) derived from the licensing of any publication rights in the Book, or any part thereof, in any form throughout the Territory shall be divided as set forth below:

United States Hardcover Rights: ___% to Author, ___% to X
First Serial Rights:
Second Serial Rights:
Foreign Translation Rights:
Book Club Rights - Paperback:
Book Club Rights - Hardcover
Book and Periodical Selection Rights:
Excerpt Rights:
Abridgement, Condensation and Digest Rights:
Textbook Rights:
Syndication Rights:
Anthology Rights:
Microfilm, Transcription, Tape & Cassette Rights:
Other Publishing rights not specifically enumerated herein:

(b) All net revenue derived from the licensing of the following performing rights shall be divided as set forth below:

Dramatic Rights: ___% to Author, ___% to X
Motion Picture Rights:
Television Rights:
Radio Rights:
Music Rights:
Commercial Rights:

(c) X shall the right right to license the photographing, microfilming, taping, reproduction in Braille or other publication of the Book, in whole or in part, for sale to the physically handicapped, without compensation therefor.

(d) The term "net revenue" shall mean all sums actually received from the licensing of publication and performing rights in the Book less any commission to sales agents or other direct expenses (other than normal overhead expenses) incurred by X in disposing of such rights.

179

━━━━━━━━━━

[Obviously, if you retain the rights to do the screenplay, teleplay, abridgement or whatever, you will want to be paid for that without sharing any money with X. Sometimes, you can argue for a 10%(Publisher)/90%(Author) split, particularly with regard to rights a publisher does not understand, such as database exploitation, or where you are going to exploit the right. But since the publisher is retaining a percentage, you should also insist that the publisher agree to at least advertise your exploited right along with the ads promoting the book, or, even better, serve as a distributor. Unenumerated rights should be excluded, particularly if they can be construed as including future rights, such as software publishing rights.]

━━━━━━━━━━

10. ACCOUNTING; STATEMENTS: Commencing with the first full accounting period (January 1 - June 30 or July 1 - December 31) following the publication of the Book, X shall render semi-annual statements of account as of June 30th and December 31st, and shall mail such statements to Author during the September and March following, together with the payment of the amounts due thereon. In rendering any statement of sales, X shall have the right to withhold a reasonable reserve against returns of the Book.

If in any accounting period, the total of all payments due Author is less than Forty ($40) Dollars, X may defer payment until such times as the sum of Forty ($40) Dollars or more shall be due.

Should the Author receive an overpayment of royalties on the Book, X shall have the right to deduct the amount of such over payment from royalty earnings subsequently due Author, provided that the term "overpayment" shall not apply to an unearned advance.

━━━━━━━━━━

[In this clause, X should grant to author the right to have an independent accountant enter X's premises during reasonable hours for purposes of auditing X's books as they relate to Author's sales. In this contract, that right is granted further down. Reserve for returns should be defined or at least given a cap -- what if X decides that all of the Books are going to be returned? This is also the section where the author's agent should be included if the agent is to receive the statements and royalties.]

━━━━━━━━━━

12. AUTHOR'S WARRANTIES: Author warrants and represents to X that Author owns all rights and licenses herein conveyed and purported to be conveyed, and has full and sole right and authority to convey all such rights; that the Book is

original with the Author in all respects, that no incident therein contained, and no part thereof, was taken from or based upon any other literary, dramatic or musical material or any motion picture; that the Book is or will be validly copyrighted or registered for copyright in the United States of America and likewise may be protected elsewhere so far as the laws of other places and countries provide for such protection; that a substantial part of the Book is not in the public domain; that no part of the rights or licenses herein conveyed has in any way been encumbered, conveyed, granted or otherwise disposed of and the same are free and clear of any liens or claims whatsoever in favor of any party whomsoever and said rights, and the full right to exercise the same, have not been in any way prejudiced, limited, diminished or impaired; that the title of the Book may be legally used by X in the exercise of all or any of the rights herein conveyed; that the use or reproduction of the Book or any part thereof, or the exercise of any of the rights herein granted or conveyed will not in any way infringe upon any statutory or common law copyright or constitute a libel or defamation of, or invasion of the rights of privacy or of publicity of any party; that Author has not done or will not do any act or thing that will or may in any way prevent or interfere in any manner with the full and exclusive enjoyment by X of any of the rights or licenses herein conveyed or which will or may impair, impede, invalidate or encumber any such rights or licenses; that to the knowledge of the Author there are no claims or litigation pending, outstanding or threatened which may adversely affect or may in any way prejudice X's exclusive rights in the Book or the copyright of any thereof or any of the rights or licenses herein granted or conveyed.

The warranties and representations of Author hereunder are true on the date of the execution of this agreement and shall survive the termination of this agreement. The warranties and representations contained in this paragraph 11 do not extend to drawings, illustrations or other material not furnished by Author.

[Has anything been left out? Starting at the top, the author is either conveying certain express rights or licenses, or not -- a purported conveyance can go out the window. Then, isn't there a clause somewhere earlier on talking about X copyrighting the Book? In any event, the two clauses can be shortened tremendously. Author warrants and represents that the Book is original or that he has valid rights to it or portions of it requiring such releases or licenses; and that he is not defaming anyone to the best of his knowledge.]

---

12. INDEMNITY: The Author undertakes to indemnify and hold X and its licensees, officers, agents, employees and assigns, harmless from and against any claims, charges, damages, costs, expenses (including reasonable counsel fees),

judgments, settlements, penalties, liabilities or losses of any kind or nature whatsoever, which may be incurred by X or its licensees, officers, agents, employees or assigns by reason of the breach or alleged breach of any of the representations or warranties herein contained or by reason of the publication, sale, distribution or disposition of rights in respect of the Book. X and Author shall each, with all reasonable promptness, notify the other of any suit, claim or demand brought or made on the basis of or in connection with the Book.

If any such suit, proceeding, claim or demand is brought or made against X, X shall undertake the defense thereof with counsel of its own selection, providing that Author shall have the right, but not the obligation, to have separate counsel of its own selection, it being understood, however, that the conduct of the defense shall always be under X's control, and, in any event, that Author shall cooperate with X in the defense. In the event such suit, proceeding, claim or demand is determined by judgment, abandonment or settlement without liability to X, Author shall have no responsibility for X's counsel fees or other expenses incurred by X in the defense thereof.

During the pendency of any such suit, proceeding, claim or demand, X may withhold payment due to Author under this agreement to the extent reasonably necessary to conduct the defense thereof and to satisfy any liability therein.

[Seems to imply that if X loses, author can be hit for X's legal costs, including attorney's fees. Actually, it would be better if author had the option to run the defense on his own with counsel of his choice. If author did not want to exercise that option, or if Author only wanted to participate tangentially, then X could hop in with its big, prestige law firm and take charge. But, in most instances, author will be a co-defendant. Author should be responsible for his direct liabilities, and X should be responsible for its direct liabilities. For example, what if X's law department goes over the book prior to publication and declares that nothing needs to be changed in it, and it is X's law department that makes the ultimate error in judgment? That should not be author's legal headache or expense.

[X should maintain an umbrella policy of a certain face insurable amount and agree to carry a same or similar policy for the duration of the agreement.]

---

13. OPTION ON FUTURE WORK: Author agrees to offer to X, before offering such rights directly or indirectly to any other publisher, the book rights in English to the next work of the Author. Author agrees that he shall not enter into a contract for the publication of such next work with any other publisher upon terms equal to or less favorable than those offered by X and shall give X the opportunity to acquire said rights on the best terms offered to Author by any other publisher.

[A joint option and right of first refusal. Wordy, yet leaves out some important words, such as time limits within which X must make up its mind. Many contracts add that the author shall submit his next proposal as a completed manuscript, which should be cut back to proposal. Even so, I know of houses that have kept an author dangling for months by saying they are very interested in the proposal, but would you please rewrite it just one more time.]

14. AUTHOR'S PROPERTY: Except for loss or damage due to its own willful negligence, X shall not be responsible for loss or damage to any property of Author. After publication, and on written request of Author, X agrees to forward the original manuscript and or galley and page proofs thereof, with printer's corrections to Author. If Author does not request the original manuscript and/or galley and page proofs in writing within one (1) month following publication, said manuscript and/ or galley and page proofs may be destroyed.

[Should be rephrased so that the original manuscript, galley and page proofs, and all illustrations and related materials are automatically forwarded to Author at no additional charge immediately after publication. Moreover, X should assume liability for loss and damage to any valuable materials. Since that portion of the clause is open-ended, covering pre- and post-publication, the issue arises as to X's liability if X inadvertently loses or destroys author's negatives, where author must then have a photographer shoot all over again. Moreover, in some art book cases, houses have insisted that authors pay for color separations, which can be costly. All these things should be spelled out with more clarity and a more equitable division of liabilities.]

15. AUTHOR'S COPIES: X shall furnish to Author   free copies of the mass-market paperback edition,   free copies of the quality paperback edition (if any) and   free copies of the hardcover edition (if any) of the Book. Author shall have the right to purchase additional copies of the Book at forty (40%) percent off the cover price for Author's own use and not for resale.

[No real comments necessary except for the forty percent discount for additional purchases. For example, author should be given an option to buy copies during those times when X is clearing inventory and selling at salvage levels.]

16. TERMINATION: REVERSION OF RIGHTS: (a) If X shall fail to publish the Book within the period specified in paragraph 5 hereof, this agreement shall terminate upon receipt by X of written notice to that effect from Author. In such event, Author shall be entitled, in lieu of all damages and remedies, legal or equitable, to retain all payments theretofore made to Author under this agreement.

―――――

[And X shall promptly return to author all materials, including galleys, plates, and the like. Note that the advance is made into a statement of liquidated damages.]

―――――

(b) In the event that after three (3) or more years from the date of the first publication of the Book, the same in the opinion of X shall be no longer merchantable or profitable, it may give notice to Author of its desire and intention to discontinue publication; or in the event that after five (5) years from the date of the first publication, the Book shall not be in print and for sale in any edition by X or any of its licensees and after written demand from Author shall not within nine (9) months be reprinted and offered for sale, then in either of these events, Author shall have the right to terminate this agreement, and upon written notice to that effect by Author to X, all rights granted under this agreement shall revert to Author subject to any outstanding licenses; provided, however, that X shall have the right, subject to the payment to Author of the applicable royalties thereon, to sell all copies of the Book which have been already printed or are in the process of being printed as of the date of such termination.

(c) If X is finally adjudicated a bankrupt, or if a receiver is appointed for all or a substantial part of X's assets and is not discharged within thirty (30) days from the date of appointment thereof, or if an assignment is made for the benefit of creditors, Author may, by notice in writing, terminate this agreement, subject to outstanding licenses; provided, however, that X shall have the right, subject to the payment to Author of the applicable royalties thereon, to sell all copies of the Book which have been already printed or are in the process of being printed as of the date of such termination.

―――――

[As usual, poorly drafted and one-sided. Also shows why the licensing agreements with the "others" should be signed off on by the author. They should contain a similar best efforts/termination clause. If no one is doing the job, no one should retain the rights. Inventoried work should be offered to the author at salvage values; otherwise, X will only sell inventory at salvage levels and author will thereby only receive lower or no royalty payments therefrom. Times periods should also be shorter. Note that the termination upon bankruptcy section sounds nice but is invalid as an *ipso facto* clause pursuant to federal bankruptcy law. Since the bankruptcy of a publisher can put an author in a terrible bind, a real bankruptcy clause should be drafted, covering collateralized interests and ownership rights favoring the author so that publication and distribution is not held up and so that accrued royalties are paid over or, at the least, not brought into the estate and disposed of.]

---

17. AUDIT RIGHTS: Author may, at its own expense, audit the books and records of X relating to the publication of the Book pursuant to this agreement at the place where X maintains such books and records in order to verify statements rendered to Author hereunder. Any such audit shall be conducted only by a reputable public accountant during reasonable business hours in such manner as not to interfere with X's normal business activities. In no event shall an audit with respect to any statement commence later than months from the date of dispatch to Author of such statement nor shall any audit continue for longer than five (5) consecutive business days nor shall audits be made hereunder more frequently than twice annually, nor shall the records supporting any such statements be audited more than once. All statements rendered hereunder shall be binding upon Author and not subject to objection for any reason unless such objection is made in writing stating the basis thereof and delivered to X within   months from delivery of such statement, or if an audit is commenced prior thereto, within thirty (30) days from the completion of the relative audit.

[Again, this clause should be up with the accounting clause for the sake of clarity. Also, the right should be extended to the author's agent, in the alternative, if that is one of the obligations the agent is bearing.]

---

18. ASSIGNMENT: This agreement shall bind and inure to the benefit of the parties hereto and their respective heirs, representatives, successors and assigns; provided, however, that no assignment of this agreement, voluntary or by operation of law, shall be binding upon either of the parties hereto without the prior written consent of the other.

[A repeat of a sub-clause from above, again giving X, the corporation, certain reproductive capabilities normally not associated with companies. There are some important aspects of this clause, however, with regard to mergers and acquisitions, and involuntary servitude. With regard to the former, you might want to consider what happens when X is taken over by Y conglomerate and, for some valid reason,

185

Y conglomerate is not the type of corporation you want handling your work. Involuntary servitude is the public policy statement that a personal services contract cannot be enforced in equity in the sense that you, as a writer, cannot be forced by a court to write a book (or even to tap dance). If you do not agree to an assignment, for example, you cannot be forced to write the book.]

19. CONFLICTING PUBLICATIONS: The Author shall not during the term of this agreement publish or permit to be published any material in book, pamphlet or other printed version form based upon material in the Book or which would directly compete with its sale.

[What is "directly compete" and in whose eyes is it defined?]

20. INFRINGEMENTS: Author hereby appoints X as Author's irrevocable attorney-in-fact, with the right, but not the obligation, and at X's expense, to bring and prosecute suits, actions and proceedings of any nature under or concerning the infringement of the copyright in the Book and all renewals thereof; and to take such action as X may deem advisable to enforce, protect, and/or defend any of the rights, privileges and property herein granted to X under any and all such copyrights and renewals thereof; and to litigate, collect and receipt for all damages arising from any infringement of any such rights. Any such action may be taken by X in the name of Author or otherwise, and X may join itself as a party plaintiff or defendant in any such suit, action or proceeding. If X shall not bring such action, Author may do so in its own names and at its own expense. All money damages recovered by X or Author shall be applied first to the repayment of such expense, and thereafter the balance shall be divided equally between Author and X.

[Like the indemnification clause, this clause gives X control over your life. Of course, you may want X to act as your policeman. But, assuming you have retained the copyright rights, the clause should state merely that, if X discovers an infringement or other cause of action, X should inform you promptly and then you can take it from there, if you wish. Obviously, if you opt to run the show, you get to keep the awarded damages.]

21. NOTICES: All notices which either party hereto is required or may desire to give to the other shall be given by addressing the same to the other at the address

hereinafter in this paragraph set forth, or at such other address as may be designated in writing by any such party in a notice to the other given in the manner prescribed in this paragraph. All such notices shall be sufficiently given when the same shall be deposited so addressed, postage prepaid, in the United States mail and/or when the same shall have been delivered, so addressed, to a telegraph or cable company toll prepaid and the date of said mailing or telegraphing shall be the date of the giving of such notice. The addresses to which any such notices shall be given are the following:

To X: To Author:

22. WAIVER; MODIFICATIONS: No waiver, modification or cancellation of any term or condition of this agreement shall be effective unless executed in writing by the party charged therewith. No written waiver shall excuse the performance of any act other than those specifically referred to therein.

[Actually, it should be in a writing signed by the party charged. Signatures are very important.]

23. CONSTRUCTION: This agreement shall be constructed in accordance with the laws of the State of New York, applicable to agreements to be wholly performed therein.

[Poorly constructed, but these clauses always are. Parties can contract to have the law of a certain state apply to the construction and interpretation of their agreement as long as that state has some reasonable relation to the contract. But if you really want the laws of that state to apply, you will state that the agreement shall be construed (not "constructed") and interpreted in accordance with the internal, local laws and not the conflict laws of the selected state. Otherwise, a court can go through the machinations of assessing whether, under the selected state's conflicts' rules, that state would apply its own laws or look to another state's laws.]

24. OPTION: X shall have the exclusive and irrevocable option, which it is under no obligation to exercise for books. If X shall exercise its option, it shall pay the

Author an advance against royalties of _____ for each of the first _____ additional books and _____ for each of the second additional books. It is understood that X shall have 60 days from receipt of each manuscript to exercise its option.

[X is trying to clarify the option it gave itself somewhere up above. Isn't this a long-winded, spread out contract? At least we have a time period here, but it doesn't really fit in with the option/right of first refusal contracted for above. These various odds and ends should be clumped together and clarified.]

25. X shall have the exclusive right to license English language rights in Australia. All revenues derived therefrom shall be divided ____% to the Author and _____% to X. If X is unable to exercise such rights within nine months after the publication of the Book, all such rights shall revert to the Author.

[Peculiar to this contract. Kept in merely to show you that it is possible to contract for anything, even strange things.]

26. The Author agrees to cause the Book to be written by _____, a pseudonym.

[But under which name shall it be published or copyrighted? This essential question has been completely overlooked by X and the author. The book shall be written by author but published under author's pseudonym. Moreover, author may want to protect himself in that he may not want anyone other than the editor and the editor's lawyer to know he is that pseudonym. Thus, a confidentiality clause is necessary.]

27. X agrees that it shall treat the Book as a lead book in the month of its publication.

[An extremely vague best efforts clause. This is where X's obligations with regard to advertising, promotion, book awards, competitions and the like should be spelled out. Same with regard to any license agreements with "others." Compare this to the clause above clumping rights in or to advertising and condensations. Note, however, that most contracts will not even have this clause.]

═══════════════

IN WITNESS WHEREOF, the parties hereto have duly executed this agreement the day and year first above written.

═══════════════

[Nothing on the witness clause, but some general comments. Note that the contract does not spell out anything with regard to reprints, sequels, or reissues (for example, timed to the release of the motion picture).]

═══════════════

X   Author

By: _____   _____

Title: _____

MOVIE AGREEMENTS

Following are sample Option and Production Agreements, excluding guild clauses. They should be read wearing sunglasses.

═══════════════

OPTION AGREEMENT

AGREEMENT as of _____ , 19__ , entered into between _____ , also known as _____ , residing at _____ (hereinafter, the "Author"); and _____ residing and doing business at _____ (hereinafter, the "Purchaser").

═══════════════

[In this agreement, the author makes clear at the top that he has a pseudonym. The residing and doing business phrase with regard to the purchaser was because the purchaser was an individual who did business from his home address.]

═══════════════

WHEREAS the Purchaser desires an option on certain rights to the script treatment entitled "_____" (hereinafter, the "Screenplay"), as detailed below;

THEREFORE, the parties hereto for good and valuable consideration given and pursuant to the terms, conditions and covenants herein, hereby agree as follows.

1. The Author warrants and represents that he is the author and has all rights, title and interest in the Screenplay.

═══════════════

[Pithier than the publishing agreement, this sentence declares that the author is the author and retains the rights of an author. The clause could be expanded with the additional warranty that the author can enter into this agreement.]

═══════════════

2. The Purchaser, by payment of $_____ to the Author contemporaneously with the execution of this Agreement, receipt of which is hereby acknowledged by the Author, does hereby purchase the following rights:
    (a) the right to an irrevocable option (the "Option") to purchase the motion

picture rights (the "Rights") to the Screenplay for a period of one calendar year from the date hereinabove given to midnight of the last day of such calendar year (hereinafter, the "Option Period"), said Rights being defined in a certain production agreement annexed hereto as Attachment A (the "Production Agreement");

(b) the right to have the Author refrain from assigning, encumbering, or otherwise committing the Rights to the Screenplay to any other individual or entity, however organized, during the Option Period, except that nothing herein shall be deemed to impair or limit the Author's remaining or reserved rights in the Screenplay or to impair or limit the Author's right to show the Screenplay to potential purchasers in the event the Purchaser herein does not exercise his Option during the Option Period.

═══════════

[The option granted is irrevocable and exclusive. What the clauses make clear, however, is that the option speaks only to the option and not to any other rights the author is reserving. One important right is the right to show the screenplay to others during the time of the option. This will prevent the purchaser from tying up the property for a year and then dropping it cold. On the other hand, this right should probably be limited somewhat, such as to the last two months of the option period. The reason for that is because a wholesale mailing of the screenplay could lead to it being stolen.

[Production companies nowadays have authors sign agreements prior to the submission of screenplays. These agreements are typically one page in length and are a declaration that the screenplay is original with the author, the author is submitting it for a reading, and the author acknowledges that the production company, after rejecting a screenplay, may well produce or release a film that appears similar to the submitted screenplay. There is a real problem here, in the sense that screenplays do get stolen, but in many cases, films are released that appear very similar to another person's screenplay, yet there really was no attempt to copy. The fact is that many movies follow the same plots and themes and have the same type of characters -- that's just the market.]

═══════════

3. Concurrently herewith, the parties have executed the Production Agreement. The Production Agreement shall not become binding upon the parties unless and until the Purchaser exercises the Option pursuant to the terms and conditions of this Agreement.

4. The Option shall be exercisable by the Purchaser giving written notice by registered mail, return receipt requested, on or before the expiration date of the Option Period, addressed to the Author at the address above given, or such address as the Author

may hereafter provide to the Purchaser for such purpose.

5. If the Purchaser fails to exercise the Option during the Option Period, all rights hereunder shall cease and the Production Agreement shall be null and void.

6. In the event the Purchaser exercises the Option, a closing shall be held within _____ days thereafter or, if the day is a Saturday, Sunday, or holiday, the first business day thereafter, at such address in [city] as the Author shall designate to the Purchaser (hereinafter, the "Closing").

7. At the Closing, the Purchaser shall pay to the Author such sums as may be due pursuant to the Production Agreement, which agreement shall thereupon become effective and binding between the parties, and the rights stated in the Production Agreement to be granted to the Purchaser shall vest in the Purchaser as of that date.

8. This Agreement shall inure to the benefit of, and shall be binding upon, the Author's and the Purchaser's heirs, legal representatives, designees, assigns and successors.

9. This Agreement represents the entire Agreement between the parties hereto, supersedes all prior or contemporaneous agreements, whether written or oral, between the parties, and cannot be changed orally or by a writing of any sort unless by a writing signed by all the parties hereto, with the following exceptions:

(a) in the event the Option is exercised within the Option Period, this Agreement shall merge with the Production Agreement; and,

(b) a notice of a change of address shall not be considered a modification of this Agreement.

10. This Agreement shall be construed and interpreted in accordance with the local, internal law, and not the conflicts law, of the State of New York.

11. Notice shall be given to the parties at their respective addresses hereinabove given, unless another address has been subsequently given by any of the parties. Unless otherwise specified in this Agreement, notice shall be deemed sufficient if given in a writing mailed by first class United States mail, postage paid.

12. If any part of this Agreement is found violative of any law or otherwise legally defective, this Agreement shall be construed and interpreted as if such part were not contained herein.

[A clause missing in the publishing agreement. It means that if any part of the contract is struck, what remains will serve as the contract.]

━━━━━━━━━━━━━━━

WHEREFORE, in witness hereof, the parties hereby enter into this Agreement as of the day and date first hereinabove given.

Purchaser   Author

_____   _____

[Attachment A]

PRODUCTION AGREEMENT

AGREEMENT made this _____ day of _____, 19__ between _____,
also known as _____, residing at _____, (hereinafter, "Author"); and _____, residing and doing business at _____
(hereinafter, the "Purchaser").

WHEREAS, the Purchaser has exercised his rights pursuant to the terms and
conditions of a certain option agreement executed on the _____ day of
_____ (hereinafter, the "Option Agreement");

THEREFORE, the Purchaser and the Author, for good and valuable consideration
given and pursuant to the terms, conditions and covenants contained herein, hereby
agree as follows.

1. The Author is the author and has the rights, title and interest, including the
copyright worldwide and any extensions or renewals thereof, in a certain screenplay
entitled "X" (hereinafter, the "Screenplay").

———————————

[A bit more lengthy than the warranty and representation given in the Option
Agreement. As you will find, the Production Agreement contains the nuts and bolts
of the overall film agreement.]

———————————

2. The Author hereby assigns to the Purchaser certain exclusive motion picture rights
in and to the Screenplay (the "Rights"). The Rights consist of the following:
    (a) the exclusive right to produce on film of [16, super 16, 35, 70] millimeter, one
motion picture based upon or adapted from or suggested by the Screenplay (the
"Film");

———————————

[The Purchaser wants to be able to make a film based in part or in whole on the
screenplay. He does not want to contract that he has to produce a film that is word
for word from the screenplay. Unlike the production of a book, which is really among
a writer, editor and market analyst, the production of a film can involve hundreds of
people. The director will want to rewrite and shoot in his style. The actors will want
to act in their styles and perhaps ad lib. The camera and sound crew may want to work

in their style. The film editor will want to cut in his style. The producer and the executive producer will want to kibbitz and perhaps give their wives or daughters starring roles. The financing bank may want to have a financial officer standing by.

[On the other hand, note that in this clause, it is suggested that an author could negotiate the medium. This sort of agreement is similar to that mentioned in annotations to the publishing agreement with regard to spec sheets. It is doubtful, however, that a producer would want to be tied in to an established method. But I think nowadays, a screenwriter should have some idea as to how the final product will look, and that depends upon the how the film is shot (film, 1" broadcast quality video, HDV), and what kind of post-production facilities are available.]

(b) the exclusive right to produce foreign language versions of said Film;

(c) the exclusive right to produce and distribute trailers or other shortened versions of the Film for exhibition in theaters in advance of the exhibition of the Film;

(d) the exclusive right to use the title "X" as the title or titles of the Film;

(e) the exclusive right to secure copyright registration in the Film worldwide in the Purchaser's own name or otherwise;

(f) the exclusive right to prepare and use excerpts and summaries not exceeding five thousand (5,000) words from and of the Film in heralds, booklets, programs, posters, lobby displays, press books, newspapers, and periodicals, for the purpose of advertising and exploiting the Film;

(g) the exclusive right to distribute, sell, lease, and exhibit the Film worldwide; and

(h) the exclusive right to distribute, sell, lease, exhibit or otherwise commercially exploit the Film with regard to the videocassette, videodisc, television and cable markets worldwide.

[In the above clauses, a number of rights are listed, all of which can be bargained over. Where the purchaser obtains or wants broad rights covering "electronic media," be careful with regard to software rights.]

---

3. The assignment of rights specified in Paragraph 2 above is exclusive and specific; and all rights not assigned remain the sole property of the Author, including, but not limited to, the right to have the Screenplay published as a book and/or short story or serial; the right to the Screenplay for use as a motion picture remake or sequel; the right to the Screenplay for use as or in a television or cable television pilot or pilots, or series, or play; the right to the Screenplay for use as or in a stage play or musical; and the right to commercially exploit the Screenplay, and the characters, plot, incidents and situations contained therein, and the title "X," for purposes of the

consumer goods market worldwide.

[The author is specifying that he retains the rights in a variety of valuable areas. It is doubtful that most purchasers would accept such a long list of rights. On the other hand, note that if the screenplay were derived from a published book, between the rights reserved by the publishing house and the rights generally taken by the production company, the author would be left with nothing and a bread basket.]

---

4. The Purchaser shall state or cause to be stated on the Film, each copy thereof, and every herald, booklet, program, poster, lobby display, press book, newspaper, periodical, or other publication, the name "_____," or such other name as the Author may provide to the Purchaser prior to the shooting of the credits of the Film, as the author of the Screenplay in a size, type and format not less than seventy percent that of the producer, executive producer, or director of the Film, whichever is largest, with the exception specified in Paragraph 5 below.

[Where your name appears is the big game in town these days. But if you don't also talk about size, your name will appear in print finer than any found in an insurance contract. Note also that the author is concerned with his name and pseudonyms. The reason will become clear later.]

---

5. In producing the Film, the Purchaser shall have the right to make such changes in, additions to and eliminations from, the Screenplay, and to include in the Film such language, song, music, choreography, characters, plot, incidents and situations as the Purchaser in his sole discretion may deem advisable, except that the Author shall be shown the final cut of the Film prior to distribution and the Author, within ____ days thereafter or, if the ____ th day falls on a Saturday, Sunday, or holiday, on the first business day thereafter, may notify the Purchaser in writing as to the size, type and form of credit and billing the Author desires based upon said final cut, although said size shall in no even be larger than that specified in paragraph 4 above.

[As noted above, the production company will require full control over the film's content and style. So, unlike a final edit clause in the publishing agreement, the author is trying to protect himself from embarrassment by contracting for the right to withdraw one of his known names and substituting a name he will make up on the spot. Some screenwriters eventually withhold the use of any of their names after seeing the final cut. Later, if the film does well and/or receives acclaim, the author will "leak" that he was the screenwriter.]

================

6. As consideration for the Rights herein granted by the Author to the Purchaser, the Purchaser shall pay to the Author the following:

(a) $_____ simultaneously herewith, receipt of which is hereby acknowledged by the Author, and which sum represents the consideration given for the exercise of the Option Agreement;

(b) _____ percent (___%) of the final production budget for the Film, minus the $_____ paid in subparagraph 6(a) above, but in no event shall the Author receive less than $_____ or more than $_____ pursuant to this subparagraph and subparagraph 6(a), the final amount to be paid within _____ days of the final cut of the Film and based upon an accounting prepared by an independent, certified accountant. The Purchaser shall pay for the accounting and shall include a true copy thereof with said payment;

================

[In this instance, the purchaser wanted a cap on what amounts to a guaranteed cash payment for use of the screenplay. The author wanted a floor. Thus, the compromise.]

================

(c) _____ percent (_____%) of any and all net revenues accruing from distribution of the Film in any manner as described herein and permitted and granted to the Purchaser, to be paid quarterly based on the calendar year.

(d) _____ percent (_____%) of any and all gross profits received from the sale, licensing, leasing, or other commercial exploitation of the Film with regard to videocassette, videodisc, television or cable in any manner as described herein and permitted and granted to the Purchaser, to be paid upon receipt by the Purchaser; and,

(e) _____ dollars an hour, plus expenses, in the event the Author is requested to and agrees to revise the Screenplay in whole or in part, or confer on or about the Screenplay or the Film or any aspect thereof.

================

[The agreement should define net revenues and gross profits, or at least state that those terms are to be understood pursuant to generally accepted accounting procedures. No clause requiring anyone to call in the screenwriter, which is a thought. But at least, if the screenwriter is called in, the fee is already defined.]

================

7. Where any payment specified herein is based upon revenues or profits, the Author has the right to request of the Purchaser an accounting performed by an independent, certified accountant to be paid for by the Author, or the right to request access to the books, account records, and similar documents of the Purchaser during reasonable business hours for the purpose of an accounting, twice each calendar year upon _____ days written notice to either of the Purchaser. In the event of any discrepancy between the amounts paid to the Author and the amounts the Author should have received, the Purchaser shall pay to the Author the difference plus interest thereon at the highest rate then permitted by law from the date payment should have been made to the date payment is made.

[The last sentence will not appear in many production agreements. The various versions of accountings, payment enforcement and penalties is geared more towards the major studios. The old saying in the business is, If you aren't paid up front, you ain't never gonna be paid. Also, the clause may serve as a liquidated damages clause, in which case the purchaser would want that specified, thereby limiting the author's other rights and remedies.]

8. The Purchaser, and his assignees or successors-in-interest, shall be jointly and severally liable for the payments due to the Author. Every agreement, contract, or writing entered into by the Purchaser with regard to the Rights shall be deemed to create a direct obligation of payment to the Author in the event of a default or other breach by the Purchaser and acceptance of the terms, conditions and covenants of this Agreement so that the Author, whether or not this Agreement is physically annexed to or otherwise incorporated or merged into such agreements, contracts, or writings, shall be considered either a third party beneficiary or assignee of the Purchaser's rights (but not of his liabilities or obligations) therein. In the event of any default or other breach by the Purchaser, his assignees or successors-in-interest, pursuant to the terms and conditions of this Agreement, that remain uncured for a period of more than _____ days after the giving of written notice of such default or other breach by the Author to the Purchaser, all of the rights granted and assigned herein by the Author to the Purchaser shall immediately and without further notice revest in or be deemed assigned to the Author.

[A further attempt at pinning liability for non-payment on everyone involved in the project. Again, favors the author so will not typically be stomached by a major studio; may be acceptable to an independent who does not know what he is doing.]

9. This Agreement constitutes the entire understanding of the parties hereto and supersedes any and all prior or contemporaneous representations or agreements, whether written or oral, between the parties, and cannot be changed or modified unless in a writing signed by all the parties hereto, with the exceptions that:

(a) the Option Agreement is merged into this Agreement; and

(b) a notice of change of address is not a modification or change of this Agreement.

10. This Agreement shall inure to the benefit of, and shall be binding upon, the Author's and the Purchaser's heirs, legal representatives, administrators, executors, assigns, and successors.

11. This Agreement shall be interpreted and construed in accordance with the local, internal law, and not the conflicts laws, of the State of New York.

12. If any part of this Agreement is found violative of any law or is found to be otherwise legally defective, this Agreement shall be construed and interpreted without reference to such part.

13. Notice shall be given to the parties at their respective addresses hereinabove given, unless another address has been given by any such party, by first class United States mail, postage paid, unless the form and type of notice has been otherwise specified.

WHEREFORE, in witness hereof, the parties hereby enter into this Agreement as of the day and date first hereinabove given.

Purchaser   Author

_____   _____

AGENCY AGREEMENTS

As stated in the text, the normal course with a literary agent is for the agent to orally state the general terms of the relationship. In that case, you should follow up with a brief letter stating: "Pursuant to our discussion of [date], you will represent me with regard to [works; market]. You will receive a commission of ___ % in the domestic market, and _____ % in the foreign market," so on and so on. If the letter is too detailed, the agent will become antzy and either revert to an oral agreement or drop you.

Although I think it is wonderful when people can have an oral arrangement or one based on a short letter, we do not really live in a world of blue blood and handshakes anymore. Some agents recognize this and at times write their own letters to writers -- but the value of these is not that great either. Below is one such letter with annotations.

═══════════════

Literary Representative

Writer

Dear   :

This letter shall serve as the agreement between us with regard to my acting as literary agent for those written works you submit to me for placement in the commercial publishing community, effective as of the date set forth below. By "commercial publishing community" or "publisher," I mean the general trade press as opposed to the scholarly, academic, university press.

═══════════════

[Relatively good clarification of the markets covered and excluded. The scholarly press is never part of an agent's territory, since there is no money in it.]

═══════════════

I agree to act as your literary agent vis a vis the commercial publishing community; to make contacts with appropriate publishers and editors to alert them to your forth-coming works; to submit those works and/or outlines and/or sample chapters

201

thereof to such publishers and editors with the purpose of promoting them for publication; and to consult with you with regard to the initial negotiations involving the terms of sale of such works, at which point you may either request that I conclude such negotiations or that I work in conjunction with an attorney of your choice, or that an attorney of your choice follow through such negotiations to an executed contract.

———

[Somewhat jumbled but makes clear the duties of the agent and the right of the author to have an attorney. Sometimes, agents, being overly helpful, state that they will handle all legal negotiations. If the agent is an old salt and really does keep with changes in the law, you might want the agent to handle the contracts for you. Otherwise, you need to seek legal advice.]

———

In no event am I authorized to bind you to any contractual under taking without your express approval, given in a writing signed by you. If the terms of any final contract executed by you calls for me to follow up on and collect all monies, fees and royalties due to you from any such publisher, I shall do so as specified in such final contract, promptly paying you such monies, fees and royalties after the deduction of my commission, as defined here in.

———

[As with the publishing agreement, you don't want anyone to be authorized to sign anything for you without your seeing it first.]

———

In return for my services, I will receive a ten (10%) percent commission of all monies, fees and royalties due to you resulting from any placement of your work through me with a publisher that leads to an executed contract.

———

[Overbroad and ambiguous in the sense that it does not make clear whether the commission is only from placement with the publisher or includes every other sale flowing therefrom.]

———

In the event the executed contract permits me to place the foreign rights to the work and I do place such foreign rights through a subagent and such placement leads to an executed contract, I shall receive a fifteen (15%) percent commission of all monies, fees and royalties due to you resulting from such foreign placement.

═══════════════

[Narrower, in that it acknowledges that the publisher might take care of the sale of foreign rights.]

═══════════════

This agreement may be terminated by either one of us at any time by written request, except that my commission shall remain in force through the term of any contract already executed by you with any publisher where such contract was achieved through my efforts, as specified herein.

═══════════════

[Fair is fair, except that here, too, there is an ambiguity with regard to receipt of commissions on sales or licensing of remaining rights resulting from the efforts of the publisher which is carrying the book.]

═══════════════

If the above accurately reflects your understanding of the terms we have agreed upon, please sign below in the indicated space.

Sincerely,

Literary Agent

Author:

_____

Dated: _____

═══════════════

[The letter agreement covers some areas of concern and totally neglects other areas, such as whether the commission remains the same where the agent does not serve as your "accountant" with regard to the publishing; whether the commission vests on all further sales and licenses, whether or not brought about by the agent; whether the agent swallows costs such as xeroxing, postage, messengers, overhead, and the like.]

OTHER FORMS AND SOURCES

There are a variety of forms available that you can get if you would like to further research the types of clauses which can be included in the contracts discussed above. A "form" is a pre-printed legal document. You should look in your local legal stationery store, your local law school library (if they let you in), or ask for model contracts from an author's group or society.

If you are ambitious, you might also read Title 17, United States Code, otherwise popularly known as the Copyright Act. At this writing, you can still receive a free copy of the statute, along with an extremely helpful packet of additional information and copyright registration forms, from the Copyright Office in Washington, D.C. A good explanatory text is House Report No. 94-1476, 94th Cong. 2d Sess. (1976), issued by the Committee on the Judiciary.

If you have a relative who is a lawyer, bug the poor soul to have him send you things that might interest you. Lawyers always receive mailings about new law publications, seminars, and forms, and also peruse changes in case law. You should make yourself aware of the same matters.

"Remember your rights before you succumb to fame and your time may not be fleeting" -- all of which reminds me that I forgot to mention the fortune cookie market.

INDEX

Standard publishing agreements typically contain the infamous index clause. This clause comes into effect when the author, exhausted from the tedious process of trying to maintain a semblance of sanity while his or her work is edited into oblivion, and suddenly realizing that the automatic indexer contained in the word processor is useless since the pagination of the galleys is completely different from the original print-out, crawls into the editor's office and the editor says, "Where's the index? And remember to do it using the Fremelhammer style."

Thus, the professional indexer, someone who is short, pasty and unused to the sunlight. This person knows the Fremelhammer style inside and out. He dwells in sets, subsets and see also's. He loves indents and italics and dual columns. And he is paid approximately two thousand dollars a book. All houses charge either the entire amount or half of it against the author's royalties.

Now, these indices are more often than not well done. It is when the frazzled author takes over the task that real problems arise. The major one is that the author, sick and tired of reviewing his book, and having become utterly confused about the topic, will often draft an index of a dozen words and most of those words will be referencing some other book he has written. Or, the author will decide that most index words actually belong under other headings or sub-headings, and the *see*'s will outnumber the words and one heading will suddenly accumulate every other index word beneath it. This is the clump effect denoting the author's utter frustration with the process of publication.

For the purpose of circumventing every index concern an author can have, I hereby demonstrate a new standard.